Neurodiversity in Higher Education

Neurodiversity in Higher Education

Positive Responses to Specific Learning Differences

Edited by

David Pollak
De Montfort University Leicester, UK

⊛WILEY-BLACKWELL

A John Wiley & Sons, Ltd., Publication

This edition first published 2009
© 2009 John Wiley & Sons Ltd.

Wiley-Blackwell is an imprint of John Wiley & Sons, formed by the merger of Wiley's global Scientific, Technical, and Medical business with Blackwell Publishing.

Registered Office
John Wiley & Sons Ltd, The Atrium, Southern Gate, Chichester, West Sussex, PO19 8SQ, UK

Editorial Offices
The Atrium, Southern Gate, Chichester, West Sussex, PO19 8SQ, UK
9600 Garsington Road, Oxford, OX4 2DQ, UK
350 Main Street, Malden, MA 02148-5020, USA

For details of our global editorial offices, for customer services, and for information about how to apply for permission to reuse the copyright material in this book please see our website at www.wiley.com/wiley-blackwell.

Library of Congress Cataloging-in-Publication Data

Neurodiversity in higher education : positive responses to specific learning differences / edited by David Pollak.
        p.   cm.
    Includes bibliographical references and index.
    ISBN 978-0-470-74159-7 (cloth) – ISBN 978-0-470-99753-6 (pbk.)   1. Learning disabled–Education (Higher)   2. College students with disabilities.   3. Learning–Physiological aspects.   I. Pollak, David.
    LC4818.38.N48 2009
    371.9'0474 – dc22

                                                                        2008052047

A catalogue record for this book is available from the British Library.

Set in 10/13 pt Futura by SNP Best-set Typesetter Ltd., Hong Kong
Printed in Singapore by Utopia Press Pte Ltd

1   2009

Contents

Notes on Contributors   ix

Foreword   xv

Illustrations   xvii

1. **Introduction**   1
    David Pollak

2. **Neurodiversity, Disability, Legislation and
    Policy Development in the United Kingdom**   13
    Alan Hurst

3. **The Psychological Assessment of Neurodiversity**   33
    David Grant

4. **Dyslexia**   63
    Ross Cooper

5. **Dyspraxia**   91
    Sharon Drew

6. **Dyscalculia**   125
    Clare Trott

7. **Asperger Syndrome: Empathy Is a
    Two-Way Street**   149
    Nicola Martin

8. **Attention Deficit (Hyperactivity)
    Disorder – AD(H)D**   169
    Mary Colley

9. **Mental Well-Being**   195
    Kitty McCrea

10. **Assistive Technology**   217
    E.A. Draffan

11. **Teaching, Learning and Assessment: 'It's Not
    Like You Think'**   243
    Heather Symonds

12. **Conclusion: Constructing the Whole Picture and
    Looking Forward**   269
    David Pollak

Index   295

Contents

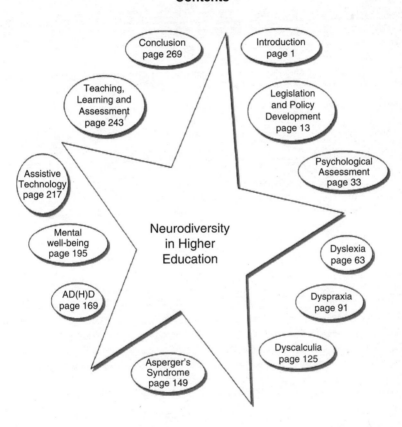

Conclusion
page 269

Introduction
page 1

Teaching,
Learning and
Assessment
page 243

Legislation
and Policy
Development
page 13

Assistive
Technology
page 217

Psychological
Assessment
page 33

Mental
well-being
page 195

Neurodiversity
in Higher
Education

Dyslexia
page 63

AD(H)D
page 169

Dyspraxia
page 91

Dyscalculia
page 125

Asperger's
Syndrome
page 149

Notes on Contributors

Mary Colley has a degree in Mediaeval History and a Postgraduate Diploma in Librarianship. She found out that she had developmental dyspraxia as well as AD(H)D and dyslexia in her mid-forties. She helped set up the UK Dyspraxia Foundation Adult Support Group and also achieved a Diploma in Specific Learning Difficulties in 1997. Mary coordinated the support group for about six years, running a helpline and organizing workshops and conferences on adult dyspraxia. In 2000, her book, *Living with Dyspraxia – a Guide for Adults with Dyspraxia*, was published with much help from the rest of the group. She works to raise awareness of dyspraxia by addressing a wide range of audiences, both in person and in print. Lately, she has also spoken on neurodiversity and sits on the steering or advisory groups of several national projects. Mary and others became aware of how frequently specific learning differences overlap, and in 2003 set up the charity DANDA – Developmental Adult Neuro-Diversity Association. In 2006, Jessica Kingsley published the 4th edition of her book on dyspraxia in adults, of which a total of 5,000 copies have been sold at the time of writing.

Ross Cooper is a principal lecturer at London South Bank University, course director of the MA in adult dyslexia diagnosis and support, and assistant director of LLU+, a national consultancy and professional development centre for staff working in the areas of literacy, numeracy, dyslexia, family learning and English for Speakers of Other Languages. He has worked in special schools, as well as further and higher education, and has a PhD in the sociology of education. Ross was an inclusive learning quality facilitator for the Inclusive Learning Quality Initiative and the learning and teaching coordinator for the widening participation project at Southampton University. He continues to promote the benefits of inclusive learning through consultancy, research, projects and workshops. Ross is a member of PATOSS (the Professional Association of Teachers of

Students with Specific Learning Difficulties) and SASC (the national committee for standards in SpLD assessment, training and practice). He, along with most of his family, is dyslexic.

E.A. Draffan trained as a speech and language therapist, before specializing in the field of assistive technologies. She has since worked with disabled students in further and higher education, set up an Assistive Technology Centre and developed a database of assistive technologies. E.A. has contributed to the work of TechDis (an educational advisory service working across the United Kingdom in the fields of accessibility and inclusion) and many other institutions and groups. She is now a Research Fellow at the University of Southampton.

Sharon Drew currently works as an independent consultant and trainer within the educational sector. She is an occupational therapist and teacher by background, with many years of experience working with adults and young people with neuro-developmental disorders. She lectures widely to professional and nonprofessional audiences across the United Kingdom and has written a number of textbooks and articles.

David Grant is a chartered psychologist and writer who, since 1999, has specialized in diagnosing students with specific learning differences. His research record includes publications in *Child Development* and *Neuropsychologia*. His recent publications include *That's the Way I Think: Dyslexia and Dyspraxia Explained*, and a commissioned handbook on neurodiversity for members of the National Association of Disability Practitioners. Before becoming a diagnostician, David spent over 30 years working in higher education. His experiences range from being a laboratory technician in a chemistry research laboratory to a lecturer in Psychology to Associate Dean of Students (Special Needs). David was the first non-American to serve on the board of the College Consortium of International Students. He has always enjoyed lecturing and new ways of working with students. This is reflected in his leading a Design and Media Management course team to a National Partnership Prize for Innovations in Teaching.

Alan Hurst, formerly Professor in the Department of Education, University of Central Lancashire, is a trustee of Skill: National Bureau for Students with Disabilities and chairs its Higher Education Working Party. He has published books and articles, and has been invited to lecture and lead workshops on disability in higher education in many countries. He was awarded an honorary doctorate by the Open University in June 2005 for his contribution to developing policy and provision for disabled students. His most recent publication is a handbook for mainstream staff developers on supporting disabled students. Having retired from the University, he is currently working with many organizations and institutions in both the United Kingdom and abroad on developing high-quality inclusive policies and provision. He is a member of the group established by the Higher Education Funding Council for England to review its policies on disabled students since 1997, and of the group set up by the UK Quality Assurance Agency to devise an updated version of its Code of Practice.

Kitty McCrea held the post of Head of Counselling and Personal Support at De Montfort University, Leicester from 2001 to 2007 where she was responsible for student counselling, mental health and learning diversity support. She is a Senior Accredited Member of the British Association for Counselling and Psychotherapy and a UKCP Registered Psychotherapist. Kitty previously had a 17-year career in teaching and management spanning the secondary, further, adult and higher education sectors. She is now practising as a cognitive-behavioural therapist and supervisor in private practice in Devon and continues to have a particular interest in the use of CORE Outcome Measures to evaluate the effectiveness of counselling. She is Chair of the CORE User Network Steering Group and is CORE User Network Development Consultant for CORE IMS, a company that supplies training, software support, and data analysis and benchmarking services to users of the CORE system.

Nicola Martin is Principal Lecturer in Inclusive Practice at Sheffield Hallam University and takes a lead role in the Autism Centre. She is the author of 'REAL services to assist university students who have Asperger syndrome', which was published by the National Association of Disability Practitioners (NADP) in May 2008. The work is based on a research project which looked into ways of making university a better place for students who have AS and is also informed by Nicola's doctoral research. Nicola is very committed to ensuring that neurodiversity is embraced as a positive aspect of society. She has personal experience of the highs and lows of dyspraxia, and over 25 years' professional experience of working with disabled students in a range of settings. As Chair of NADP and editor of the *Journal of Inclusive Practice in Further and Higher Education*, Nicola is also committed to ensuring that practitioners are informed by the student voice, and that practice is influenced by emancipatory research. She has recently compiled a toolkit to assist colleges and universities to self-assess and action plan for improving provision for students who have AS.

David Pollak is Principal Lecturer in Learning Support at De Montfort University and a National Teaching Fellow (learning support). He was professionally focused on dyslexia for 30 years, in all sectors of education. Working in higher education since 1995, he has recently been acting to raise awareness of neurodiversity. At De Montfort University, he has organized a series of conferences and public lectures on dyslexia and neurodiversity, and frequently speaks at such events in the United Kingdom and on mainland Europe. David's book based on his doctoral thesis, *Dyslexia, the Self and Higher Education: Learning Life Histories of Students Identified as Dyslexic*, is published by Trentham Books. He set up the BRAIN.HE project: 'Best Resources for Achievement and Intervention re Neurodiversity in Higher Education'. He is a member of the Disability Equality Partnership 'think tank' for national disability organizations and the editorial board of the NADP *Journal of Inclusive Practice in Further and Higher Education*.

Heather Symonds is Senior Lecturer (Dyslexia Co-ordinator/Adviser) at London College of Communication, University of the Arts and has been teaching for 26 years. Her diverse audiences have included vocational students, undergraduates from social sciences, humanities and creative arts, which informs her delivery on full-time postgraduate teacher-training programmes. Her curriculum experience includes History, Sociology, Cultural Studies and Communication Skills. Grounded in practice and supported by her work as a Development Officer and as a team member of many higher education validation teams, Heather has a professional and pragmatic approach to teaching, learning and assessment. She has developed resources for accommodated assessment for students with dyslexia, supporting and enabling students to undertake oral assessments in lieu of a written dissertation. Heather held a Teaching and Learning Fellowship and has presented her viva voce research in the United Kingdom, Europe, the United States and Australia. She is a PATOSS registered assessor and is currently undertaking doctoral research.

Clare Trott is a Mathematics Support Tutor within the Mathematics Education Centre at Loughborough University. The Mathematics Education Centre is a designated Centre for Excellence for Teaching and Learning. She specializes in the provision of one-to-one mathematics support for students with dyscalculia and dyslexia. Students are from a range of the University's departments, but all experience difficulties in the mathematical or statistical aspects of their course as a result of their neurodiversity. The teaching involves developing specific techniques and materials for mathematics. Clare's current research interests focus on mathematics and neurodiversity in higher education, particularly dyscalculia and the development of a first-line screener for dyscalculia. Clare has been instrumental in establishing the Dyscalculia and Dyslexia Interest Group, which she continues to coordinate, and The Eureka Centre for Mathematical Confidence, the first such centre in the United Kingdom. Clare is also co-tutor on the Postgraduate Certificate in Mathematics Support and Dyslexia/Dyscalculia in FE/HE.

Foreword

In recent years, we have made significant advances in working towards inclusivity in our approaches to supporting students' learning in universities and colleges, triggered at least partially by legislative drivers in the United Kingdom, the United States, Australia, New Zealand and elsewhere. Initially, we were striving to ensure we did what we had to do, but increasingly we are aiming to go beyond compliance to ensure that students and staff with all kinds of disability are welcomed, challenged and supported to achieve their maximum potential.

That is why I really welcome this contribution to the literature on inclusivity, with its focus on neurodiversity, approached here as a trigger for action rather than a label or diagnosis. Once we move away from seeing *difference* as problematic, we can start welcoming diversity as positive enrichment. Universities have long been havens for neurodiverse individuals, who can find their alternative approaches accepted as tokens of ability rather than markers of deviance, as long as they can survive the rites of passage necessary to graduate and attain higher degrees. The clichés of 'absent-minded professors' and 'brainy boffins' unable to manage day-to-day interactions have their origins in the behaviours of highly intelligent, unconventional people who choose to work in contexts where eccentricity is no bar to achievement. However, the needs of all neurodiverse students need to be recognized and met if we are to provide truly inclusive learning environments.

Much has been written on inclusivity in the last decade, but nothing quite like this radical and ground-breaking edited collection brings together chapters on a range of what are traditionally described as impairments. It is enormously helpful that the text is supported by a website (www.brainhe.com) where illustrations (such as assistive technology) can be viewed. This book is not only for disability specialists; everyone who works to support learning and teaching in higher education (and indeed further education) will benefit from reading and referring students to this volume.

Sally Brown
Pro-Vice-Chancellor
Professor of Diversity of Learning and Teaching in Higher Education
Leeds Metropolitan University
May 2008

Illustrations

Chapter 1
Figure 1.1 UK HESA statistics: selected types of disabled students, 2003–2007   2

Chapter 3
Figure 3.1 Holly's WRAT-IV Reading and Spelling scores and her 4 WAIS-III scores expressed as mean percentile scores   52
Figure 3.2 David's BAS Reading and Spelling scores and his 4 WAIS-III scores expressed as mean percentile scores   53
Figure 3.3 Terry's WRAT-IV Reading and Spelling scores and his 4 WAIS-III scores expressed as mean percentile scores   53
Figure 3.4 Jimmy's WRAT-IV Reading and Spelling scores and his 4 WAIS-III scores expressed as mean percentile scores   54
Figure 3.5 Georgina's WRAT-IV Reading and Spelling scores and her 4 WAIS-III scores expressed as mean percentile scores   55
Figure 3.6 Peter's WRAT-IV Reading and Spelling scores and his 4 WAIS-III scores expressed as mean percentile scores   57
Figure 3.7 Sandra's WRAT-IV Reading and Spelling scores and her 4 WAIS-III scores expressed as mean percentile scores   58
Figure 3.8 Leo's WRAT-IV Reading and Spelling scores and his 4 WAIS-III scores expressed as mean percentile scores   59

Chapter 4
Figure 4.1 Dyslexia in Higher Education   63

Chapter 5
Figure 5.A.1 Penagain   115
Figure 5.A.2 Stabilo pen   116

Figure 5.A.3 Yoro pen   116
Figure 5.A.4 Soft pen/pencil grips   117
Figure 5.A.5 Angled writing surface (and integral file)   117
Figure 5.A.6 Ruler clipboard   118
Figure 5.A.7 Rulers   118
Figure 5.A.8 Scissors   119
Figure 5.A.9 Voice recording pens   119

Chapter 10

Figure 10.1 Mapping the areas that need to be considered
when making assistive technology choices   219
Figure 10.2 Smart Hal   222
Figure 10.3 CapturaTalk   222
Figure 10.4 Olympus DS-40   223
Figure 10.5 Audio Notetaker   224
Figure 10.6 Using Microsoft Word Spell Checker   225
Figure 10.7 Microsoft OneNote   226
Figure 10.8 Laptop with mobile phone   227
Figure 10.9 Laptop stand   227
Figure 10.10 Rivers of text   229
Figure 10.11 VTM Line Reader   229
Figure 10.12 ClaroView   229
Figure 10.13 ReadAble   230
Figure 10.14 ClaroRead for Mac   231
Figure 10.15 Texthelp Read and Write Gold   232
Figure 10.16 Screenshot Reader   233
Figure 10.17 Mind maps made with Inspiration, Mind Genius
and Spark Learner   234
Figure 10.18 ieSpell used with an online text editor   236
Figure 10.19 Tag Cloud   237
Figure 10.20 Tab groups   238

Chapter 11

Table 11.1 Checklist for adjustments to assessment   250
Figure 11.1 Sequence of the design process   254

Chapter 1

Introduction

David Pollak

Why Is This Book Needed and for Whom Is It Intended?

This book is about a variety of types of brain. It comes at an opportune moment in the evolution of higher education (HE), as a growing number of neurodiverse students enter our universities. We can see this if we take dyslexia as an example. Between 1995 and 2005, numbers of known dyslexic students in UK HE increased by a factor of 10 (HESA, 2008a). Anecdotally, similar increases have been noted in the United States, Canada and Australia, although such detailed centralized statistics are not recorded in those countries. In the United Kingdom, the chain of events leading to this increase began with the expansion of awareness since the 1981 Education Act, which led to improved support for school students. From 1993 to 1995, the Higher Education Funding Council financed large numbers of special initiatives aimed at improving provision for students defined as disabled. Dyslexic people ceased to believe that HE was not for them. The flexible university arrangements, which seemed so far-fetched when proposed by a UK working party report in the 1970s (Kershaw, 1974), began to become a reality.

Subsequent legislation has continued this process. The United Kingdom followed the model of the Americans with Disabilities Act 1990 when it passed the Disability Discrimination Act (DDA) 1995 (HMSO, 1995). Dyslexia (or 'learning disability' in the United States) was included under the heading of disability. When this legislation was extended in the United Kingdom explicitly to apply to educational institutions (in the DDA Part 4, HMSO, 2001), it became illegal for these to discriminate against disabled students; higher education institutions (HEIs) began to come to terms with the need for 'reasonable adjustments'.

The experience of dyslexic students, and of universities in responding to their increased presence, is now true of a much wider range of students identified with specific learning differences. Writing of the treatment of autistic school students, Powell (2003, p. 4) states: 'Individuals who less than 20 years ago would have been described by those in authority as mystifyingly odd, and who would have had little formal schooling of an appropriate kind, and therefore little opportunity of progressing into further or higher education, are now ... proving themselves able to gain access to higher education, and potentially to be successful within it.' Universities in the United States, Canada and Australia, as well as in the United Kingdom, are enrolling ever-increasing numbers of people identified with Asperger's Syndrome. The same applies to students who need support with mental well-being. UK statistics (HESA, 2008a) show the increases (see Figure 1.1).

Numbers of UK-domiciled HE students known to be on the autistic spectrum increased by a factor of almost six over this period. There are various limitations to these statistics:

- They refer to UK-domiciled students only.
- They include only those who have disclosed a disability to their universities.
- Other types of learning difference, such as dyspraxia, are included under the broad category of 'other disability', which includes health issues such as diabetes and epilepsy.

Nevertheless, the trend is clear. Where is the HE sector to turn for information about these students? Publications about learning differences have tended to be focused on children. Recent years have seen some books on dyslexia in HE (Riddick, Farmer and Sterling, 1997; Hunter-

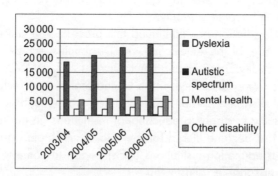

Figure 1.1 UK HESA statistics: selected types of disabled students, 2003–2007

Carsch and Herrington, 2001; Farmer, Riddick and Sterling, 2002; Pollak, 2005) and a practical handbook on Asperger's Syndrome (Jamieson and Jamieson, 2004). Internet information has been collated by a UK-based project (BRAIN.HE, 2008), which includes online conference papers on many of the types of students covered by this book; the number (and location) of visitors received by the project web site shows that there is worldwide interest in neurodiversity in HE. The project also carried out qualitative research with a wide variety of students (Griffin and Pollak, 2008). One theme running through the interview data was the extent to which the HE experiences of students identified with many types of learning difference were similar; another was the need for greater staff awareness of learning differences in general and inclusive practices in particular (see Chapters 11 and 12).

But there is not enough accessible information focused on neurodiversity in HE. This book is therefore for lecturers, support staff, HE managers and policy makers. It is unique in bringing together information about such a wide range of students.

The HE Context

In the academic year 1995–1996, there were approximately 1.5 million students in HE in the United Kingdom; by 2005–2006, numbers had risen to 2.5 million (HESA, 2008b). In Australia, total numbers increased from 634,000 in 1996 to almost one million in 2003 (Universitiesaustralia 2005). Anecdotal evidence suggests that similar increases are taking place in the United States. During the same period, the United States, Canada, Australia, New Zealand and the United Kingdom all enacted significant and wide-reaching legislation concerning disability, both in society in general and in education. This has had the effect of 'raising the profile' of inclusivity issues. The current trend is towards the unification of equality and diversity legislation and policy; the UK Equality Act (HMSO, 2006) was passed in 2006, and the Higher Education Academy has a Single Equality Scheme (HEA, 2008).

Such national initiatives also have the effect of provoking a re-examination of the very nature of HE, but this comes at a time when staff morale is being undermined, not only by increased student numbers but also by managerialism and marketization, with its concomitant bureaucracy. Equality and disability legislation also has the potential to conflict with academic and professional competency standards, an issue which will be examined in Chapter 12.

Language

This area will be discussed at some length, because it reveals a great deal about attitudes and beliefs.

The term 'neurodiversity' is relatively new. It was coined by autistic people in the United States in the 1990s (Harmon, 2004), with the aim of suggesting that far from being disabled or abnormal, people with atypical brain 'wiring' are as entitled to respect as anyone else, and that everyone can be placed on a range of spectrums. This book uses the term for that reason, and also because it believes in the adage 'nothing about us without us'. If the people concerned prefer the term neurodiversity, then those writing about them should adopt it; more importantly, those writing about the subject should be people who experience it themselves (and several of the authors in this book do). There is another reason for using the word 'neurodiversity': it is possible to include more types of student within its definition than are covered by the expression 'specific learning difference'. For example, the current view proposed by influential publications such as the Diagnostic and Statistical Manual of Mental Disorders (American Psychiatric Association, 1994) is that Asperger's Syndrome and Attention Deficit (Hyperactivity) Disorder (AD(H)D) are not learning differences but developmental disorders. In the mid-twentieth century, dyslexia was viewed in that way (Miles and Miles, 1999) – that is, as a medical matter rather than an educational one. This book proposes that in terms of HE, all types of neurodiversity constitute learning differences.

The value of the term 'neurodiversity' has been a cause of some disagreement among autistic people, centred on a polarization between those who seek some kind of 'cure' for autism and those who reject such thinking (www.neurodiversity.com). Anecdotally, there are some in HE in the United Kingdom who doubt the validity of the term, either on the basis that it does not avoid sounding medical, or because it is too 'liberal' and potentially distracts attention from the needs of a group of disabled people.

Language in the field of disability and learning difference is rightly seen as a highly sensitive matter. As with a medical model of disability, people identified with learning differences can be described as having 'disorders', 'deficits' and 'dysfunctions' – their differences can be seen as within-person problems, which they have to overcome (e.g. Snowling, 2000 in respect of dyslexia). On the other hand, a social model of learning difference proposes that if there is a problem, it is one for educational institutions; the disability of neurodiversity is socially constructed by the practices of HEIs and indeed by society in general (BRAIN.HE, 2008; DANDA, 2008). That is broadly speaking the stance adopted by this book, and is also the reason why the expression 'specific learning *difference*' is used, rather than 'specific learning *difficulty*'. The use of the word 'difficulty' places the problem within the person.

The definition of neurodiversity offered by Grant (Chapter 3) is comprehensive. Definitions of that kind will, however, always tend to be 'work in progress'. It may be that in the future, terminology preferred by those outside the world of education speaks of 'specific processing differences' or 'specific cognitive differences'.

However, just as the social model of disability does not deny the existence of impairments (Oliver, 1990), this book does not seek to suggest that all aspects of the experience of neurodiversity are easy for people to live with. It remains essential to give careful consideration to the way these things are described. Etymologically, the word 'impairment' is derived from the Latin for 'worsen', and is generally taken to refer to a diminution of strength, value or quality. In the context of disability, Barnes (1996) explains that while the earlier construction of the term focused on physical mechanisms, the definition has broadened to include learning and mental well-being issues. (For a different interpretation of the ideological aspects of the use of the word 'impairment', see Chapter 7.) Nevertheless, there are those who believe that use of the term 'neurodiversity' implies equal respect for all to the extent that the word 'impairment' is not required. In this field, there is virtually no vocabulary which has universal support, but there is agreement that under a social model, disability results from social organization, whether a person is a wheelchair user, partially sighted or dyspraxic.

Another term which is sometimes controversial is the word 'diagnosis'. For most people, this is a word associated with a medical context, but educational psychologists and other professionals have been using it for decades in connection with the identification of learning difference. The *Shorter Oxford English Dictionary* (Trumble, 2002) ('shorter' in that it consists of only two weighty tomes rather than 12) gives the chief definition of 'diagnosis' as 'the process of determining the nature of a disease'. But it also offers a figurative definition: '(a conclusion from) analysis', which is tolerable by those who favour a social model. Nevertheless, in the context of neurodiversity, it is easy to substitute the word 'identification'.

The same professionals often use the term 'comorbidity' to refer to a person identified with more than one learning difference. Etymologically, that means 'having more than one illness', and hence will not be used in this book. Another word which will not be used is 'suffering', as in 'suffering from dyspraxia'. A more dignified alternative is 'experiencing'. Similarly, the word 'indicators' will be used rather than 'symptoms'.

Many types of neurodiversity are referred to as 'conditions'. This is a term which also sounds medical, and the *Oxford Dictionary* indeed gives a specific definition of 'condition' as 'a state resulting from a physical or mental illness'. However, the lead definition for that strand of the entry is 'state, mode of being', and as such it is acceptable.

Sometimes, the effort to avoid language which pathologizes people can result in the clumsy use of extra words (and of course the decision as to what makes for clumsiness is subjective). Does the expression 'dyspraxic person' put the dyspraxia first and the person second, semantically as well as syntactically? Is it therefore better to say 'person with dyspraxia'? This raises the issue of the word 'with', as this is again quasi-medical, resembling as it does expressions such as 'man with tuberculosis'. An important factor is the nature of the speaker (or writer). Ross Cooper (see Chapter 4) uses the term 'dyslexics', but he is dyslexic himself; it can appear offensive for someone who is not dyslexic to generalize about people in that way.

In some cases, the people involved have again coined their own terms. Some Americans identified with Asperger's Syndrome refer to themselves as 'Aspies' (Willey, 1999), just as other Americans prefer 'ADDers' to 'people with Attention Deficit Disorder'. These terms do not meet with universal approval; those who regard themselves as disabled (and hence entitled to any adjustments prescribed by law) tend to dismiss language which sounds 'liberal' or what is known in the United Kingdom as 'politically correct'. At a UK conference on mental health in HE (UUK/HEA, 2006), it was suggested by some of the students present that they preferred to speak of 'mental well-being' rather than 'mental illness'. This raises a problem as regards ways of referring to people. It is currently fashionable in the United Kingdom to use the word 'issues', as in 'he has mental health issues' rather than 'he is mentally ill'. The case for referring to 'service users' in this context, rather than 'patients', is clear-cut; it is simply more powerful, just as 'wheelchair user' is more powerful than the dreadful expressions 'wheelchair-bound' or even worse, 'confined to a wheelchair'. But what about 'person with mental well-being issues'? Is this akin to 'waste disposal operative'? The answer is no, because it is not a simple euphemism; it is a genuine attempt to avoid pathologizing people. But at the time of writing, the way forward remains unclear. Chapter 8 in this book uses the term 'ADDer' as both a handy abbreviation and a student-friendly locution.

In his discussion of the place of religion in society, Dawkins (2006) uses a card-playing analogy: do the sensitivities of religious people 'trump' (i.e. have superior power to) the views of nonbelievers? In the same vein, which attitude to neurodiversity language should predominate? In the case of dyspraxia and dyscalculia, there are no equivalent terms to 'ADDer' or 'Aspie' (although, as Chapter 5 shows, there is some debate about the expression 'developmental coordination disorder'). However, this book broadly favours user-friendly (or rather, neurodiversity-friendly) terminology.

It is necessary to reflect upon one further term: the adjective 'neurodiverse'. If the noun 'neurodiversity' is valuable, why not refer to individuals by such an adjective? An Internet search (in March 2008) showed that the term was being used by autistic people. Its use by others may nevertheless be problematic; in terms of 'othering' a person, is stating 'she is neurodiverse' the same as stating 'she has a specific learning difference'? Are we not all 'neurodiverse'? Readers may well recognize aspects of themselves in some chapters of this book, because individual indicators of each type of neurodiversity may be experienced by anyone. Each label applies mainly to people who experience most of its key indicators, all the time.

There are types of neurodiversity which have been omitted from this book for reasons of space: Tourette's Syndrome and stroke survival are prime examples. Students who experience these are present in HE, and there is a need for staff awareness regarding them. Psychologists seem to enjoy coining new labels for people, and some students are being labelled with 'dysgraphia' and 'dysorthographia', which are also not included in this book.

Labelling in itself has advantages and disadvantages. In respect of the label 'dyslexic', various studies have pointed out that it can serve as both an explanation and a source of hope (Miles, 1993; Riddick, Farmer and Sterling, 1997; Pollak, 2005). Several informants of the BRAIN.HE project (Griffin and Pollak, 2008) said the same about a variety of types of neurodiversity. However, a book such as this could be said to be perpetuating the use of such labels. Powell (2003, pp. 5–6) comments that a book with chapters on different types of 'special need' may serve to confirm the view that certain individuals are different, rather than promoting the concept of inclusive practice for all. On the contrary, the authors of this book agree with Powell's subsequent comment (2003, p. 6): 'If the goal of inclusion is to be attained, it will only be by considering the specifics of need as well as a pedagogy for all.' Greater awareness and understanding of such specifics, and particularly the themes which run through them, has enormous potential for increasing the ability of all educational institutions to provide truly inclusive learning and teaching. (See Chapters 11 and 12 for a discussion of the overlaps between types of neurodiversity, and of accessible and inclusive practice in HE.)

University staff have to deal with large numbers of students, who are heterogeneous in many different ways. Lecturers are of course aware of the need to retain students and to maximize their attainment. They therefore want to develop and deliver courses which meet the students' needs; they are also aware of the pressures of a number of agendas, such as the particular requirements of international students, mature students and those who have enrolled through widening participation initiatives. This book proposes not only that members of all of those groups may be 'neurodiverse'. Its principal point is that learning, teaching and assessment approaches which are inclusive of neurodiversity are beneficial to all.

Contents of the Book

The authors of this book bring a lifetime's experience to the task, in all cases in a professional context and in many cases from a personal point of view as well. The book can be read as a complete volume, but it is envisaged that many readers will prefer to select chapters which particularly interest them. There is occasional overlap between some chapters, for example, with regard to accessible learning and teaching practices and models of learning difference.

Conferences about particular types of students generally benefit from the inclusion of presentations, or panel discussions, by representatives of the kind of student under discussion. The approach taken in this book is to include the student voice in most of the chapters.

Chapters 2 and 3 set the scene by providing an overview of current policy and practice. In Chapter 2, Alan Hurst explores models of disability, policy drivers and the legal position which affects neurodiversity in HE at this time. Although the focus of this chapter is on UK disability legislation, the chapter will be of value to readers in any country where the legal position is similar. The core of Chapter 3 is the role of the chartered psychologist in providing formal identification of neurodiversity in an individual. David Grant shows how this work can be supportive for students; he uses case studies and quotations from students to explain the variety of neurocognitive profiles exhibited by the subjects of this book. Grant also proposes a definition of neurodiversity.

Chapters 4–9 are each focused on a particular type of neurodiversity. Ross Cooper (Chapter 4) presents a highly distinctive and challenging view of dyslexia. He offers what he calls a social-interactive model, calling upon universities to remove barriers to learning. Cooper's use of his own experience makes this a powerful argument. In Chapter 5, Sharon Drew gives practical examples regarding dyspraxia, which add usefully to the coverage of it in Chapter 3. She provides a concise checklist of indicators and a longer one for screening purposes. The chapter also includes many 'tips' for lecturers and advice for students on useful equipment.

Chapter 6 is a valuable addition to the paucity of information about dyscalculia in adults and in HE. The field of screening for dyscalculia in students of any age is very new; Clare Trott describes 'cutting-edge' work on a computer-based, HE-specific screening tool. She also presents plentiful examples of student voices and practical examples of supportive approaches. In Chapter 7, Nicola Martin challenges the 'triad of impairments' model of Asperger's Syndrome by suggesting that university staff might themselves exhibit such a triad in attempting to deliver good communication, flexibility and socially appropriate experiences to students. Her distinctive style of writing draws the reader into the world of an Aspie.

In Chapter 8, this book again presents an author with a distinctive style. Like Chapter 7, it offers a vivid portrayal of the experience of a type of neurodiversity, in this case AD(H)D. Mary Colley draws on her own experience in a variety of roles to explain not only the nature of AD(H)D, but also the kind of supportive practice which can be specific to it (such as medication, coaching and cognitive behavioural therapy).

Kitty McCrea (Chapter 9) covers mental well-being. Experiences such as depression have clear effects on people's ability to study, and are covered in the United Kingdom by disability legislation. The inclusion of this topic in a book on neurodiversity may be surprising, but the key point is that in the present climate, the kinds of students covered by this book often struggle to maintain their mental well-being. Chapter 9 points out that poor educational experiences before university, as well as during a course, can often lead to reduced mental well-being in a variety of ways. It makes clear that university marketing material should make positive statements about the institution's commitment to mental health, and provides many practical examples of ways in which this can be supported.

The next two chapters return to the overview stance adopted by Chapters 2 and 3. In Chapter 10, E.A. Draffan displays an encyclopaedic knowledge of the variety of assistive technology available to students, both mobile and desk-based. She includes many illustrations, informative quotations from students and a practical list of sources for the items covered. In Chapter 11, Heather Symonds addresses the potential mismatch between the way many students think and conventional approaches to learning, teaching and assessment. She picks up the theme of the UK Disability Equality Duty alluded to in Chapter 2 and relates this to curriculum design and strategies for academic assessment. Chapter 11 also covers virtual learning environments.

In the Conclusion (Chapter 12), the editor draws upon the combined insights of the authors to sum up the issues raised in the book. The chapter examines the themes of diversity and inclusion, overlaps between types of neurodiversity, admission and transition, identification, learning and teaching practices, and staff development. It also looks towards the future.

References

American Psychiatric Association (1994) *DSM IV. Diagnostic and Statistical Manual of Mental Disorders* 4th revised edition, A.P.A., Washington.

Barnes, C. (1996) Theories of disability and the origins of oppression of disabled people in western society, in *Disability and Society: Emerging Issues and Insights* (ed. L. Barton), Longman, London.

BRAIN.HE (2008) *Best Resources for Achievement and Intervention re Neurodiversity in Higher Education*, www.brainhe.com (accessed 20 May 2008).

DANDA (2008) *Developmental Adult Neurodiversity Association*, www.danda.org.uk (accessed 27 March 2008).

Dawkins, R. (2006) *The God Delusion*, Houghton Mifflin, Abingdon.

Farmer, M., Riddick, B. and Sterling, C. (2002) *Dyslexia and Inclusion: Assessment and Support in Higher Education*, Wiley, Chichester.

Griffin, E. and Pollak, D. (2008) Student experiences of neurodiversity in higher education: insights from the BRAIN.HE project. *Dyslexia*, **14** (4), in press.

Harmon, A. (2004) Neurodiversity forever: the Disability Movement turns to brains. *New York Times*, 9 May, http://query.nytimes.com/gst/fullpage.html?res=9C07E0D9143CF93AA35756C0A9629C8B63 (accessed 23 May 2008).

HEA (2008) *Single Equality Scheme*, Higher Education Academy, York, www.heacademy.ac.uk (accessed 20 May 2008).

Higher Education Statistics Agency (HESA) (2008a) *Disability 1994–2007*, www.hesa.ac.uk (accessed 23 May 2008).

Higher Education Statistics Agency (HESA) (2008b) *All Students at UK HE Institutions*, www.hesa.ac.uk (accessed 23 May 2008).

HMSO (1995) *Disability Discrimination Act*. Her Majesty's Stationery Office, London.

HMSO (2001) *Special Educational Needs and Disability Act*, Her Majesty's Stationery Office, London.

HMSO (2006) *The Equality Act 2006*, Her Majesty's Stationery Office, London.

Hunter-Carsch, M. and Herrington, M. (eds) (2001) *Dyslexia and Effective Learning in Secondary and Tertiary Education*, Whurr, London.

Jamieson, J. and Jamieson, C. (2004) *Managing Asperger Syndrome at College and University*, David Fulton, London.

Kershaw, J.D. (ed.) (1974) *People With Dyslexia: a report of the British Working Party on the Needs of the Dyslexic Adult*, British Council for the Rehabilitation of the Disabled, London.

Miles, T.R. (1993) *Dyslexia – the Pattern of Difficulties*, Whurr, London.

Miles, T.R. and Miles, E. (1999) *Dyslexia a Hundred Years On*, Open University Press, Buckingham.

Oliver, M. (1990) *The Politics of Disablement*, Macmillan, Basingstoke.

Pollak, D. (2005) *Dyslexia, the Self and Higher Education*, Trentham Books, Stoke-on-Trent.

Powell, S. (ed.) (2003) *Special Teaching in Higher Education, Successful Strategies for Access and Inclusion*, Kogan Page, London.

Riddick, B., Farmer, M. and Sterling, C. (1997) *Students and Dyslexia: Growing up with a Specific Learning Difficulty*, Whurr, London.

Snowling, M. (2000) *Dyslexia*, Blackwell, Oxford.

Trumble, W. (ed.) (2002) *Shorter Oxford English Dictionary*, Oxford University Press, Oxford.

Universitiesaustralia (2005) *Student Characteristics 1996–2003*, www.universitiesaustralia.edu.au (accessed 24 May 2008).

UUK/HEA (2006) *Mental Well-Being and Learning: Exploring the Connections*, Joint Conference on HE, London.

Willey, L.H. (1999) *Pretending to be Normal: Living with Asperger's Syndrome*, Jessica Kingsley, Bristol PA.

Chapter 2

Neurodiversity, Disability, Legislation and Policy Development in the United Kingdom

Alan Hurst

Introduction

Sometimes, those working to support disabled students in higher education (HE) forget that consideration of disabled students in post-compulsory education is a relatively recent phenomenon. It was only in 1974 that the first research study of disabled students in the United Kingdom was published (National Innovations Centre, 1974) and the first specialist national conference organized (the latter leading to the establishment of the National Bureau for Handicapped Students, now known as Skill: National Bureau for Students with Disabilities). Progress has been made, but perhaps more slowly than many would want. Evidence to demonstrate the progress can be provided in several ways. For example, the overall number of students declaring that they have an impairment either on entry or during their time in HE has grown year by year (although in some institutions and within them, in some faculties and departments, there is still the need to improve participation rates). In 1995–1996, there were 448 199 undergraduates in the United Kingdom including both full- and part-time students, of whom 15 754 were known to have a disability. By 2005–2006, these figures had become 711 590, of whom 45 425 had a disability (HESA, 2007). What these basic figures disguise is that, based on HESA categories of disability, there have been slight falls in applications from most groups (e.g. blind students), while those with dyslexia and other forms of neurodiversity rose significantly.

This chapter begins with a brief consideration of factors which have prompted changes in policy. It goes on to consider some principles, which underpin the developments, before exploring anti-discrimination legislation. Following an outline of legislation in other countries, the final section reviews what has happened in the United Kingdom in the two years since the last relevant legislation was passed. Note that the focus is on an overview, which covers the full range of impairments and is not specifically focused on neurodiversity, although at some points particular reference is made to this group of students.

Policy Drivers: A Brief Overview

At the level of policy and provision, there has been a shift in focus since the mid-1990s. From access and increasing numbers, which appeared to be the major focus of the first national survey of disabled students in UK universities (NIC, 1974), the major concern has become the quality of the HE experience, especially in learning, teaching and assessment. Policy drivers for this include the projects and initiatives supported by both the English and Scottish Higher Education Funding Councils, the publication and implementation of the Quality Assurance Agency Code of Practice (QAA, 1999), and the post-Dearing introduction of the Institute for Learning and Teaching in Higher Education (ILTHE) (now the Higher Education Academy (HEA)), some of whose subject networks/subject centres have published very useful guides about the inclusion of disabled students in their curricula (e.g. in engineering, geography, hospitality/travel/tourism, social work and veterinary medicine).

Linked to this has been improved financial provision. Following the modified structure introduced in 1990, Disabled Students' Allowances have increased in line with inflation and have also been extended to encompass groups such as part-time students who had been excluded under the original system. Thus, for students entering HE in 2008–2009, the UK government has raised the amount available to support nonmedical personal assistance by 60% (from a maximum of £12420 in 2007–2008 to £20000 in 2008, while the overall maximum for post-graduates has gone from £5915 in 2007 to £10000 in 2008). On launching the increases, the then Minister for Lifelong Learning, Further and Higher Education, Bill Rammell said:

We know that there are a small number of disabled students who need a lot of support. We want these students to be able to reap the benefits of higher education. ... Through making the increases to the Disabled Students' Allowances we hope to increase students' access to the types of support which are essential for their continuing success in higher education. (Department for Innovation, Universities and Skills, 2007, Government News Network, 4 July)

In parallel, the national Funding Councils have increased their financial support. The Higher Education Funding Council for England (HEFCE) describes its contribution thus:

Between 1993 and 1999 we supported special disability funding programmes that had the broad aim of widening the participation of students with disabilities in HE. Over 100 projects worth £12 million were funded through these programmes, and significant gains were made by the sector for students with disabilities. Two further specialist funding programmes between 1999 and 2005, totalling over £11 million, supported a range of projects designed to ensure that provision for disabled students was consistent across the sector. During this time, the National Disability Team (NDT) provided hands-on support and advice both to funded projects and to institutions generally. (HEFCE, 2007)

The HEFCE also notes that additional funds have been made available to improve institutions' infrastructures and that since 2000–2001, money has been built into mainstream teaching funding. This has increased from an initial £7 million to £13 million in 2007–2008.

The final drive towards developing high-quality provision for disabled students has been the growth of anti-discrimination legislation. Before considering this in detail, it is necessary to explore some principles underpinning the development of policy and provision.

Models of Disability, Conceptions of Independence and Equality/Equity

Within the field of disabilities, since 1975, there have been important developments in the theoretical approaches which have led to consequent changes in policies and practices. Thirty years ago, the position adopted could be described as the individual/medical/deficit model, which sees all problems and challenges faced by people with impairments as their own. Impairment was viewed as an illness; people were seen as being sick or deficient in some attribute such as hearing, mobility or vision. It was left to the individuals to try to resolve any difficulties themselves, often with the help of charities, social services and the medical profession. Within HE in the early days, this was reflected in the close involvement of university medical staff in the development of policy and provision (Hurst, 1993). It is also important to note the comparative absence of reference to neurodiversity in these early days. A significant matter for neurodiversity and disabled students is that their impairment is usually not obvious to others on first meeting. This situation is often made worse by the traditional images of disability used by institutions/organizations in their publicity devised to recruit disabled students. Using pictures of wheelchair users or blind students with guide dogs is not helpful to those whose impairments are invisible.

In the late 1970s/early 1980s, a group of disabled people proposed the replacement of the original model with what was described as the social/educational/political model of disability. From this perspective, the difficulties and challenges faced by people with impairments result from the social construction of society. For example, for people with mobility impairments, problems of access to public buildings and public transport are created by the design of these facilities. This has now become recognized more widely and in the United Kingdom, anti-discrimination legislation has tried to ensure that access to public facilities is guaranteed. In more recent times, there have been criticisms of the social/educational/medical model because of its lack of recognition of the impact of an impairment on individuals, for instance, with respect to the pain and discomfort experienced by them (Shakespeare and Watson, 2001). There has also been some suggestion that the model has become the new orthodoxy and is not open to challenges (Low, 2001).

Within UK HE, there are still remnants of the individual/medical/deficit model. For example, the standard application form used by the majority of those wanting to enter universities asks applicants to indicate the nature of their impairment by using a numerical coding system. They can place themselves in various categories such as blind or D/deaf, where the term Deaf denotes those who identify with a cultural or linguistic minority. Were the system to move towards a genuine social/educational model, the categories would need to be written to allow users to indicate areas of difficulty, for example, with printed materials or oral work. Institutions would then need to consider how these difficulties might be addressed and minimized. The onus of responsibility shifts from individual students to the institutions and the staff they employ. Dyslexia provides a clear example of such a transfer. If dyslexia is regarded as a 'specific learning difficulty', the impairment is individualized. However, if following the work of Neanon (2002), dyslexia is regarded as a learning *difference*, then it becomes the responsibility of well-trained professional tutors to use and adapt their skills to meet the needs of students whose way of learning is not the same as others. Good training ought to prepare classroom practitioners for working with a wide range of learning needs and styles. A further example of the shift in the UK HE sector to a social/educational/political model is the increased focus on inclusive curriculum design and pedagogy, a matter discussed in more detail towards the end of this chapter.

With regard to conceptions of independence and independent living, two principles in particular are important: the principle of having choices and the principle of having the right to take decisions about one's own life. Firstly, it is important to ensure that disabled students experience the same levels of choice of what and where to study as their nondisabled peers. Occasionally, in connection with choice, a case is proposed for establishing 'centres of excellence'. This would mean that in every region, one institution would develop high-quality policy and provision for those with a particular impairment, while its neighbours would choose a different impairment on which to base their support facilities. Such an approach has a particular appeal when there is a focus on supposed cost-effectiveness, although this concept seems to assume that it is often the cheapest alternative and ignores the related notion of value-for-money. The overall approach is unsound and unacceptable. It places restrictions on choices. It assumes also that studying the same subject in different universities is identical in relation to subject content, core knowledge and available options.

Secondly, disabled people have the right to take decisions about their own lives. It is no longer acceptable to inform students that the institution does not think they can complete the course for which they are applying. The situation has changed, since new laws make it illegal to discriminate solely on grounds of disability. Also, each applicant must be treated on an individual basis; blanket exclusions such as 'no blind students can do chemistry' are illegal. So, if an applicant is rejected for a place on a course, it is necessary to provide sound reasons for the decision if the institution wishes to avoid possible litigation. This does not mean that there is unlimited access for those with disabilities. What it does mean is that institutions need to be very clear about why an application from a disabled person has been rejected. One approach to this is to identify the core requirements of a study programme and to investigate whether the applicant might meet these, with some modifications to the course. This is another point which will be explored further in a later section of this chapter.

Finally, as will be seen, there has been an important focus on the concept of equality. Yet, it might be argued that this is not really at the core of the changes. Rather, the latter are about equity. It is the difference between treating people the same (equally) and treating them according to their situation (fairly). Taking the simple example of a cake which has to be divided between a group of people, if slices are based on equality, all would get the same irrespective of whether the size of each slice is appropriate to the context and the individual. For instance, dividing a small sponge cake between a large group would result in everyone getting little more than crumbs. In this example, equal treatment for all could be unfair to some. Applying the principle of equity/fairness, it might be agreed that, because of their position, some will be given more than others. In relation to the example of the cake, some of the recipients may not have eaten for some time, so it would be agreed that they deserve more than others. Perhaps this is really what is at the core of the legislation and the policies to be discussed below.

The Disability Discrimination Act (DDA) 1995

Unlike other groups, such as women and people from minority communities, who might experience discrimination and who have had anti-discrimination laws protecting them since the mid-1970s, it was not until 1995 that legal protection for people with disabilities was provided. The law was needed for several reasons. Firstly, only half as many disabled people of working age are in employment compared to those without disabilities. Secondly, progressing in education and obtaining training and qualifications reduce the unemployment statistics for disabled people. Thirdly, disabled people in employment become less reliant on state benefits and in fact contribute to the state through taxation.

The UK DDA 1995 begins by defining 'disability'. According to the law, this is

a physical or mental impairment which has a substantial and long-term effect on the person's ability to carry out normal day-to-day activities.

It also defines discrimination as treating an individual unfairly compared to people without disabilities because of the person's impairment. Organizations have to make 'reasonable adjustments' in order to allow and facilitate access to their goods and services for disabled people. They also have to act in anticipatory ways rather than responding in an *ad hoc* reactive manner to a situation when it arises. For instance, while so far there might never have been the need to provide printed information in various formats, organizations need to plan for a future in which they will encounter people with visual impairments. When the Act was passed by Parliament, the main concerns were access to employment, and to goods and services. Policy and provision in education was not covered by this law, although it did require institutions to devise and publish Disability Statements. This was an attempt to improve the quality of information available to disabled people. (For a detailed review of Disability Statements, see HEFCE, 1998. This is also relevant to the discussion on the Disability Equality Schemes, which follows shortly.) It took another six years for the law to be extended to embrace policy and provision in schools, colleges and universities.

The Special Educational Needs and Disability Act (SENDA) 2001

The SENDA became law in 2001. In effect, this is Part 4 of the DDA. It uses the same definitions of disability and of discrimination, and the same requirements for 'reasonable adjustments' and anticipatory duties are now placed on schools/colleges/universities. Auxiliary aids and services and the physical environment are also included. Within HE, all services are covered by the law, including learning, teaching and assessment, distance and e-learning, and partnership and overseas provision. Discrimination can be avoided by making 'reasonable adjustments' and also by complying with the anticipatory requirement of the SENDA. Reasonable adjustments might be needed in relation to applications and admissions procedures, learning, teaching and academic assessment practices, work placements and the physical environment. Changes should not be made as a direct result of enrolling a student with a disability; rather, those responsible for the course should have planned in advance what they need to do to make the course accessible and inclusive. There is a key role here for staff training and the development of high levels of disability awareness, since the provision of such training could be central to any defence if discrimination is alleged.

There are some key questions which relate to this legislation:

1. What is the position regarding the rejection of applications from disabled
    students?
    Within the law, it remains possible to refuse entry to a student with a disability
    on a number of grounds. Firstly, the decision might be based on the need to
    maintain academic standards. However, in order not to put themselves at risk,
    course teams and admissions tutors need to be clear about the criteria used to
    select students. Secondly, the decision might stem from there being parts of
    courses which are a basic requirement but which some students with disabilities
    might be unable to complete and where 'reasonable adjustments' cannot be
    made. This is often linked to the involvement of external professional and
    regulatory bodies. Thirdly, the decision might result from 'reasonable
    adjustments' that would be 'material' and 'substantial', perhaps involving high
    costs within a very restricted budget.
2. Has discrimination occurred?
    If discrimination is alleged to have taken place, there are key issues to
    consider. Firstly, the individual needs to have a disability as defined by the
    law. Secondly, are the services covered by the law? Thirdly, has there been
    either less favourable treatment or lack of 'reasonable adjustment'? Fourthly,
    has the student disclosed a disability? If the institution can prove that the
    individual did not disclose, it is unlikely that the allegation can be sustained.
    However, institutions have a responsibility to ensure that students have several
    opportunities to disclose information about their disability. In itself this raises
    further questions, since there are issues about who the information is disclosed
    to and whether the individual asks that the information remains confidential,
    since confidentiality requests are seen as 'reasonable adjustments'. Specific
    guidance on matters relating to disclosure has been issued (DfES, 2002) as
    well as some useful general information (LSC, 2003; Skill, 2005; Rose, 2006).
3. How are individual rights and institutional responsibilities balanced?
    The law tries to balance individual rights and institutional responsibilities.
    Institutions must take reasonable steps to find out about people's disabilities
    and then respect any subsequent requests for confidentiality, even if this affects
    their ability to make reasonable adjustments. This raises the issue of disclosure.
    Institutions must encourage students to disclose their disability using as many
    opportunities as possible. They must also review what happens to the
    information and conform to data protection law. Disclosure is linked also to risk
    assessment. Some students choose not to disclose because they fear that they
    will be prevented from doing what they want because of the need to comply
    with health and safety laws. The DDA recognizes the need for risk assessment,
    but says that it should not be used in a dishonest way to avoid admitting
    students and making reasonable adjustments.
4. What can be learnt from case law and conciliation?
    Where students and institutions cannot agree on an issue in the United
    Kingdom, the former Disability Rights Commission (DRC) (now part of the

Equality and Human Rights Commission) (EHRC, 2008) was sometimes invited to become involved to seek conciliation. This has happened where reasonable adjustments have not been put in place or have not been there in time despite appropriate advance notice; conciliation has been needed where there has been a lack of sensitivity and respect for confidential information. The result has been that senior staff have been required to make a public apology, give assurances that the institution has learnt from the experience, agree to introduce formal staff development including disability equality training, review relevant policies and procedures, and pay financial compensation for distress and hurt feelings.

The DDA 2005

The most recent UK legislation is the DDA 2005 (HMSO, 2005). This includes changes to the definition of disability to cover more impairments and also changes affecting access to employment and to goods and services. There are general duties such as the ending of discrimination and of harassment, and also specific duties. The Act covers both students and staff, and so it might be seen as a 'whole-institution approach' to eliminate discrimination (ECU, 2005a). The most important specific duty for colleges and universities is that they have to compile and publish a Disability Equality Scheme (DES), a three-year plan which must involve disabled people in its compilation, and which must demonstrate how policies and provision have had an impact on disabled people and how the scheme will be checked. The DES has to be updated annually and a short report on progress has to be published. Impact assessments will have to be done on all existing policies and procedures to ensure that universities and colleges take into account any poor-quality decisions they have made in the past (see Skill, 2005 for a more detailed outline of the legislation).

The latest legislation poses several questions. To begin with, there are concerns about some concepts and definitions such as the concept of 'equality'. To return to the point made earlier, perhaps what is being sought is 'equity' in the sense of being fair. This could lead to some unequal treatment in the sense of what in the United States is called affirmative action. Indeed, the DDA 2005 suggests that there might be unequal treatment, in that higher education institutions (HEIs) must take into account disabled people's needs, even if this means treating disabled people more favourably. In that sense, the DDA contains a contradiction. Perhaps the United Kingdom should follow the example of Australia, where an important report was called 'A Fair Go' and where institutions publish equity plans to obtain funding (Shaw, 1998).

Secondly, 'involvement' – what does it mean? Can it be measured and quantified? What is it that people are involved in? Being 'involved' will mean disclosure, so what about those staff and students who prefer to keep information about their impairments confidential? (ECU, 2005c) To reiterate the point made already, this might be more significant for those in focus in this book whose impairments are unseen, but if people with unseen impairments are not involved, then the process of meeting the Disabity Equality Duty (DED) and of devising a DES will contribute to the continuation of stereotyped images of impairment.

Thirdly, there is the notion of 'impact'. Impact assessments have to be carried out, but how is impact to be measured and evaluated? How will distinctions be made between short-term and long-term and between temporary and permanent impacts?

If one looks in detail at the DED and the DES, it appears that there is a wide range of variables potentially affecting the experiences of both staff and students with impairments. Can these be recognized and taken into account? For example, there is the size and scope of the HEI, the subject/course/programme in which staff are employed and students are enrolled, the mode of employment/study (part-time, full-time), the type of impairment, the age, sex and community background of the individual.

The conclusion must be that the field is too broad to provide meaningful data. This seems to be acknowledged in guidance from the United Kingdom's Equality Challenge Unit (ECU, 2005b). Paragraph 20 says:

Disabled people are not a homogeneous group. They have multiple identities and other aspects of their identities may influence outcomes. Data on the number of disabled people with a black or ethnic minority background, the number of disabled women or the age of disabled staff, for example, will potentially be very useful when pursuing lines of enquiry about discrimination against particular groups.

Also, there is the fluidity of data. The ECU quite rightly reminds us (Paragraph 11) that:

Disability is dynamic and relative to environment so data relating to the percentage of disabled people within an institution needs to be dynamically collected and maintained.   (ECU, 2005b)

Finally, there is the monitoring of the DES, especially the annual updates which the law requires institutions to publish. As will be mentioned below, the ECU did undertake a small-scale survey in 2007, the results of which could be seen to be a cause for concern, most notably the fact that the majority of the DES's reviewed did not comply with legal requirements. Monitoring and policing the implementation of the law could be made more difficult as a result of the demise of the DRC. The question remains about whose responsibility it is to check whether institutions have devised and published their annual updates.

What Is Happening Elsewhere in the World? A Brief Outline of Developments

Finding out about what is happening in other places is helpful in three ways. Firstly, it can be used to develop and enhance the policies and practices already in place. Secondly, it can offer reassurance about possible progress. Thirdly, it involves gathering information for staff and students who might wish to take part in international exchanges.

With regard to anti-discrimination laws, there are a growing number of countries where these exist. As in the United Kingdom, these laws are concerned to ensure that disabled people enter HE on the same basis as everyone else, this basis being reached partly by making reasonable adjustments (known as 'accommodations' in some countries, although using this term in the United Kingdom could lead to confusion, since the same word is used to refer to where students live) and partly by changing attitudes, cultures and policies. Perhaps the best known is the United States of America which started legislation in the 1970s with the Rehabilitation Act 1973, then the Education of All Handicapped Children Act 1975 and, more recently, the Americans with Disabilities Act 1990. The key part of the latter is Section 504, which states:

> *No otherwise qualified individual with a disability shall, solely by reason of his or her disability, be excluded from participation in, be denied the benefits of, or be subjected to discrimination under any program or activity of a public entity.* (Americans with Disabilities Act 1990)

'Otherwise qualified' means that the individual must meet all the other criteria for admission to the study programme.

Other countries have followed the American example, although progress has also been made using other legislation. For instance, in New Zealand, a group of students (note that this was a class action rather than an individual student) successfully used the Human Rights Act against the University of Wellington concerning the location of a session in a room that was inaccessible to a disabled student. In Ireland, there has been a series of laws since 1998, all of which impact on policy and provision for disabled students. The earliest of these was the Employment Equality Act 1998 (revised 2004), followed by the Qualifications (Education and Training) Act 1999, the Equal Status Act (revised 2004), the Education for Persons with Special Needs Act 2004 and finally the Disability Act 2005.

As in the United Kingdom, some countries have devised codes of practice. A code of practice on working with disabled students was published in Australia in 1998. This contains examples from named institutions of good practices on several aspects of provision (e.g. admissions and record keeping). The Code of Practice published by the Quality Assurance Agency (QAA) for Higher Education in England appeared in 1999 and offers general advice based on a collection of basic precepts with no illustrative examples. Both codes are permissive rather than compulsory although in the United Kingdom, if there is a dispute between an institution and a student and the former has not implemented the Code of Practice, it might be required to justify its decision. The QAA Code of Practice is being updated at the time of writing.

Moving to national coordination, probably the first country to appoint a national coordinator was Sweden in 1996, followed shortly afterwards by Scotland. The approach in England was to appoint a small team of experienced staff whose main responsibility was to monitor the special initiative projects funded by the HEFCE. This developed into the National Disability Team, which was disbanded at the end of 2005; its work is being taken forward by the HE Academy, the ECU and the Action on Access Team.

Developments in Policy and Provision 2005–2007

Following the approach adopted by Professor Will Swan when opening the Open University's annual staff conference for those working with disabled students in November 2007, this section might be called more appropriately, using the title of a song by Ian Dury and the Blockheads, 'Reasons to be Cheerful'. Indeed, for the immediate future, there are a number of developments that hold promise for the continuing development of high-quality policy and provision for disabled students.

Firstly, despite the abolition of the National Disability Team in England in 2005–2006, policy makers have continued to demonstrate strong interest in disabled students. As part of mainstreaming as many policies as possible, responsibility for monitoring and promoting the interests of disabled students is shared between three bodies: Action on Access (whose remit is about widening participation more generally rather than working with disabled students only), the ECU (an organization set up in 2001 as a joint enterprise between universities and the national funding councils; as with Action on Access, it embraces all dimensions of equality/inequality), and the HEA (which took on the responsibilities of the former ILTHE and the subject networks, and has appointed specialist advisers on disability). Action on Access produces and circulates a regular news bulletin, while the HEA works closely with its subject centres and its Centres of Excellence in Teaching and Learning to ensure that the needs of disabled learners are not overlooked.

Arguably, the ECU has been the most obviously active of the three partners by publishing a number of guides advising institutions on how to meet the requirements of the new anti-discrimination legislation. More recently, the ECU was given responsibility for a small-scale evaluation of a sample of Disability Equality Schemes (ECU, 2007). The latter is important since many wondered what would happen to the institutions' DES after publication. The study found much to celebrate (e.g. the collection of accurate statistics on admission, retention and progression of disabled students, successful ways of undertaking impact assessments, and the active involvement of disabled students, disabled staff and disabled people in the local community in the process of compiling the DES). However, of the sample of 21 DESs, 13 were found not to comply with the legal requirement, for example, by failing to indicate the priorities raised by disabled people and by failing to show how impact assessment would be addressed. The report considers four major topics: involvement, information gathering, impact assessment and action planning. The report ends by noting that by December 2007, institutions should be reviewing their original DES and action plan, and publishing a progress report and an updated version.

Moving to the second 'reason to be cheerful', the role of the ECU in the DES process was linked closely to the work of the DRC. Shortly before its abolition, the DRC published two important documents: a revised Code of Practice for Post-16 Education Providers (DRC, 2007a) and a guide for colleges, universities and adult community learning providers on the DDA (DRC, 2007b). The DRC itself was abolished in autumn 2007 and merged with the Commission for Equality and Human Rights (CEHR). Alongside this, institutions and organizations are working now on the creation of single equality schemes. One might argue that the DRC was abolished too soon and that within the new CEHR, disability issues could be swamped by concerns about other aspects of equality which involve greater numbers of people (e.g. age, ethnic grouping, gender). Perhaps the unification should be seen as a source of strength, in that it could draw attention to many shared aspects of disadvantage and then become more effective through the power of numbers involved.

The third potentially positive development is the creation of the Office of the Independent Adjudicator for Higher Education (OIAHE). This was set up by the government in response to concerns about the operation of complaints systems in HE. It is interesting to note that in the OIAHE *Annual Report 2006*, disability issues appear at several points. For example, in the opening comments, which consider the extent to which the OIAHE has met its objectives, the Adjudicator says:

> We note that while discrimination and harassment issues rarely feature in complaints, disability remains a major factor. We have found some universities uncertain about the nature of the duties placed on them by the legislation. Essentially, there is insufficient understanding about where responsibility lies for ascertaining disability and what adjustments are required.   (OIAHE, 2006, p. 7)

Subsequently, more is said about disability and the nature of the cases that have involved the OIAHE:

> As access to university has widened, it is only to be expected that, mirroring the general population, more students with disabilities will be present in the universities. The disability most commonly raised in complaints to the OIA is dyslexia. ... New regulations made under the DDA came into force in September 2006. The justification for different treatment that was called 'academic standards' changed to 'competence standards', and the burden of proof was reversed. Under the amended law, the universities are required to plan ahead for the needs of disabled students and to be proactive in encouraging the disclosure of a disability.   (OIAHE, 2006. p. 9)

The OIAHE also provides information about the impairments disclosed by those students who used the OIAHE services. Given the focus of this book, it is interesting to note that over 70% of individuals had impairments relating to neurodiversity (e.g. dyslexia and mental health service users).

Fourthly, it is pleasing to note the growth of interest in disabled students as shown by the research community and those who fund it. In addition to the growing number of papers published in learned journals and to the publication of collected papers, full-scale research investigations have taken place. In Scotland, for example, Sheila Riddell and her team investigated the experiences of disabled students in universities, a project funded by the prestigious Economic and Social Research Council (Riddell, Tinklin and Wilson, 2005). More recently, a Teaching and Learning Research Programme project, involving four institutions and focusing in particular on the learning experiences of disabled students, is coming to an end. Already a number of papers stemming from this have been published (e.g. Fuller, Bradley and Healey, 2004). Shortly before its demise, the DRC itself commissioned some small-scale investigations, for example, about disclosure and access to professions such as nursing, social work and schoolteaching (Stanley *et al.*, 2007). The growing body of research provides valid quantitative and qualitative data on which further progress can be built rather than relying on random, anecdotal data. All of the sources named offer significant information about students with neurologically-based impairments. Remaining with research but looking at a different aspect of it: the various national research funding councils have also been working to ensure that disabled students are not disadvantaged in the competition to secure research awards and that when undertaking research, they have appropriate support. New guidance about research students with disabilities is to be published in 2009.

Following on from the comments on the supervision of research students, the fifth cause to be optimistic about the future is the increased attention being given to what happens in learning and teaching contexts. The impetus for this in the United Kingdom was the Dearing Report (Dearing, 1997) and its desire to achieve a more appropriate balance between the status of research and of teaching in HE. (For a detailed discussion of the Dearing Report's implications for disabled students, see Hurst, 1999.) On the basis of the recommendations, most institutions have made greater efforts to ensure that members of the teaching staff have more opportunities for basic training and for in-service professional development. In many institutions, it is now compulsory for those new to teaching to undergo basic training. More specialist source materials are becoming available to support both initial and continuing professional development, some of which are linked to supporting the kind of students who form the focus of this book (e.g. Hurst,

2006). Often, the basic introductory programmes include aspects of inclusive pedagogy. Alongside this, there have been a number of initiatives designed with a particular focus on disabled students. Perhaps the best known and most successful and effective of these is the 'Teachability' programme funded by the Scottish Higher Education Funding Council (SHEFC) and led by Anne Simpson, Graham Charters and a team based at the University of Strathclyde. Because of its significance, more should be said about this initiative, which at its core is about universal design.

According to Smith and Sowers (2003), the idea of universal design came from architecture and planning, which were concerned to make environments as accessible as possible to all potential users. They cite the example of automatic doors at the entrance to buildings; research showed that when shoppers did not have to struggle to open doors while carrying their purchases, they actually bought more things because they no longer had to worry about leaving the shops.

Returning to universal design and its applicability to education, the 'Teachability' project began in Scotland in the mid-1990s (SHEFC, 2004). It was intended to prompt academic staff to consider ways in which their current classroom practices help or hinder the full participation of students with a range of impairments in their subjects/courses/programmes of study. Staff were reminded that some barriers might stem from the requirements and nature of the subject/course/study programmes themselves. Others might be created as a result of the strategies chosen for use in routine approaches to teaching and learning (e.g. using audio-visual materials and their accessibility to students with sensory impairments). Finally, there are those barriers to participation which result from an unconscious approach to what is done in classrooms as part of the routine daily practices and which might be changed by maintaining heightened levels of sensitivity/awareness (e.g. continuing to talk when turning round to write on the board destroys communication for any students who lip-read).

The 'Teachability' project worked with staff from different academic departments, who were asked to do the following:

1. identify ways in which the subject/course/programme for which they were responsible or with which they were associated closely is accessible to students with a range of impairments;
2. identify barriers to prevent the participation of students with a range of impairments;
3. suggest how these barriers might be overcome;
4. consider what needs to be done in order to implement the strategies identified for overcoming the barriers; and

5. think of ways to draw attention in an honest way to the possibilities and
    challenges posed by subjects/courses/programmes of study.

Experience in Scotland suggested that sometimes staff needed some
assistance at the start of the task. If this was the case, then the initial task
was to agree on what are considered to be the core requirements/core
skills which all should have on completing the subject/course/programme
of study successfully and which are nonnegotiable. (For more details, see
SHEFC, 2004.) Staff were encouraged to think about access to the
curriculum at the point of course design, so that the need for reasonable
adjustments would diminish. Arguably, what the 'Teachability' project did
not give sufficient stress to was the potential power and influence of those
groups responsible for initial validation of courses and for any periodic
reviews. (For more on this, see Chapter 11.) Where this might involve
working in partnership with professional bodies external to the institution, it
is important to note that these bodies are also subject to the requirements
of anti-discrimination law.

The sixth development that could lead to improved policy and provision
is the creation and promotion of an organization for staff working with
disabled students in post-compulsory education. Given that many of these
colleagues work alongside others such as careers advisers and counsellors
who have their own professional organizations, UK staff working with
disabled students lacked a structure and framework within which to base
their practices. However, as a result of a HEFCE-funded special initiative
project, the National Association of Disability Officers was established
(now the National Association of Disability Professionals). The organization
remains comparatively young, but it has the potential to contribute
significantly to the development of policy and provision in the future. In
moving to this position, its members will need to devise strategies allowing
them to escape from their current heavy burden – often associated with
'firefighting' and crisis management – to a role in which they operate at a
more strategic level. After all:

> If we do not change the direction we are headed, we will end up
> where we are going. (Chinese proverb quoted by Jodi Picoult, 2007,
> as the frontispiece of the novel *Nineteen Minutes*)

Finally, towards the end of 2007, the HEFCE announced that it would be
undertaking a review of the impact of its policies and provision. In
particular, it is acknowledged that the study undertaken in the late 1990s
to try to establish a baseline level of provision for all institutions and which

has been very useful indeed to many (including some working in other countries) needs to be updated (HEFCE, 1999). An important objective of the study was to try to outline what support disabled students should receive as part of an institution's routine responsibilities and what they need to procure for themselves using the Disabled Students' Allowance. Since the baseline study was first published, much has happened which ought to mean that the level of baseline provision has risen. Some of these stem from the legislation outlined above, some stem from the work of organizations such as the national funding councils and some from other sources such as the QAA Code of Practice, Section 3.

Closing Comments: Into the Unknown

It would be wrong to create a picture suggesting that, in the future, policy and provision for disabled students will have reached a state of high quality in almost all HEIs. Indeed, in contrast to the previous section, there are some developments which constitute a cause for concern. Most result from government policies concerning overall policy and provision rather than being directed specifically towards students with disabilities, an approach which could have serious and deleterious consequences for this group. The proposed developments include a rethinking of the structure of education and moving towards a system based on a 14–19-year-old structure; the further spread of foundation degrees and the possibility of degree-awarding powers being given more widely to colleges specializing currently in further education; the continuing impact of tuition fees on students; and the introduction of post-qualification admissions.

It might have been possible to ignore these changes and their potential negative consequences had the position regarding the mainstreaming of accessible pedagogy been more successful on a widespread and firmly embedded basis. To achieve this requires a change in cultures in most HEIs – a process that is very difficult to accomplish. The importance of cultural change has been identified by Mary Johnson in the United States. At the start of her book about disability rights, she says: 'A law cannot guarantee what a culture will not give' (Johnson, 2003).

So there is no time for complacency and for excessive celebration of the progress made. The struggle to ensure that the interests of disabled students are not forgotten must continue. Real progress will have been made only when disability services in post-compulsory education are seen as value-added provision and a routine part of all activities (especially the creation and validation of learning programmes), and not as an optional source of additional expense and an additional demand on staff time.

References

Americans with Disabilities Act (1990) Pub. L. No. 101-336, sect. 504 USC.

Dearing, R. (1997) *Higher Education in the Learning Society*. Report of the National Committee of Inquiry into Higher Education, HMSO, Norwich.

Department for Education and Science (DfES) (2002) *Finding Out about People's Disabilities: A Good Practice Guide*, DfES, London.

Department for Innovation, Universities and Skills (DIUS) (2007) *Big Increase in Disabled Students Allowances – Rammell*. Government News Network, London, www.gnn.gov.uk (accessed 5 July 2007)

Disability Rights Commission (DRC) (2007a) *Code of Practice (Revised) for Providers of Post-16 Education and Related Services*, Her Majesty's Stationery Office (HMSO), London.

DRC (2007b) *Understanding the Disability Discrimination Act: A Guide for Colleges, Universities and Adult Community Learning Providers*, DRC in association with LSN and Skill, London.

Equality Challenge Unit (ECU) (2005a) *Promoting Equality – The Public Sector Duty on Disability: Suggested First Steps for HEI*, ECU, London.

ECU (2005b) *Update 06/05*, Equality Challenge Unit, London.

ECU (2005c) *Disability Equality Schemes: Collecting and Improving Baseline Data and the Importance of Involving Disabled People*, Equality Challenge Unit, London.

ECU (2007) *Meeting the Duty: An Assessment of Higher Education Institutions' Performance in Relation to the Disability Equality Duty*, Equality Challenge Unit, London.

Equality and Human Rights Commission (UK) (EHRC) (2008) Equality and Human Rights www.equalityhumanrights.com (accessed 20 May 2008).

Fuller, M., Bradley, A. and Healey, M. (2004) Incorporating disabled students within an inclusive higher education environment. *Disability and Society*, **19** (5), 455–68.

Higher Education Funding Council for England (HEFCE) (1998) *Disability Statements: A Guide to Good Practice*, HEFCE, Bristol.

HEFCE (1999) *Guidance on Base-Level Provision for Disabled Students in Higher Education Institutions*, HEFCE, Bristol.

HEFCE (2007) *Circular Letter 31/2007 Review of HEFCE Policy as It Relates to Disabled Students*, HEFCE, Bristol.

Higher Education Statistics Agency (HESA) (2007) Disability 2005/6 www.hesa.ac.uk.

HMSO (2005) *Disability Discrimination Act 2005*, Her Majesty's Stationery Office, London.

Hurst, A. (1993) *Steps towards Graduation: Access to Higher Education and People with Disabilities*, Avebury, Aldershot.

Hurst, A. (1999) The Dearing Report and students with disabilities. *Disability and Society*, **14** (1), 65–84.

Hurst, A. (2006) *Towards Inclusive Learning for Disabled Students in Higher Education – Staff Development: A Practical Guide*, Skill/UCLan/HEFCE, London.

Johnson, M. (2003) *Make Them Go Away: Clint Eastwood, Christopher Reeve and the Case against Disability Rights*, Advocado Press, Louisville, Kentucky.

Learning and Skills Council (LSC) (2003) *Disclosure, Confidentiality and Passing on Information*, LSC, London.

Low, C. (2001) *Have Disability Rights Gone Too Far?* Insight Lecture, City University, London, April.

National Innovations Centre (NIC) (1974) *Disabled Students in Higher Education*, NIC, London.

Neanon, C. (2002) *How to Identify and Support Children with Dyslexia in the Primary School*, Learning Development Aids (LDA), Cambridge.

Office of the Independent Adjudicator for Higher Education (OIAHE) (2006) *Annual Report 2006*, OIAHE, Reading.

Picoult, J. (2007) *Nineteen Minutes*, Hodder & Stoughton, London.

Quality Assurance Agency for Higher Education (QAA) (1999) *Code of Practice Section 3: Students with Disabilities*, QAA, Gloucester.

Riddell, S., Tinklin, T. and Wilson, A. (2005) *Disabled Students in Higher Education: Perspectives on Widening Access and Changing Policy*, Routledge Falmer, London.

Rose, C. (2006) *Do You Have a Disability – Yes or No? Or Is There a Better Way of Asking? Guidance on Disability Disclosure and Respecting Confidentiality*, LSDA, London.

Scottish Higher Education Funding Council (SHEFC) (2004–2005) *Teachability: Creating an Accessible Curriculum for Students with Disabilities*, 2nd edn (available from Anne Simpson, Disability Services, University of Strathclyde, Floor 4 Graham Hills Building, 50 George Street, Glasgow G1 1QE).

Shakespeare, T. and Watson, N. (2001) The social model of disability: an outdated ideology. *Research in Social Science and Disability*, **2**, 9–28.

Shaw, J. (1998) 'A fair go' – the impact of the Disability Discrimination Act 1992 on tertiary education in Australia, in *Higher Education and Disabilities: International Approaches* (ed. A. Hurst), Ashgate, Aldershot.

Skill (revised 2005) *A Guide to the Disability Discrimination Act for Institutions of Further and Higher Education*, Skill, London.

Smith, M. and Sowers, J.-A. (2003) *A Day in the Life of Health Science Students: Faculty In-service Training Guide*, Oregon Health and Science University, Portland, Oregon.

Stanley, N., Ridley, J., Manthorpe, J. *et al.* (2007) *Disclosing Disability: Disabled Students and Practitioners in Social Work, Nursing and Teaching*, Disability Rights Commission, London.

Chapter 3

The Psychological Assessment of Neurodiversity

David Grant

A diagnostic assessment has the potential to be both empowering and enabling. By empowering, I am referring to both an increase in understanding as to why some aspects of behaviour and experience differ from many others, and to an increase in self-esteem. By enabling, I am referring to the adoption of strategies and techniques that result in an increase in performance which more closely reflects an inherent ability. These twin features of empowerment and enablement are captured in Carol's e-mail some months after her diagnostic assessment: 'Seeing you made me realise that lots of things I thought were my own idiocies were because of dyspraxia, and feel much more confident before finals. On your recommendation I was given extra time in finals which made an incredible difference – for the first time ever exams seemed manageable. Somehow I got a first and was the highest performing woman in my year.'

Carol's reference to 'my own idiocies' reveals very clearly a sense of self-negativity, a factor often encountered in individuals with an undiagnosed specific learning difference. Although her assessment enabled Carol to understand that her forgetfulness, her difficulties with time management, her slowness at taking in information, her proneness to bumping into things and knocking things over, are typically dyspraxic and attributable to her neurocognitive profile, her comment 'somehow I got a first' reveals that even some months after her assessment, she had still not fully grasped just how intellectually able she is. The process of empowerment, of understanding and of enhancement of self-esteem, takes time. Her assessment was also an enabling one for it resulted in appropriate exam accommodations being made (and also the provision of study support advice).

The twin process of empowerment and enablement are achieved when a diagnostic assessment is much more than an exercise in labelling. It is not sufficient to inform an individual that they are dyslexic, dyspraxic or an ADDer. It is necessary to chart and discuss with them their profile of strengths and weaknesses, and to map these on to their own everyday experiences, behaviours and preferences. It is this additional process, the debriefing process of interpretation, that transforms a diagnostic assessment into a psychological assessment.

The neurocognitive profile for all individuals is complex, and when a specific learning difference is present, this complexity can be inadvertently masked by a diagnostic label. For example, dyslexia and dyspraxia are defined as very different experiences: difficulties with acquiring literacy skills in the case of dyslexia, difficulties with motor control in the case of dyspraxia. In spite of dyslexia and dyspraxia appearing to be completely unrelated, the neurocognitive profiles of dyslexics and dyspraxics frequently reveal a very high degree of similarity, including strengths in verbal and visual reasoning skills, and relative weaknesses in working memory, processing speed and grapho-motor speed. By undertaking an assessment within a framework of neurodiversity, the narrowness of specific diagnostic categorization can be overcome.

The term neurodiversity is quite a recent one, and appears to have been first used by Singer (1998) as a positive way of referring to being autistic. At its simplest, the concept of neurodiversity was first used to describe the 'wiring' of the brain of an autistic person as being different from that of neurotypical individuals. Rather than perceiving this difference as a dysfunctional one requiring 'curing', this difference was to be appreciated and accepted. Within a relatively short period of time, the concept was adopted as being one that also included a wide range of other specific learning differences, including dyslexia, dyspraxia, dyscalculia, Attention Deficit (Hyperactivity) Disorder (AD(H)D) and Tourette's Syndrome.

Possibly because of its newness, and its adoption as a positive statement of difference, there is a lack of operational definitions of what neurodiversity is. While it is the case that diagnostic categories such as dyslexia and dyspraxia are often interpreted in a very narrow way, they do have a practical value in that there is a reasonable degree of consensus internationally as to what is understood by these terms, and how they are to be identified. This is not yet the case for neurodiversity. There is also a major difficulty with the concept: it implies there is a body of individuals who are neurotypical, with the implicit assumption that their neurocognitive profile does not vary significantly. This is a highly questionable assumption. The definition I offer below is designed to avoid this assumption:

Neurodiversity is present when an exceptional degree of variation between neurocognitive processes results in noticeable and unexpected weaknesses in the performance of some everyday tasks when compared with much higher performances on a subset of measures of verbal and/or visual abilities for a given individual. These everyday tasks, which are dependent on the neurocognitive processing of information, include tasks of learning and remembering, time management, social interaction and attention span, as well as tasks requiring fine and gross motor movements.

It is an umbrella term for it encompasses a range of specific learning differences, including dyslexia, dyspraxia, dyscalculia, ADD/ AD(H)D, and Asperger's. One or more specific learning differences may be present simultaneously, and it is possible for some forms of neurodiversity, such as a weakness only in working memory, to lack a well-known diagnostic category, such as dyslexia. Neurocognitive variation may be inherited (i.e. developmental in origin), and/or acquired (e.g. through perinatal or postnatal cerebral trauma). In most instances, neurocognitive variation is lifelong. Neurodiversity is a positive statement of differentiation, for while it explicitly refers to individuals whose everyday ways of thinking and behaving differ in certain key aspects from the majority of people, it rejects the assumption that these differences are dysfunctional and are to be 'cured'. Instead, there is a societal obligation that others make suitable adjustments and accommodations to enable inherent potential to be fully realized.

This definition allows for there to be variation in neurocognitive information processing that do not result in noticeable weaknesses (indeed, some unexpected variation, such as the ability to visualize, may be perceived as positive). The use of the term 'noticeable' requires that others, other than the individual, have drawn attention to an unexpected weakness. That is, in spite of being effective in the performance of some tasks, there are nevertheless one or more weaknesses. (DANDA (2008), a UK-based organization for neurodiverse adults, describes neurodiverse individuals as having 'a very uneven spread of strengths and weaknesses in comparison with non NDs'.)

The definition also requires that objective measures are taken (using both psychometric and achievement tasks, and where appropriate, standardized behavioural checklists), and that any recorded disparities exceed standard limits. Furthermore, such disparity has to be mapped onto the everyday experiences of an individual. An assessment to determine whether neurodiversity is present therefore requires the targeted and detailed taking of a life history, plus, minimally, the administration of psychometric and educational achievement tasks.

While it would be easy to describe this definition as being a deficit model, it is important to distinguish between a medical concept of specific learning difficulties, with its emphasis on dysfunctionality and being 'cured', and an information-processing psychological model of specific learning differences. Many psychometric forms of assessment are designed to capture very specific forms of cognitive processes, such as short-term auditory memory and speed of visual coding at a basic level. The definition proposed above is an attempt to capture the concept of neurodiversity in terms of variations in a wide variety of cognitive processes.

I would argue it is only through understanding the interface between the cognitive requirements of specific tasks and social situations and the cognitive profiles of individuals that meaningful steps can be taken to bring about positive change. This is essentially a human-factors engineering approach. A social (or sociological) model of disability wills that societal change should occur. An information-processing model provides a means for understanding how to bring about that change in terms of design of educational experiences and the design of everyday objects and environments.

As a generalization, if a range of psychometric and achievement tasks results in a profile that reveals relatively little variation, neurotypicality is present. However, if there is a high degree of variation, it is probably the case that neurodiversity is present. Such a profile, when presented visually, appears spiky in appearance, with the peaks and troughs representing relative strengths and weaknesses in performance. While some profiles are associated with specific learning differences, it would be a mistake to assume that there is just one profile characteristic of dyslexia, and one profile characteristic of dyspraxia. Dyslexia and dyspraxia are themselves umbrella terms, and there are significant profile differences between dyslexics as well as between dyspraxics. One value of the neurodiversity concept is the focus on an individual's profile rather than the diagnostic category.

The wider focus that neurodiversity encourages can be illustrated by considering the underlying reasons for five similar answers to a simple question. The question: 'Can you provide an estimate of the total number of books you have read for pleasure in your life from cover to cover (excluding textbooks)?' can be a very revealing one, provided the answer is then explored. The answers provided by five students are given below in Table 3.1, along with diagnostic outcomes. An answer of 'less than five'

Table 3.1 Number of books read for pleasure in life from cover to cover and diagnostic outcome

Student	Total number of books	Diagnosis
Carol	2	dyslexia
Maria	0	AD(H)D
Daniel	<10	dyspraxia
Ranjit	<5	visual stress
Apurva	<5	working memory deficit

by a 20-year-old student might be perceived as being a strong sign of dyslexia. In the case of Carol, a biology student at a university of excellence, her response of 'two' (one of which was *The Selfish Gene*), did indeed coincide with a diagnosis of dyslexia. This is not the case for the other four students.

Maria's response of zero is directly attributable to her difficulties with maintaining attention for long enough to finish a book. It is not that she does not want to read for pleasure, for she has started a large number of books. Nor is it the case that Maria lacks skills of reading accuracy, for they are congruent with her level of verbal reasoning (42nd percentile versus 58th percentile).

Daniel, in spite of excellent scores on tests of reading accuracy and spelling, and a very high verbal reasoning ability, experiences major difficulties with reading for comprehension due to the combination of a slow processing speed and a weak working memory. Being dyspraxic frequently results in dyslexic-type experiences, for these weaknesses are frequently observed in dyslexics as well.

Ranjit replied that he has never read for pleasure, and estimated his total as being below five. His speed of reading was exceptionally slow, approximately 60% below the undergraduate norm. However, when Ranjit made use of a grey-tinted overlay, his speed of reading increased by almost 40%. When using this overlay he commented: 'I can see spaces between lines – the words are separate.' His neuropsychological profile revealed no meaningful variations. Ranjit's dislike of reading stems primarily from the presence of visual stress, a barrier that can be easily ameliorated through using tinted overlays and tinted reading glasses.

Apurva, who estimated he has read just five books in total, said 'I rapidly forget what I have just read.' His level of performance on a test of reading accuracy was impressive, well above his level of verbal reasoning skills (86th percentile versus 58th percentile). However, Apurva's psychometric assessment revealed a major working memory weakness (9th percentile). As a consequence of this, as soon as he started to read, he quickly lost the thread of what he was reading.

The diversity of diagnostic outcomes for these five students reveals very clearly the necessity to gather appropriate data about personal experiences and preferences, to enable achievement data to be correctly interpreted. Reading difficulties are not exclusive to dyslexia. Nor are reading difficulties present only when skills of word recognition are unexpectedly low. It is essential, when undertaking a diagnostic/psychological assessment, to ensure that sufficient information is gathered to enable a variety of diagnostic outcomes to be actively explored. This is a process of both elimination and confirmation; dyspraxia, AD(H)D and dyscalculia are estimated to occur with approximately the same frequency as dyslexia, and frequently occur in combination.

Estimating the frequency of specific learning differences is fraught with major methodological problems. For example, in a study by Lauth, Heubeck and Mackowiask (2006), 11% of 569 primary school children (aged 7 to 11) were reported as showing clear signs of AD(H)D by their teachers. This identification process was based on criteria taken from the Diagnostic and Statistical Manual of Mental Disorders (DSM) Version III-R of the American Psychiatric Association (2000). While the survey by Lauth, Heubeck and Mackowiask (2006) is important for being conducted in everyday classroom settings across a number of schools, it does not address the question, as the authors indeed acknowledge, of whether pupils who are inattentive in class, and also frequently hyperactive, are ADDers. Difficulties with maintaining attention are frequently reported by both dyslexics and dyspraxics. In addition, AD(H)D frequently occurs in conjunction with other specific learning differences, such as dyspraxia (e.g. Kadesjo and Gillberg, 2001).

As there is no one test for any of these specific learning differences, population surveys such as those carried out by Lauth, Heubeck and Mackowiask (2006) and Kadesjo and Gillberg (1998, 2001), while very important, are inevitably limited because they lack the real depth of questioning and quantitative testing that are the central ingredients of a psychological assessment. In spite of major difficulties in determining with a high degree of precision the frequency of occurrence of any specific learning difference, there appears to be a consensus that each form occurs with a frequency of approximately 5–7%, and this holds true worldwide, whether the specific learning difference is AD(H)D (Faraone *et al.*, 2003), reading difficulties (Stevenson *et al.*, 1982), dyspraxia (Kirby and Drew, 2003) or dyscalculia (Desoete, 2006).

There are two significant implications that flow from survey findings of an approximate 1 in 20 frequency for any given specific learning difference and a high incidence of co-concurrence. Firstly, a student referred for diagnostic assessment because of a suspected specific learning difference is as likely to be dyspraxic, dyscalculic or an ADDer as to be dyslexic. Secondly, there is a high probability that if one form of learning difference is present, then another is also present. This is why it is so important that a diagnostic assessment is conducted in a framework of neurodiversity. It is my experience that the assessment reality differs. All too frequently, I find a previous diagnostic assessment has been blind to an existing specific learning difference, such as dyspraxia and/or AD(H)D. Secondly, many psychologists, at least in the United Kingdom, do not undertake diagnostic assessments for dyspraxia and AD(H)D even when very willing to carry out assessments for dyslexia.

This bias is clearly reflected in the available literature. A topic search on amazon.co.uk (27 October 2007) yielded the following: 864 books on dyslexia, 455 on AD(H)D, 63 on dyspraxia (plus a further 11 on developmental coordination disorder) and 15 on dyscalculia. That is, in spite of dyspraxia, dyscalculia and AD(H)D occurring with approximately the same frequency as dyslexia, and in various combinations, there are approximately twice as many books on dyslexia as on AD(H)D, and 11.6 times as many books on dyslexia as on the combined numbers for dyspraxia and Developmental Coordination Disorder (DCD). The ratio for dyscalculia is even more skewed: 57.8 books on dyslexia for every one book on dyscalculia.

In spite of this bias, there is nevertheless a duty of care to ensure that whenever a diagnostic assessment is carried out, it should be carried out with due diligence. That is, it is necessary to systematically consider all possible explanations for suspected learning differences. The key step towards achieving this objective is to ensure that a detailed personal history is taken. In my experience, this is all too often perfunctory. The taking of a detailed personal history does take time (minimally one hour in my experience), but if it is sufficiently broad, then small but telling details can be captured. When a specific learning difference is present, it colours and shapes a surprisingly wide range of everyday behaviours and experiences; a key part of a psychological assessment is, as it were, akin to collecting pieces for a jigsaw and then mapping these onto the neurocognitive and achievement profile.

As an example of this process, the next section presents a detailed personal history for Louise, a mature student, along with comments on why specific questions need to be asked. Louise was first diagnosed as being dyslexic when she was 20. However, a careful reading of her personal history reveals clear signs of both dyspraxia and AD(H)D, signs that were completely overlooked at her first diagnostic assessment.

Louise was born in South Africa to English-speaking parents. Her birth was beset by complications. It was induced and her shoulders were dislocated during delivery. Louise was born with the umbilical cord around her neck and it was six to eight minutes before she began breathing. She believes her walking and talking developed on time.

Questions about birthplace and first language are crucial to determining cultural history and whether English is a first or additional language. Children of first-generation immigrants frequently report that the first language they learnt was that of their parents, and it was not until they began nursery that they were required to learn English for the first time. As many of these children also have to attend weekend schools to help them maintain and develop the language of their parents, and skills of reading and spelling, their experiences of learning to read and spell in a language other than English can also be questioned. Care has to be exercised over assuming that children born to English-speaking parents are necessarily exposed from birth to English. I have encountered children who have spent a considerable period of time with nannies who use their own mother tongue, such as Cantonese or Swahili, with their charges.

Birthing experiences can provide vital early clues. Of the students I have assessed, about 60–70% of those who report birthing difficulties, such as a difficult labour or an overdue birth that was induced, are also dyspraxic. Early prematurity, especially very early prematurity, is another clue that a specific learning difference is likely to be present. For example, intra-cerebral haemorrhage in a very early premature neonate can result in a neurocognitive profile of much greater verbal than visual reasoning skills (the neurocognitive profile that can lead to a diagnosis of a nonverbal learning disorder (NVLD)).

Apart from bouts of depression during her mid-20s, Louise has enjoyed good health throughout her life. There are no known allergies, but she suffers from dermatitis on her fingers, which is most severe when she is under stress (e.g. during exam times). Louise has broken bones on a number of occasions. She broke her nose when she was a baby through falling out of her cot and when she was about 12, she broke her left arm. About a year ago she broke a toe walking upstairs and chipped a kneecap in a separate incident. (Louise pointed out that during a lecture on statistics, when the lecturer asked the group of about 130 students about the number of times people had broken bones, only two other students had done so on four different occasions.)

Questions about health are very important for two very different reasons. Some medical conditions, such as epilepsy, can result in weaknesses in working memory and impact on intellectual ability. Others, such as glandular fever or chronic fatigue syndrome, are often responses to stress – stress which may reflect an undiagnosed specific learning difference. This is highly likely to be the case if the onset of glandular fever or chronic fatigue syndrome coincides with a period of important exams in mid- to late teens. The same is true of bouts of depression. When a medical condition such as diabetes is present, additional care has to be taken over the pacing of an assessment.

The deceptively simple question: 'Is there a history of broken bones?' can be quite revealing. Occasionally, the list can be quite extensive. A history of broken bones and/or being accident-prone is a sign of dyspraxia, and has clear health and safety implications for those students who need to work in workshops or labs.

Louise attended two primary schools, changing at the end of Year 1 because her parents moved home. She found learning to read and spell a very difficult process, and did not begin reading for pleasure until she was in her early 20s. She has a vague memory of being provided with tutors by her primary school to help improve her reading and spelling skills. Louise said that a major difficulty for her is forgetting very quickly what she has just read. She also described herself as being a very slow reader. She pointed out that when she was diagnosed as being dyslexic she was provided with light orange/brown-tinted glasses, which have made reading an easier process for her. Without her glasses words 'move', and a page of text appears as if it has rivers of white running through it. Louise found it impossible to estimate how many books she has read for pleasure over the past 10 years, but said it was 'a good few'.

If there are changes of schools, it is important to know why. For example, a change because a child is being bullied, or underperforming, or moved into the private sector, can all be read as potential signs of an undiagnosed specific learning difference. A significant number of dyspraxic students report being bullied.

It is not sufficient to note whether reading and spelling difficulties were present. It is important to try to identify the source of difficulties. For example, some students report being able to read fast but not take anything in. Others find it difficult to read with fluency because they still stumble over words. Yet others report becoming tired quite quickly (a sign of visual stress). It is surprising how few psychologists screen for visual stress, yet it can be a highly significant factor influencing skills of reading, including sight-reading of music notation. Louise explained that she first became aware of her visual stress when she pointed out to a friend that it was 'very clever how they got words to move about' when viewing a van with slogans on its side. When her friend pointed out the words did not move, she sought advice and this resulted in her being diagnosed as being dyslexic. Once Louise began wearing her tinted glasses she began reading for pleasure.

> Louise described herself as 'quite enjoying' learning handwriting skills and said she can write neatly as long as she can write slowly. However, under pressure it becomes messy. On being asked about her speed of copying information down from the blackboard at school, Louise said she was 'one of the last to finish'. She has found it 'really difficult' to take notes in lectures as she cannot listen and write at the same time.

Being one of the last to be permitted to use a pen at school is indicative of grapho-motor difficulties, while reasons for slowness with taking notes can range from a slow grapho-motor speed to poor spelling abilities to forgetfulness. All these factors will result in difficulties with taking notes in lectures. For example, a weak working memory often results in lecture notes that consist of 'lots of half-finished sentences'.

> Louise described herself as 'hating maths – it was really difficult' at both primary and secondary school. She struggled with learning the times tables ('I don't know them'), and disliked mental arithmetic. A series of numbers was read out and Louise said she remembered them by repeating them to herself.

Maths difficulties may reflect poor teaching. However, difficulties with learning the times tables and with undertaking mental arithmetic may reflect a working memory weakness, particularly if the same person then describes herself as being good at higher maths skills, such as algebra and differentiation. Continuing difficulties with maths across secondary education may reflect a relative weakness in visual reasoning abilities and raises the question of whether dyscalculia may be present.

The question about how a series of numbers is remembered may seem surprising. However, if a student reports being able to 'see them', it is important to know this; if a strong visualization ability is present, that can make it difficult to interpret the outcome of the Digit Span test of working memory. It can also provide a clue as to the presence of synaesthesia. As synaesthesia occurs with a frequency of 4% (Simner *et al.*, 2006; Grant, 2007), and can impact in negative ways on academic performance, it is a sensory experience that needs to be considered.

On being asked whether she was well-coordinated or clumsy as a child, Louise said that while she had, and still has, very good balance, she is still 'a bit clumsy – always dropping things, knocking things over'. As a consequence of her clumsiness, she now buys only plastic glasses for home use. She is constantly bruising herself, especially her legs. However, when applying make-up she has good fine hand–eye coordination. In spite of her good balance, she dislikes having to walk down stairs, especially when the treads are metal ones with a grid pattern. Louise said she 'liked sports' at school. When asked about her skill at catching and throwing, she replied, 'I was not so good at catching', but judged her throwing skills were better. Louise is still very keen on being physically active, and regularly attends gym and yoga sessions. She also cycles. She said she finds taking part in physical activities essential for running off excess energy.

Clumsiness and difficulties with motor coordination are classic soft signs of the presence of dyspraxia. They are often more muted in adult life than in childhood. However, when clumsiness intrudes on everyday life to such an extent that the student has to take precautionary measures, such as buying plastic glasses because of a history of breakages, and frequently finds unexplained bruises, then these constitute good evidence of continuing clumsiness. It is important to remember that dyspraxia takes different forms, so fine motor coordination skills may be good when compared with poor gross motor skills. Everyday activities, such as difficulties with putting on make-up, especially eyeliner, and messy eating skills, are clues to the presence of poor fine motor skills.

While many dyspraxic students report disliking having to take part in sports at school, a small minority report a liking for some sports activities, particularly swimming. I have met two dyspraxic students who have represented their country at rowing, so exceptional sports achievements are not completely out of the reach of dyspraxic students. Louise's comment about 'running off excess energy' may be indicative of AD(H)D, for a number of ADDers report how, by taking part in regular active exercise, they are better able to maintain focus.

Two other deceptively simple questions concern whether the student has ever lost a mobile phone, and whether they are prone to dropping it. For example, Tom, a dyslexic and dyspraxic student, reported that as he has lost several mobile phones to date, he now 'constantly re-checks' that he has key items with him. He said he also has a tendency to drop his phone and has broken an MP3 player through dropping it. (The number of lost mobile phones, and phones broken through being constantly dropped, can be staggeringly high, and once again helps to bring to life a neurocognitive profile.)

Louise attended the same secondary school from the age of 11 until just before she was 16. The school had seven levels and she was initially placed in Level 4, but finished up in Level 6. The only activity she recalled being good at was Drama. She would try to avoid being required to read aloud in class. Louise was required to study Afrikaans and said she found this 'a difficult subject'. On being asked about using a ruler and compass in Maths and Science classes, Louise replied that she would have to press down on the ruler 'very hard', otherwise it would slip. Louise enjoyed Art at school, apart from when she had to undertake projects that involved proportionality.

Drama was Louise's favourite subject, particularly when allowed to improvise. She did not encounter problems with learning lines as she was given small parts. Her school reports often said 'she tries hard'. Louise recalled that her teachers were puzzled as to why her educational performance did not match her ability to discuss ideas. Louise took the Year 10 state exams prior to leaving school and has a memory of performing badly in them.

Secondary schools often place pupils according to perceived ability. When this is done on a subject basis, disparities such as being placed in the top set for Science, the second set for Maths, and sets 5 for French and

English, can reflect literacy difficulties very clearly. When pupils reach a point at which they can exercise a choice of which subjects to study, preferences can be very revealing. For example, a number of students explain that they prefer Maths and Physics to English and History, for these subjects do not require the writing of essays, nor do they require the learning of a sustainable body of factual information, as answers can be arrived at from first principles. On the other hand, when a student described French, English and History as being their favourite subjects, and added 'I can't draw', this is atypical of dyslexia and is strongly indicative of weak right-hemisphere function.

Comments made by teachers over a period of time also help to reveal strengths and weaknesses. All too frequently, teachers make comments such as 'Sue could do better if she tried harder', a very dispiriting comment given that Sue has been trying her hardest and has no idea why, in spite of working harder than her friends, she finds it so difficult to match their grades. Comments about poor time keeping, poor spelling and grammar, and untidiness, can also be useful clues as to long-standing difficulties.

On leaving school, Louise obtained employment straight away, working as a retail assistant in a pastry shop at a mainline railway station. After about six months, she left this job for another position as a retail assistant in a shoe shop. Once again, she left this position after a short period of time and has since worked in a range of different jobs, including at a butcher's (retail assistant), childcare and bar work. Following a very short and disastrous spell in an office (e.g. filing was an impossible task), Louise has avoided applying for office work. She explained she changed jobs quite frequently as she becomes 'bored very easily'.

When Louise was in her early 20s she was diagnosed as dyslexic. Following this assessment she was provided with tinted glasses, which she found very helpful when reading. She then embarked on a four-year hairdressing apprenticeship. During the first two years, she attended college on a day-release basis. She described herself as 'hating' having to take exams. She said she learnt best through watching others: 'I'm a very good visual learner.' She spent the remaining two years of her apprenticeship working in a number of salons. She described herself as being prone to misplacing and dropping items such as scissors and hairgrips. Although Louise successfully completed her apprenticeship, she became very sensitive to the chemicals used in hairdressing when her immune system weakened, and had to abandon hairdressing. Louise left South Africa about three years ago. Over this three-year period she has worked as a carer in a residential home for the elderly, and as a retail assistant in a number of shops.

The career path followed by a mature student can provide a number of clues as to whether a specific learning difficulty is present, and if so, what form this might take. For example, Louise's frequent changing of jobs is indicative of AD(H)D, while her disastrous office spell (less than two weeks) reveals continuing difficulties with sequencing and literacy tasks.

Surprising as it may seem, even the type of university or college a student attends can reflect an underlying learning difference. When dyslexia and/or dyspraxia are present, students frequently prefer undergraduate courses that minimize the need to write essays, do not require the learning of lots of facts, and have few if any timed exams. Tom, a dyspraxic student, having performed poorly when he studied Law at high school, summed up his experiences: 'Law combined the worst aspects of English and History – lots of writing of essays and lots of learning of facts.' Maths and Physics are often appealing to students who find the writing of essays and learning of facts difficult.

The taking of a personal history can give rise to ethical questions, for students often divulge very personal data, such as time spent in prison, mental illness, the taking of drugs, reliance on friends when completing coursework and messy personal relationships. It is necessary to establish with the student at this point what will and will not appear in a report. Very sensitive information, unless it is of critical importance to substantiating a diagnosis, has to be left out.

It should also be stressed that the diagnostic report, in the first instance, is for the eyes of the student alone. There are times when it is necessary to ask sensitive questions. For example, NVLD gives rise to pseudo-signs of autism. Questions about whether difficulties have been experienced in forming and maintaining friendships and personal relationships are necessary to arriving at a diagnosis.

A couple of weeks after her diagnosis, Louise e-mailed me: 'I must also say that the diagnosis has helped me to be a lot kinder to myself, and I can laugh at the silly things I do and the simple things I have trouble with. I have more of an understanding now why some things are difficult for me and I can let it go, I don't get so frustrated. It has also given my husband a better understanding of me too … You have burst my little bubble of secret hatred and self-loathing.'

A psychological diagnosis has the potential to be life-changing, but to achieve this requires time and care over the collection of information and its interpretation. It must always be remembered that a diagnostic report will be read by a range of people other than the student, so there is a real need to write a report in a manner that enables others to understand how an outcome has been reached, and how the neurocognitive profile shapes and colours everyday life and academic performance.

In some instances, the world experienced is strikingly different from that of many others. Hollingham (2004) describes each individual as living in their own sensory world. When that world is one where most information – even verbal information – is recalled visually, or synaesthesia is present, the taking of a personal history is essential to capture this sensory world, for visualization, and/or synaesthesia, can result in very striking variations in performance.

By visualization I am referring to the ability to generate and/or recall a visual image. This may include an ability to 'see' a series of numbers when they are read out, creating a detailed visual image of a story when reading and being able to 'see' revision notes in an exam. Synaesthesia refers to the automatic triggering of one sense modality by another sense modality. For example, the word Monday might be accompanied by the brief sensation of yellow, while Tuesday might be accompanied by the brief sensation of green, and Wednesday by the sensation of red. Synaesthesia takes many different forms, ranging from number-colour synaesthesia and grapheme-colour synaesthesia to music-colour synaesthesia and vision-taste synaesthesia.

Although the dividing line can be hard to draw on occasions, visualization and synaesthesia occur independently of each other. It is my experience that most visualizers and synaesthetes are unaware that their sensory experiences are different from those of most people. Consequently, it requires sophisticated questioning to tease out their sensory world experiences.

When either visualization or synaesthesia is present, it is sometimes the case that the impact is strong enough to mask an underlying working memory weakness. The Wechsler Adult Intelligence Scale (WAIS-III; Wechsler, 1999) contains three separate subtests of auditory short-term memory capacity: Arithmetic, Digit Span and Letter-Number Sequencing (see Appendix 3.A). These three different means of capturing working memory capacity are important, for unexpected variation is often an indication that something other than auditory short-term memory is being captured, and there is a need to question why.

This was the case with June, a postgraduate dyspraxic social science student. Her excellent score of 16 for Digit Span was much higher than her average score of 10 for Arithmetic. She scored 13 for Letter-Number Sequencing. At the start of the Digit Span test, June closed her eyes to enable her to 'see' the numbers. She also made use of visualization on the Letter-Number Sequencing subtest.

June's enhanced performance on the Digit Span subtest is not exceptional. Seventeen of forty-two synaesthetes seen by me reported using visualization when administered the Working Memory subtests and, on average, their subtest scores for Digit Span and Letter-Number Sequencing were over one standard deviation higher the scores recorded for the nonvisualizers. (The two groups had virtually identical scores on the subtests of Arithmetic and Similarities.)

In my experience, when visualization results in an enhanced figure for the Index of Working Memory (see Appendix 3.A), it is wise to avoid concluding that there is no evidence of a Working Memory weakness. Rather, it is much more meaningful to ask whether the presence of visualization masks a substantial working memory weakness.

This is a question that all diagnosticians need to be alert to, for the recording of the presence of visualization and/or synaesthesia is not a rare occurrence. For example, the 42 synaesthetes were identified over a 33-month period of carrying out diagnostic assessments, and represent 8.6% of students seen over that period of time. While this incidence of 1 in 11.6 may appear high, I strongly suspect it is still an underestimate, for my skills at identifying the presence of synaesthesia are still developing. As visualization also occurs without synaesthesia being present, and is even more common, this ratio has to be viewed as being a very conservative one.

This incidence means it is inevitable that all those who undertake assessments will encounter synaesthetes and/or visualizers, and that some data and conclusions will be compromised if these features are not recognized. As a working memory weakness is associated with a range of specific learning differences, and is a key factor underlying such everyday experiences as forgetfulness, difficulties with structuring essays, 'going off at tangents' and slowness when learning, it is very important when recording working memory capacity to have confidence in the validity of measurement.

As a psychological assessment is one that steps beyond psychometric data, an awareness of how visualization and synaesthesia can and do result in very different sensory experiences is vital to achieving this objective. It is not sufficient to rely upon personal history as the source of information. It is also necessary to ask questions throughout the total course of the assessment. The extracts below for Andrea, Karen and Luke reveal just how visual the cognitive world of some students can be.

Andrea's personal history initially revealed the ability to visualize and the presence of synaesthesia. For example, when reading a fiction book Andrea builds up a fairly detailed visual image of the story: 'I can see the person'. This mental image is detailed enough to enable her to 'see the jacket, coat, shoes, personality' of characters. Andrea's visualization extended far beyond being able to 'see' a story when reading. She also 'sees' words when someone is speaking to her, a form of visualization known as ticker-tape synaesthesia. Her ability to 'see' words is also a spelling aid, for it is as if she can just copy a word down; this was reflected in her much higher percentile for Spelling (47) than for Reading Accuracy (16).

Andrea's visualization and synaesthetic experiences are far from unique. Karen, a design student, also creates (unconsciously) a very detailed series of visual images when reading a fiction story. This mental image is detailed enough to enable her not only to 'see' the characters but also 'hear their voices' and 'sense the smells' in a setting. She described herself as being 'inside the story'.

During the course of her assessment, Karen pointed out that when someone is speaking to her, she often does not look at the person but looks away. She said this is because she tends not to listen to each word. Rather, 'I pick up on some words and build up a story in my head.' Karen's behaviour of looking up to her left when someone is speaking to her was observed throughout the course of her assessment.

Luke's sensory experiences are even more complex. In addition to experiencing a different colour for each day of the week, Luke described the colour as being 'just the tip of the iceberg', for each weekday name was 'just the start of the laying of images and emotions'. For example, Monday was not just blue (he could see the word 'Monday'), but also evoked images of rain and umbrellas, with the images 'flying in, flying out' of his vision. Luke said even small words, such as 'was', evoke emotions (for example, of loss). As a consequence of his constant flurry of images and emotions, he finds it necessary to take breaks when someone is talking, particularly when they are talking quickly.

Luke's responses to general knowledge questions, including Information subtest questions, were embedded in images and 'snippets of sound'. When asked about the capital city of Brazil, he initially 'saw' a world map, followed by flashes of images associated with the travels of friends and musical sounds. Luke is a jazz music student and his synaesthesia is an integral part of his sensory experiences and response to music. While the clapping of a rhythm provides him with 'a voyage through images and emotions', an individual note takes on 'a completely different character' depending on which instrument it is being played on. Consequently, Luke's synaesthesia influences the types of music he prefers, as some result in a sensory overload.

Luke's account of his sensory experiences is very important, since it addresses the question of whether synaesthesia is always a positive experience. For a number of students the answer is yes, but it is not inevitably the case. For some it results in a sensory overload, and it is not that surprising that of the 42 synaesthetes, AD(H)D was a diagnostic outcome in 32% of instances.

This sense of being overloaded is echoed in an e-mail to me from Sophie:

It gets very busy in my mind seeing words/numbers in colour and I wish I didn't have synaesthesia. I didn't notice it half as much before in my time away from studying and it certainly didn't interfere with my life in the way it does now. The only real benefit I can think of is my ability to remember things like names, places, film titles, etc., as when I cruise through the alphabet in my mind the colour of the first letter of the forgotten word jumps out at me which then narrows my alphabetic search down.

I also find my synaesthesia a hindrance to my studies rather than an asset, especially when it comes to my module titles and days of the week. For example, I might have a yellow module on a red day (Tues or Thurs) and a red module on a yellow day (Wed) but I have got mixed up several times and brought the wrong books in to Uni based solely on the colour confusion dominating my thoughts. I have to double check my timetable every day.

Sophie, like Andrea, Karen and Luke, had never realized there was anything unusual about her way of experiencing the world. This is the case in over 90% of students who are synaesthetes or are visualizers. It is unwise to assume that being a synaesthete, or being able to visualize, are automatically positive experiences. While in many instances there are substantial benefits (e.g. 'picturing' a story or song may be the key to being a film/video director, while 'seeing' words can result in enhanced spelling skills, and abstract paintings by painters such as Jackson Pollock are experienced as emotions and movement), there can be negative experiences as well, such as an inability to 'picture' a research article when reading it, or difficulties with mastering an academic abstract vocabulary.

The taking of a personal history is a vital first stage in arriving at a diagnostic outcome. Without this information the interpretation of achievement and psychometric data, and/or checklist responses gathered in the next stages of an assessment, is fraught with major problems, and it is impossible to arrive at a valid diagnosis. This stage enables hypotheses to be generated, and these in turn will influence the final choice of tests and checklists. For example, if AD(H)D is suspected, then it is essential to use an appropriate checklist, while if dyscalculia is suspected, then measures of mathematical competence need to be administered. When Asperger's Syndrome is suspected, then the personal history is the most compelling source of diagnostic evidence. However, as NVLD is usually accompanied by signs of both Asperger's and dyspraxia, it is essential that a neurocognitive profile is available in order to arrive at an appropriate diagnosis.

While the choice of tests can appear bewildering, the web site of the Educational Testing Service (www.ets.org) maintains an up-to-date listing of appropriate tests. In addition, they provide guidance on the range of evidence that needs to be provided in a diagnostic report. A more limited service is available from the UK web site of the Professional Association of Teachers of Students with Specific Learning Difficulties (PATOSS) organization (www.patoss-dyslexia.org).

Probably the best known of the batteries of psychometric assessments is the WAIS, although www.ets.org lists five acceptable alternatives to it. The current version, the third edition, consists of 14 subtests, 11 of which are core subtests. Provided all 11 are administered, then individual figures for the four Indices can be calculated. The Indices are Verbal Comprehension, Working Memory, Perceptual Organization and Processing Speed. It is important to note that this battery of subtests has been designed to ensure that there is a high level of commonality of performance across all 14 subtests. That is, high performance on one subtest, such as Vocabulary, will ordinarily be echoed by high scores across all the subtests (such as Digit Span, Block Design and Symbol Search). Some degree of variation is to be expected, but when large variations are recorded, these may be indicative of a specific learning difference.

It is vital always to remember that while cognitive and educational achievement data are important to reaching a diagnosis, such data do not constitute a diagnosis in their own right. They provide key information that must be interpreted within the context of the personal history. Nor can subtest or Index figures always be accepted at face value. For example, if visual stress is present and has not been controlled for, there is a very high probability that reading speed will be underestimated and there will be a question mark over any measure of reading accuracy or speed of phonological processing. For example, Karen, whose speed of reading increased by 40% when using a blue overlay, described how the target words in the reading test became 'embedded in the paper' when using a blue overlay. Without the blue overlay, it was as if the words 'were floating on top – it's like looking at noise'.

The process of arriving at a diagnosis is not an easy one and it is essential it should be as transparent as possible. This requires that a diagnostic report must contain a definition of the diagnostic label and show how the diagnostic criteria have been satisfied. For example, the British Dyslexia Association definition of dyslexia (only part is cited below) reflects an appreciation of dyslexia as a complex cognitive processing system and also draws attention to specific difficulties: 'Dyslexia is a combination of abilities and difficulties that affect the learning process in one or more of reading, spelling and writing. It is a persistent condition.' Accompanying weaknesses may be identified in areas of speed of processing, short-term memory, sequencing, spoken language and motor skills. There may be difficulties with auditory and/or visual perception. It is particularly related to mastering and using written language, which may include alphabetic, numeric and musical notation (Tresman, 2006, p. 7).

A crucial feature of this definition is that it allows for variations in cognitive profiles, and the three examples given below reflect the kinds of variation that may be encountered. A failure of this definition is the conflating of dyslexia with dysorthographia (unexpectedly poor spelling) and dysgraphia (difficulties with handwriting and forming marks on paper). Reading and spelling skills are quite different cognitive processes and can and do exist independently of each other. This is also true of handwriting skills.

Holly's profile (Figure 3.1) is a typical dyslexic 'spiky' profile. Her profile reveals considerable strengths in those forms of verbal skills as measured by the WAIS, and quite reasonable visual skills. In contrast, her

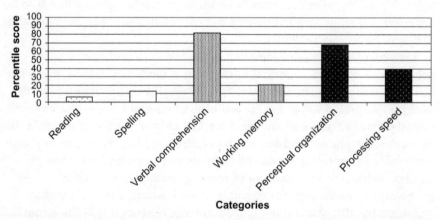

Figure 3.1 Holly's WRAT-IV Reading and Spelling scores and her 4 WAIS-III scores expressed as mean percentile scores

performance on measures of Reading Accuracy, Spelling, Working Memory and Processing Speed is noticeably lower. The variation in Holly's WAIS-III profile has been reported by many others (e.g. Ramus *et al.*, 2003; Ingesson, 2006).

There are variations on this characteristic pattern. For example, in David's case (Figure 3.2), the major cognitive weakness is one of quite limited Working Memory capacity. In Terry's case (Figure 3.3), the major cognitive weakness is one of a slow Processing Speed. The disparity in

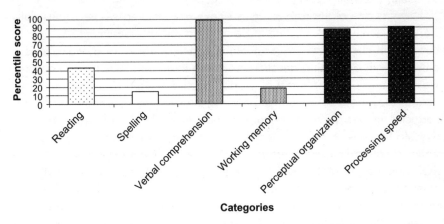

Figure 3.2 David's British Ability Scales (BAS) Reading and Spelling scores and his 4 WAIS-III scores expressed as mean percentile scores

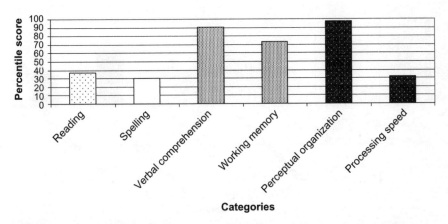

Figure 3.3 Terry's WRAT-IV Reading and Spelling scores and his 4 WAIS-III scores expressed as mean percentile scores

Processing Speed between these two students helps explain why Terry can only complete about 60% of an exam paper without an additional time allowance, while David hardly ever makes use of his time allowance of 25% additional time.

While a neurocognitive profile renders variations in cognitive functioning explicit, it would be a mistake to believe that dyslexia is the result of this neurocognitive variation, for such variations are also associated with other specific learning differences as well. Jimmy's WAIS-III profile (Figure 3.4) is also a 'spiky' one. In spite of his reading and spelling skills being excellent, his Maths Computation test score places him in the bottom 13%.

Jimmy is one of the rare students I have encountered whose Maths skills were sufficiently weak for him to be referred for an assessment. As Butterworth (1999) has argued that the defining feature of dyscalculia is a difficulty with answering questions of 'more than' and 'less than', Jimmy was given a very simple test of proportionality devised by me. As he was able to arrange a series of numbers into their correct ascending order, and correctly answer questions about who has 'more than' and 'less than', pure dyscalculia could be discounted. However, Jimmy's inability to solve on paper simple arithmetic questions, such as 210 divided by 5, was replicated on the Math Computation test. Jimmy left unanswered anything other than the most basic questions. Although Jimmy's WAIS-III profile reveals weaknesses in both Working Memory and Processing Speed, these are not sufficient in themselves to explain why his Maths skills are so weak.

Temple (1997), while defining developmental dyscalculia as being 'a disorder of mathematical ability, seen in children of normal intelligence',

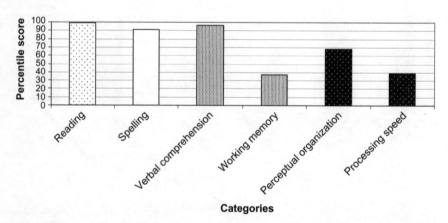

Figure 3.4 Jimmy's WRAT-IV Reading and Spelling scores and his 4 WAIS-III scores expressed as mean percentile scores

also makes the case for there being developmental dyscalculias. While there is a high degree of consensus that the mastering of mathematical skills is a complex process, there is very little consensus as to what the dyscalculic subtypes are, which is why the term specific maths weakness (my diagnosis for Jimmy) is one I prefer.

It is very important to differentiate between an inability to understand a mathematical concept and a difficulty with following a procedure due to limitations imposed by a limited working memory capacity. For example, it is not unusual to encounter dyslexic and dyspraxic Maths and Physics students with high-level mathematical skills who make simple errors on tasks of mental arithmetic, and are prone to missing out a step when undertaking a long mathematical procedure. It does not appear sensible to opt for a possible diagnosis of dyscalculia in such instances.

Like dyslexia and dyscalculia, the diagnostic category of dyspraxia is another umbrella term. While the core defining features of dyspraxia is 'an impairment or immaturity of the organization of movement', the Dyspraxia Foundation's definition also notes that 'there may be problems of language, perception and thought' (Dyspraxia Foundation, 2008). In contrast, the concept of DCD is focused purely on movement (Drew, 2005).

The profile for Georgina (Figure 3.5) is more indicative of the presence of dyspraxia than dyslexia, for it reveals a noticeably higher performance on Verbal Comprehension than for Perceptual Origination, and a very low figure for Processing Speed, a pattern of variation that is reflected in her everyday life.

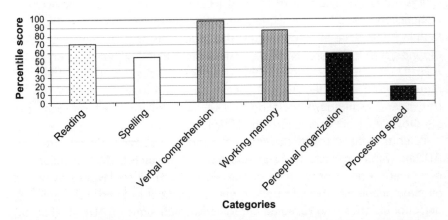

Figure 3.5 Georgina's WRAT-IV Reading and Spelling scores and her 4 WAIS-III scores expressed as mean percentile scores

Georgina's educational history revealed a consistent pattern of slowness, including learning to spell and with Maths. She recalled being 'one of the last to finish' when tested on knowledge of the times tables. Because of poor exam performances, Georgina had to repeat the first year of her Sixth Form course. She was also required to retake her first undergraduate year. When her exam performance was discussed with Georgina, she said she always runs out of time in exams: 'I can only complete 60%.'

While there is a long and continuing history of clumsiness and being accident-prone, there is also a high degree of neurocognitive variation that colours and shapes Georgina's everyday life.

So far, the emphasis has been on the need to integrate details from a personal history with educational achievement data and cognitive psychometric data. However, no assessment is complete unless the behaviour of a student is closely observed. This is especially important when considering whether Attention Deficit Disorder (ADD) or Attention Deficit Disorder with Hyperactivity/Impulsivity (AD(H)D) is present. Restlessness, sudden lapses in attention and starting a test before told to start, are all typical behaviours that should alert a diagnostician to the possibility that ADD or AD(H)D may be present.

While the identification of ADD is not easy, this is not a reason for being unaware of ADD being a possible diagnostic outcome, particularly as there is significant evidence that ADD is more likely to occur in conjunction with other specific learning differences than as a pure form in its own right. For example, Kadesjo and Gillberg (1998) argue that Disorders of Attention, Movement and Perception, a combination of AD(H)D and DCD, 'may be a valid diagnostic construct'.

It is my experience that ADD or AD(H)D occurs more frequently in conjunction with other specific learning differences than as a specific learning difference in its own right. This places an onus on any diagnostician to be prepared to consider the possibility that ADD or AD(H)D may be present even if their diagnostic focus is dyslexia. This requires using either the AD(H)D checklist, derived from the DSM-IV (American Psychiatric Association, 2000), or an alternative form such as the Brown AD(H)D Scales (Brown, 1996).

Peter, a creative sound student, and Sandra, a science student, are two ADDers with Hyperactivity. Peter said eight of the nine DSM Inattention items were a good description of himself, as were all six Hyperactivity and all three Impulsivity items (a pattern almost identical to Sandra's). Their personal histories also revealed characteristic soft signs of AD(H)D. For example, Peter recalled his parents describing him as being a hyperactive child who was 'always getting into trouble'. As a mature student, Peter experienced significant difficulties with completing projects on time and with maintaining concentration during lectures.

Sandra also experienced problems at school; in secondary school she was placed in the remedial class on occasions 'for being naughty'. Her inattention and restlessness impacted on family activities as well, for she has always found it hard to watch a film without taking a break. This resulted in her father being reluctant to take her to the cinema when she was a child because of her difficulties with viewing a film. Sandra, like a number of ADDers, is also a synaesthete and visualizer; this is reflected, for example, in her higher percentile for Spelling than for Reading Accuracy (see Figure 3.7).

It is my experience that psychometric assessment also has a valuable role to play, and my own data have revealed two very distinct profiles for ADDers: spiky and flat, with a Processing Speed weakness being recorded in the majority of instances. The profiles for Peter (Figure 3.6) and Sandra (Figure 3.7) reveal this divergence very clearly. While relative weaknesses in Working Memory and Processing Speed give rise to some signs of ADD, such as forgetfulness and being distracted easily by extraneous sounds or movement, it cannot be argued these are the sources of ADD. That is a complex question still very much open to debate and research.

Throughout this chapter I have stressed the need for diagnosticians to work within a neurodiversity perspective. This requires always questioning previous diagnoses even when they have been arrived at by highly competent professionals, for there are occasions when a narrow focus can result in the broader picture being missed. This was the case for Leo, a TV

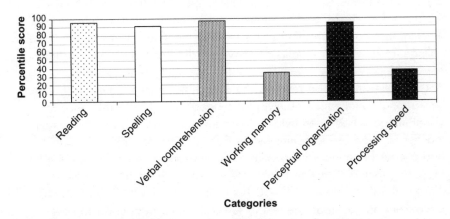

Figure 3.6 Peter's WRAT-IV Reading and Spelling scores and his 4 WAIS-III scores expressed as mean percentile scores

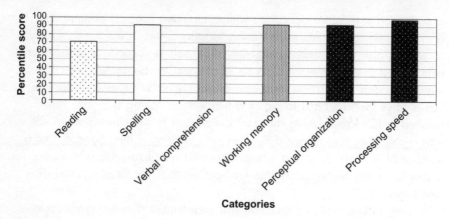

Figure 3.7 Sandra's WRAT-IV Reading and Spelling scores and her 4 WAIS-III scores expressed as mean percentile scores

production student. Leo was first diagnosed with high-functioning Asperger's when he was at primary school. Since then he has been taught how to read nonverbal behaviours and pay attention to others; during the assessment he was able to maintain eye contact.

When taking Leo's personal history, care was taken to look for evidence of the classic defining features of Asperger's, such as repetitive behaviours, avoidance of new situations, difficulties with interpreting the intentions and moods of others, a dislike of ambiguity and a tendency to be unconcerned about social conventions.

Leo's history revealed a number of characteristic behaviours, such as always having the same sandwich filling, spending hours perfecting a skateboarding move, and constantly calculating the time to achieve a task, whether that be the brushing of his teeth or the time it takes him to travel to college. However, his ritualistic behaviours did not include such actions as always being early to a lecture to obtain the same seat.

Leo's assessment also revealed he was dyslexic (see Figure 3.8), with a very strong visualization ability, plus synaesthesia. Leo's preference for visual imagery had been evident for many years since a primary school teacher allowed Leo to communicate through cartoon strips. Leo said he had always been more interested in the illustrations in books than the text, preferring factual to fiction books. He estimated that while he looked through the illustrations of 40–50 books in primary school, and 20–40 since then, he had read the text of fewer than 10 from cover to cover. When someone is speaking, Leo 'sees images', which he 'plays out as a story in my head'. Even silent thoughts are represented by a series of

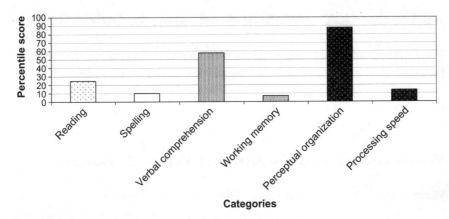

Figure 3.8 Leo's WRAT-IV Reading and Spelling scores and his 4 WAIS-III scores expressed as mean percentile scores

images. He sees finished college projects as red, while ongoing projects are white. It was as if Leo's first language was visual imagery, with English being a weak additional language.

To be more certain that Asperger's Syndrome is a valid diagnosis, it is important to rule out an alternative diagnosis of NVLD (sometimes referred to as Right Hemisphere Dysfunction), for this is characterized by signs of both autism and dyspraxia. This can only be achieved through neurocognitive profiling. When the Index figures for Verbal Comprehension and Working Memory are higher than those for Perceptual Organization and Processing Speed, this is indicative of a stronger functioning left than right hemisphere. Leo's profile is not an NVLD profile.

A diagnosis has the potential to transform an individual's life. A good psychological assessment is one that empowers and enables. In my experience this cannot be accomplished in less than four hours, and frequently takes longer. A well-informed neurodiverse student is one who becomes his or her own best advocate for change. That is the real key to enabling the social model of disability to be driven forward.

Acknowledgements

To my parents for providing me with the space to learn what I was best at.

To those students who have allowed me to learn about the many different ways of experiencing the everyday world.

Appendix 3.A   WAIS-III Subtests – a Quick Guide

The current (i.e. 1998) version of the WAIS–III has 14 subtests. Eleven of these are required to calculate the four Index scores. A brief description of what each subtest requires is given below, under the heading of each Index.

Verbal Comprehension: Assesses Verbal Reasoning

Vocabulary	knowledge of the meanings of words
Similarities	identifying how sets of words are linked conceptually
Information	general knowledge

Working Memory: Assesses Active Use of Auditory Short-Term Memory

Arithmetic	mental arithmetic problems
Digit Span	remembering strings of digits in forward and reverse order
Number-Letter Sequencing	mentally unscrambling a mixture of numbers and letters

Perceptual Organization: Assesses Visual Reasoning Skills

Picture Completion	spotting missing details from pictures
Block Design	a visuospatial task using patterned blocks to copy patterns
Matrix Reasoning	completing complex visual patterns logically

Processing Speed: Assesses Speed of Visual Processing

Digit-Symbol Coding	drawing the symbol that belongs with a number as quickly as possible
Symbol Search	looking to see whether an array contains target symbols

12th, 13th and 14th Subtests

The calculation of Verbal IQ requires the inclusion of the subtest of Comprehension and the exclusion of Letter-Number Sequencing. (Comprehension requires an explanation of a variety of policies.)

Performance IQ requires the inclusion of Picture Arrangement (a storyboard type of task) and the exclusion of Symbol Search.

The 14th subtest, Object Assembly, is very seldom used, and is primarily for use as a visual reasoning back-up task.

References

American Psychiatric Association (2000) *Diagnostic and Statistical Manual of Mental Disorders, 4th edn*, American Psychiatric Association, Washington, DC.

Brown, T.E. (1996) *Brown Attention Deficit Disorder Scales*, Harcourt Brace, San Antonio, TX.

Butterworth, B. (1999) *True Grit*. Interview with A. Moluk, *New Scientist*, **2193**, 3 July, p. 46.

DANDA (2008) *Developmental Adult Neurodiversity Association*, www.danda.org.uk (accessed 20 March 2008).

Desoete, A. (2006) *Dyscalculia in Belgium: Definition, Prevalence, Subtypes, Comorbidity, and Assessment*. Keynote paper prepared for the Dyscalculia and Dyslexia Interest Group conference, April 5, Loughborough University, UK.

Drew, S. (2005) *Developmental Co-ordination Disorder in Adults*, Whurr, London.

Dyspraxia Foundation (2008) What Is Dyspraxia? www.dyspraxiafoundation.org.uk (accessed 20 March 2008).

Faraone, S.V., Sergeant, J., Gillberg, C. and Biederman, J. (2003) The worldwide prevalence of AD(H)D: is it an American condition? *World Psychiatry*, **2**, 104–13.

Grant, D. (2007) Incidence of synaesthesia and its diagnostic implications in adults referred for suspected specific learning difficulties during a 2-year period. *Newsletter of the UK Synaesthesia Association*, **4** (1), 3.

Hollingham, R. (2004) In the realm of your senses. *New Scientist*, 31 January, **181**, 40–42.

Ingesson, S.G. (2006) Stability of IQ measures in teenagers and young adults with developmental dyslexia. *Dyslexia*, **12**, 81–95.

Kadesjö, B. and Gillberg, C. (1998) Attention deficits and clumsiness in Swedish 7-year-old children. *Developmental Medicine and Child Neurology*, **40**, 796–804.

Kadesjö, B. and Gillberg, C. (2001) The comorbidity of AD(H)D in the general population of Swedish school-aged children. *Journal of Child Psychology and Psychiatry and Allied Disciplines*, **42**, 487–92.

Kirby, A. and Drew, S. (2003) *Guide to Dyspraxia and Developmental Coordination Disorders*, David Fulton, London.

Lauth, G.W., Heubeck, B.G. and Mackowiask, K. (2006) Observation of children with attention-deficit hyperactivity (AD(H)D) problems in three natural classroom contexts. *British Journal of Educational Psychology*, **76**, 385–402.

Ramus, F., Rosen, S., Dakin, S.C. *et al.* (2003) Theories of developmental dyslexia: insights from a multiple case study of dyslexic adults. *Brain*, **126**, 841–65.

Simner, J., Mulvenna, C., Sagiv, N. *et al.* (2006) Synaesthesia: the prevalence of atypical cross-modal experiences. *Perception*, **35**, 1023–33.

Singer, J. (1998) *Odd People In: The Birth of Community amongst People on the Autistic Spectrum: A Personal Exploration of a New Social Movement Based on Neurological Diversity*. Honours dissertation, University of Technology, Sydney, www.neurodiversity.com.au/lightdark.htm (accessed 20 March 2008).

Stevenson, H.W., Stigler, J.W., Lucker, G.W. and Lee, S. (1982) Reading disabilities: the case of Chinese, Japanese and English. *Child Development*, **53**, 1164–81.

Temple, C. (1997) *Developmental Cognitive Neuropsychology*, Psychology Press, Hove.

Tresman, S. (2006) What is dyslexia? in *The Dyslexia Handbook* (eds S. Tresman and A. Cooke), British Dyslexia Association, Reading.

Wechsler, D. (1999) *Wechsler Adult Intelligence Scale*, Third UK edition *(WAIS-III UK)*, Pearson Education, Harlow.

Chapter 4

Dyslexia

Ross Cooper

This chapter will consider how to improve the learning experience of dyslexic learners in higher education (HE), using a social-interactive paradigm of dyslexia based on the social model of disability (Oliver, 1990).

Key elements in the analysis are shown in Figure 4.1.

The interaction between these elements determines the degree of achievement for the learner, or the apparent 'disability'. I shall consider each element before exemplifying strategies for successful inclusion.

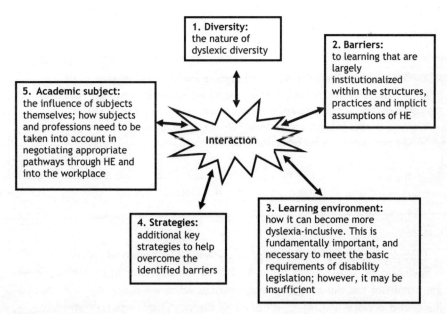

Figure 4.1 Dyslexia in higher education

Diversity

In the social-interactive model (Herrington and Hunter-Carch, 2001), dyslexia is a social construct; we are all neurodiverse. The social context determines whether or not the neurodiversity is perceived as a disability.

The concept and experience of dyslexia arise from the social development of schooling and particular forms of literacy. What we know as 'dyslexia' began to be recognized through interactions in that social context. Social constructs can also be concrete and include material objects (such as books, or schools), but more importantly ways of seeing (or interpreting) material constructs, the design assumptions made in their construction (such as the use of phonics or left-to-right scansion), required behaviours and emergent difficulties. Perceiving a difficulty as an individual deficit, rather than a difficulty presented by circumstance, is itself a social construct.

Doctors, psychologists, academics, teachers and dyslexics themselves have been puzzling over the nature of dyslexia for 130 years (Thomson, 1990). Yet it is only relatively recently that the voices of dyslexics themselves have begun to be heard (Morgan and Klein, 2000).

Dyslexia is not something that has happened to me, it is intrinsic to who I am. Take away the 'dyslexia' and I would no longer be me. I am 'dyslexic' not 'a person with dyslexia'; it means much more than having difficulty with literacy. In recognizing my dyslexic identity, it becomes empowering and I would not choose to be other than 'dyslexic'.

Ross Cooper (RC)

I would argue that the concept of dyslexia first emerged as an articulation of 'unexpected difficulties' with literacy. This led to research into the nature of the difficulty and debate over what we mean by 'unexpected' (Rice and Brooks, 2004). The nature of literacy itself was conveniently taken for granted.

> I am probably ... unnecessarily paranoid about exposure of my weaknesses,
> as it will take more than one assessment to recover from many and repeated
> experiences of perceived unexplained inadequacy.
>
> Mature student

There have been various well-documented fashions in research circles
(DfES and NIACE, 2004; Rice and Brooks, 2004), from 'word blindness'
(Orton, 1925), to phonological awareness deficits (e.g. Snowling, 2000),
to the double deficit (Wolf and O'Brien, 2001), to visual deficits again
(Stein, 2001), to automaticity deficits (Fawcett and Nicolson, 2001). All of
these academic theorists have looked at dyslexia as a form of deficit.
Although there are many models of dyslexia, they all tend to fall within a
single deficit (medical) paradigm. Despite extensive research, there remains
no consensus about causes, or about the full range of difficulties to include
in the definition of dyslexia.

I argue that trying to understand the nature of dyslexia by examining the
apparent weaknesses, or difficulties, is like trying to understand the nature
of left-handedness by examining the weaknesses, or difficulties, that such
individuals have with using their right hand. This tells us very little about the
nature of being left-handed.

> Labels are irrelevant, but being able to rethink how I work and learn is
> invaluable.
>
> Mature first year student, recently diagnosed as dyslexic

The difficulties that dyslexic people experience may be indelible, but
they only tell half the story, based on the negative imprint on our lives of
social interactions and expectations. We are only just beginning to
articulate the other half of the story, the range of differences that are not in
themselves negative at all, that lead through social interactions to the
impression and experience of disability.

> I know that I would have given up the course before asking for a dyslexia
> assessment, without having had the opportunity to talk about it and untangle
> it all in my head in a much slower way.
>
> First year undergraduate

There have been very few definitions or descriptions of dyslexia from the social model of disability perspective (Riddick, 2001). I have argued that:

> *We challenge the deficit models of dyslexia in favour of a social model that maintains that we are not 'disabled' by our dyslexia, but by the expectations of the world we live in. There is nothing 'wrong' with being dyslexic per se.*
>
> *We would argue that dyslexia is an experience that arises out of natural human diversity on the one hand and a world on the other where the early learning of literacy, and good personal organisation and working memory is mistakenly used as a marker of 'intelligence'. The problem here is seeing difference incorrectly as 'deficit'.*
> *(Cooper, 2006a)*

Some of the characteristics of being dyslexic in HE include:

- Approaching academic issues from unusual perspectives;
- Making unusual connections;
- Being creative and producing new ideas easily;
- Being particularly good at dissecting arguments in discussions;
- Being good at 'what if' problematics; and
- Being good at following passionate interest.

Many of these characteristics are associated with processing information holistically, rather than sequentially, and thinking visually, rather than verbally (Krupska and Klein, 1995; Morgan and Klein, 2000). My research in tertiary education (Cooper, 2006b) found that 80% of dyslexic learners preferred to problem-solve visually rather than verbally; 33% of dyslexics never thought verbally at all. This is almost seven times more likely for those diagnosed as dyslexic than those who are not (5%) and can feel like living in an alien world (Morgan and Klein, 2000).

My tutor ... is slowly coming round to the idea that people really can be visual learners without it being less than writing! For that matter I am finally starting to feel less that I need to cover it up so people don't find out that I need to change the way information is presented to make it make sense.

Mature postgraduate student

Many characteristic difficulties can be perceived as a direct result of the false assumption that all people think verbally and sequentially. Difficulties with these also form the basis of both diagnostic assessment and screening procedures.

The notion of diagnosis is sometimes deplored as the language of the deficit, medical paradigm. However, the concept of diagnosis pre-dates the medical paradigm and focuses on understanding the reasons for experiences, behaviours and difficulties. The concept of diagnostic assessment can therefore be an important element in the social model of dyslexia, enabling us to create a structure that facilitates explicit discussion of the difficulties without implying deficit.

Many dyslexic learners still hide their difficulties, making it difficult to develop strategies to overcome the barriers. I would therefore argue that both assessment and screening are extremely important within a dyslexia-friendly organization.

I always went to great lengths to hide my difficulties with writing, pretending that I spent much less time than I did. Everyone else seemed to be able to dash essays off, when it would take me weeks and many drafts before I would even consider letting anyone see it. Then I would pretend it was my first draft to cover myself. Some tutors thought I was lazy when I was working so hard! I thought that if someone found out, I would be thrown off my course. It was only when I began to realise that I was not alone, that all these famous people were dyslexic, that I began to think differently.

Second year undergraduate, Humanities

Working to a timed schedule also creates difficulties, including:

- sense of the passage of time;
- sequence over time; and
- planning time (which also relates to organization).

The stronger the preference for visual thinking and holistic processing, the more difficult it is to keep track of time. Time dilation effects, where minutes seem like hours (and vice versa), can be extreme. Visual thinking is so fast and emotionally immediate (or 'hot'), that keeping track of time while thinking is not possible. This makes it extremely difficult to be anywhere on time, or to estimate how long work may take. At university, this can be problematic (Herrington, 2001, p. 187).

> My own strategy to achieve punctuality is to have made myself extremely stressed about being late, which can 'jerk' me out of my thoughts regularly enough to avoid lateness, sufficiently often to get by. It is not a strategy I would recommend, since the emotional cost is high.
>
> RC

Barriers

Dyslexic learners are disabled by educational expectations and assumptions. These take many forms, and individuals are unique in their responses. Typical features include:

- An obvious differential between conceptual understanding and argument on the one hand, and written expression, organizational structure and writing on the other.
- The need for time keeping and deadlines.
- The expectation of accurate spelling, although some have overcome this difficulty.
- University life also makes great demands on personal organization, which many dyslexics find difficult.
- Listening to long explanations is extremely difficult for most dyslexic learners, who usually experience lectures as a very poor form of education.
- In contrast, some find the cut and thrust of seminars very useful, although others will find it very difficult to process a conversation where different individuals may interrupt each other.
- Reading: some find difficulty decoding unknown words, some find difficulty in taking in what they read. Most find long reading lists counterproductive and need to find a way of focusing the reading. There is a serious lack of electronic versions of key texts.

> I normally read well, but it depends. I remember spending six hours reading one paragraph. Who would believe that?
>
> Social Science student who achieved a 1st

Accessing courses

Rational university entry criteria would identify the skills and abilities that a candidate needs in order to undertake and complete a course successfully, and which will not be taught during the course. Identifying them allows the criteria to be questioned. Unfortunately, this rarely happens. In the UK, specified A-level grades are the norm, even though there is only a 40% correlation between A-level grades and degree success (Black and Wiliam, 2002). A levels are therefore an unnecessary barrier to university entrance. They appear to be retained because universities are judged by the standard of A-level results that students achieve before enrolling. This is analogous to judging a hospital on the basis of the health of the patients on arrival.

One consequence is that some UK universities then waive the necessity of achieving the A-level grades for dyslexic candidates. Unfortunately, A levels are not replaced with more meaningful criteria that enable candidates to judge whether they are ready to manage the course. When candidates do not manage, some academics imagine that this is evidence of lack of 'ability' 'mislabelled as dyslexia'. Once again, the debate centres on the individual when the real issues are a lack of:

- Clear entry criteria matched to the requirements of the course; and
- Effective study skills support to enable the required skills.

Requiring high-level sequencing skills

Perceptual processing difficulties

It is generally considered a defining characteristic of dyslexia to experience 'processing difficulties' when bringing meaning to auditory or visual sequential information such as language or writing (Klein, 2003). This requires good sequential and working memory skills to hold on to the strings of information. In contrast, processing information holistically makes these skills less crucial. Therefore, an apparent 'processing difficulty' is a consequence of the requirement to process sequences of perceptual information. Visual holistic learners can succeed with a limited capacity for these skills. Requiring learning to involve these skills presents a sophisticated barrier to achievement.

Reproducing linear sequence

Nowhere is the disabling effect of implicit assumptions more devastating than through academic assessment.

> I have a friend who has gone way beyond the call of duty and lets me verbalise my ideas until I can work out some kind of order on the page.
>
> Visual thinker

It is entirely arbitrary to assess learning through essays (Pollak, 2005). In Bourdieu's terms, this is oppression through the imposition of a 'cultural arbitrary' (Bourdieu and Passeron, 1977).

> The hardest thing I find is that nothing other than academic written work is actually measured. I got a 1st on my practical placement before Christmas, but this isn't graded, and I do great in class and skills sessions but these aren't marked. We have to do a verbal/visual presentation on a research theme but this isn't assessed, only the written version of the same material. It is very hard that the things I can do are 'irrelevant' and the things I can't do are the only things that have any value. It does get me quite down some days.
>
> Rosa, Postgraduate, mature student

Assuming that everyone can take in and remember sequences of information (particularly auditory information) is disabling and entirely unnecessary. The point is to understand and use, not to remember.

> Where my visual approach to information and explaining what I have learnt is always regarded as very positive, the thought of being able to present my learning in this way for assessment is not even worthy of discussion. Linear text, and ONLY this form, is a valid way in the current system of measuring learning, even more so in a postgraduate environment. It rarely improves my learning (or application thereof) to write it down, as this has already taken place in the holistic visual way that I use to make sense of the material. All the writing bit does is make me very stressed, exhausted and thoroughly miserable. Even my tutor has said (in an attempt to encourage me!) that post qualification no one is likely to care whether I am able to write an academic-style piece of writing, just whether I am able to fulfil the requirements of the job: SO WHY IS IT THE ONLY WAY YOU MEASURE ME! The sooner the notion in the academic world that competency and academic writing are not one entity, the better as far as I am concerned!
>
> Mature learner

Social interaction

Dealing with barriers to learning leads to stress (Miles and Varma, 1995), but this is rarely acknowledged in Assessment of Need reports or indeed the support systems in HE. Stress can arise from such issues as work overload due to the need to spend more time reading and producing written documents.

There is also emerging evidence of wider difficulties with social and informal interactions, currently described as 'pragmatic abilities', or 'meaning in interaction' (Thomas, 1995). Smith-Sparke *et al.* (2001) also found indications of attentional difficulties, memory and miscellaneous slips. Griffiths (2007), in her pilot study, identifies evidence of a range of 'pragmatic difficulties' experienced by 'well-compensated adults with dyslexia'. These include difficulties with processing language in social situations, missing jokes and inferences. This can place additional stress on the relationships which can form informal support networks.

Learning Environment

This section is intended to outline a range of good practice, to reduce barriers to learning for dyslexic learners. The more inclusive the learning environment, the fewer additional support strategies are necessary.

> I am very sad that during the 13-year gap when I have done everything in my power to avoid education, very little seems to have changed.
> Mature postgraduate learner

I asked a group of dyslexic learners who were aspiring to university what the most important aspects of teaching were to them. They all wanted to:

- Know why they were expected to do what they were doing; and
- See teachers/lecturers owning up to 'making mistakes'.

The modelling of making mistakes as part of the learning process is important for two reasons:

1. Many dyslexics have learned to feel acutely embarrassed about making mistakes (apparent and stressful evidence of their 'inabilities') and carry this burden into new learning environments.
2. Feeling able to make mistakes is also part of valuing diversity and a key element of an inclusive learning environment.

Entry criteria

Universities would become more inclusive if they provided clear and meaningful entry criteria based on a thorough course analysis that identifies the nature of the learning journey, the learning environment and the capacity of the organization to respond to diversity. Much of this knowledge is rarely open to candidates. An understanding of the nature of the course would be improved by knowing:

*   What will learners be expected to be able to do on arrival?
*   Do the entry criteria reflect these expectations?
*   Are the necessary study skills taught here?
*   What is the nature of the teaching?
*   How do lecturers modify teaching to be inclusive?
*   How will learners be assessed?
*   How do tutors/lecturers modify assessment to be inclusive?
*   Will learners be able to follow their passionate interests?
*   How far is creativity in this subject encouraged?

Screening for dyslexia

The UK National Research and Development Centre review of dyslexia research states:

> Screening tests, whether behavioural checklists, cognitive batteries or hybrid methods, have one purpose: to reduce the time and expense of diagnosis.   (Rice and Brooks, 2004, p. 165)

Having a screening process for dyslexia also provides a clear message that the university expects dyslexics to be among their students. In addition to the ethical and legal reasons for being proactive (Disability Discrimination Act (DDA), 2005), there are also financial advantages for UK universities. Each student who receives the Disabled Students' Allowance brings into their university an additional 50% of their Higher Educational Funding Council funds each year, while reducing pressure on information technology resources and library books. Providing access to diagnostic procedures following the screening also communicates the message that the university supports and values dyslexic learners; that we belong.

An effective screening has two further purposes. It can:

1. Prioritize those identified, so that those most in need can benefit from a diagnostic assessment first; and
2. Inform individuals (confidentially) of the likelihood of being dyslexic. If this includes referral information and feedback about strengths and difficulties, it can empower students' learning and they can choose to find out more.

Some screening materials focus on limited aspects of dyslexia such as phonological difficulties, but ignore visual processing or motor integration difficulties (James, 2004; Price and Skinner, 2007). Others, like the free Adult Dyslexia Organisation (ADO) questionnaire (Cooper and Miles, 2006), take an empirical approach by matching the responses against those who have been diagnosed already as dyslexic. Any question that is found empirically to discriminate between dyslexics and non-dyslexics becomes a legitimate screening question. Such questionnaires are interesting, because the questions that prove to be the best discriminators are about the difficulties experienced with sequencing of different kinds. We might then theorize why this is, but the effectiveness of the tool is established empirically.

Part of the difficulty of gauging the accuracy of a screening tool is that it is difficult to know what you are measuring this against. There remains no agreed 'gold standard' of diagnostic assessment. In the United Kingdom, the Specific Learning Difficulties Working Group (2005) has attempted to work towards this. Part of the problem is that assessment involves judgement about the evidence, which is not value-free, and there remains no guarantee that two assessors will always agree who is, or is not, dyslexic.

Learning and teaching strategies

The main challenge here is not what individual lecturers can do; this has been established (brainhe.com). The real challenge is designing a whole-organizational approach that is fit for purpose, that implements the requirements of disability legislation and ensures that lecturers can change their practice. Unfortunately, there appears to be little effective leverage for internal change, except through linking staff development to appraisal.

There is a risk of stereotyping dyslexic learners when generalizing about strengths and weaknesses and learning strategies. All dyslexics are unique, even if most have much in common.

The importance of the big picture

Most learners need to know the big picture when learning (DfES, 2004). Most dyslexic learners cannot learn at all without it (Cooper, 2007).

If I can't see the big picture, I can't do it!

Second year economics student

The big picture can be provided in many ways. The purpose can be made clear, or, even better, learners can be allowed to follow their own purpose; this is one reason why problem-solving approaches, which intrinsically provide a meaningful purpose, are effective.

Mind-maps can be excellent for displaying overviews, connections and the organizing principle of teaching. Analogies and metaphors can capture key messages (visual information can be expressed verbally in this way), or even better encourage learners to develop their own (Williams, 1983). Without an overview or purpose to the learning activity, learners focus on trying to work it out for themselves, reducing their ability to retain strings of verbal information. An overview should also provide clarity about parameters and expectations in the learning environment. What are the expectations, entitlements and obligations? What are the ground rules and expected behaviour? Once these are clear, some of the anxiety can be removed from the learning situation and the expectations and assumptions become open to scrutiny.

Visual and verbal thinking

Academics often assume that everyone thinks verbally (Fraser, 2006) – that thought requires vocabulary to think it. This presumption seems extremely strange to most dyslexic learners, 80% of whom prefer to problem-solve visually (Cooper, 2006b). Perhaps more surprisingly, 55% of non-dyslexic learners also prefer to problem-solve visually (Cooper, 2006b).

Most people (91%) are capable of thinking verbally (in a similar way to right-handed people being capable of using their left hands). But when it comes to problem-solving, or really making sense of something, most do this visually. However, there is a difference of degree: 33% dyslexics can *only* do this visually compared to 5% of nondyslexics (Cooper, 2006b).

Ensuring that verbal communication does not create a barrier to visual learning is an important consideration. There are many ways this can be avoided. Some strategies relate to big-picture processes, since visual thinking relies on the creation and manipulation of whole pictures, using spatial organization to map priorities, connections and meaning. This can be supported by real materials and contexts, and colour-coding of meaning. Analogies (visual narrative and parallels), metaphors and overviews are all conducive to generating visual meaning. Similarly, work experience that enables 'seeing' the purpose of work within real, if complex, contexts can be very helpful.

It is incorrect to assume that visual thinking is necessarily concrete. It often involves symbols to represent abstract concepts, like Faraday's 'lines of flux' (West, 1991). But abstract language can present particular difficulties unless these are exemplified. Visual thinkers need to 'see' what something means. If teaching cannot meet that need, learners need to find a way to meet it themselves.

Dyslexic diversity

It is often incorrectly assumed that all dyslexics think visually. My research (Cooper, 2006b) indicates that although most do, 8% of dyslexics never problem-solve visually, which is over double the percentage of the 'nondyslexic' group (3.5%). In other words, dyslexic learners populate the extremes in problem-solving visually and verbally. This may be one reason that 'dyslexia-friendly is learner-friendly' (ADO), since the full range of cognitive and perceptual processes must be included. However, I have found that those dyslexics who think verbally tend to be more responsive to sequential strategies, arrive on time and relate to rules (Cooper, 1997). There is some evidence to suggest that those who think verbally are more likely to progress to university.[1]

If dyslexic learners have no choice but to problem-solve visually or verbally (rather than engage both modes of thinking), and in addition experience difficulties with a range of 'processing difficulties', it clearly becomes the responsibility of educators to avoid limiting teaching to a single mode. Requiring extended periods of listening to lectures will

---

[1]Fifty-five per cent of dyslexic learners at a university college were found to problem-solve verbally rather than visually.

disadvantage and discriminate against anyone with a difficulty with processing auditory information (or, indeed, anyone who is deaf or hearing impaired).

Inclusive learning

There is a consensus that multisensory learning is particularly beneficial to dyslexic learners, while also being beneficial to all (Cottrell, 2001; DfES and NIACE, 2004; Price and Skinner, 2007), arguing that providing multiple perceptual pathways strengthens memory. However, scaffolding 'weak memory' is the least of three reasons why it is effective. Multi-sensory teaching also:

1. Avoids perceptual barriers to learning; and
2. Allows learners to make meaning either sequentially or holistically.

> I managed to turn a whole chapter of dense information into a four-part colour-coded picture, blu-tacked to the wall in stages to talk the group through it. Before I did the course last year I would have done that for myself, but would never have had the confidence to use it in such an academic context – but it worked well and people really got it.
>
> Mature first year undergraduate student

Active learning, where the learner is engaged in learning activities such as problem-solving, is always more effective than passive listening (Hattie, 1999), yet this remains the dominant mode of teaching in universities.

> One lecturer did not let us take notes while we were listening. He made us listen for 15 minutes and then gave us 5 minutes to take notes and compare with a neighbour. It made us all really think about what we were learning.
>
> Business studies undergraduate

Most dyslexic learners at university do not take up additional support. For example, at my current university, with over 1200 identified dyslexics (almost 80% of all students with disabilities), only 10% accept the support being offered to them, beyond receiving their assistive technology and a technical crash course in its use.

In contrast, at a previous university college, which took a whole-organizational approach to widening participation, 48% received support. Furthermore, it was found that those who received support were slightly more likely to pass their degrees than nondyslexic students, whereas those who did not receive support were much more likely to drop out or fail than nondyslexic learners.[2] Tutors therefore can play an important role in advocating appropriate support, particularly the use of assistive technology.

> Audio Notetaker is an excellent new tool to enable audio files to be organised visually, edited and labelled. Making sense of lectures is much easier.
>
> Dyslexic tutor involved in study support

Lecturers can be proactive in encouraging all learners to record their lectures, and provide PowerPoint notes that learners can download.

> I always feel too embarrassed to record lectures and miss most of it.
> Postgraduate student

Staff can insist on avoiding bleached white paper, which causes visual stress for at least 20% of learners (Evans, 2001). They can develop an open personal style that exemplifies the learning process and opens debate, involving learners more actively in learning. They can think in a more focused way about what they want learners to learn and how to facilitate this, rather than simply 'lecture'.

> In all my years of running workshops on creative teaching, I have never had a single lecturer state that they would prefer to go back to the way they used to teach.
>
> RC

Assessment for learning (formerly known as formative assessment) is designed to improve the learning process by identifying strengths and how the learning performance can be improved (Black and Wiliam, 1998).

---

[2]Internal documentation, New College, 2001–2003.

Such strategies are particularly important for dyslexic learners, who may have missed critical cues about what is expected.

> I was constantly confused and frustrated at the feedback of 'come on there is clearly no reason why you can't do this, as you understand everything perfectly well, so obviously you just need to relax more'. I always knew that there was more to it than this, but could not articulate what that was.
>
> Mature postgraduate

> I was once told that my submission had 300 spelling mistakes; could I please correct them? This was useless feedback. I did not know where they were.
>
> RC

Essays can create particular difficulties for those making meaning holistically, since unlike an essay, holistic meaning has no beginning, middle or end. An organizing principle to convert holistic visual meaning into sequential verbal writing is rarely taught (or even understood by tutors). Yet it is critical for academic success in our universities. Good teaching about mind- or concept-mapping can provide this and the tools to facilitate it.

> I was unable to write academic essays until I could see what one looked like, and understand how it should be structured.
>
> RC

> I used to try and write essays by writing my ideas out – the whole picture. It was like trying to write out a dream of a complex and active 3D universe, which took place in 360 degrees. Further, the more I tried to pin bits down in careful linear language, the more the overall universe slipped away from me. No wonder what I wrote didn't make much sense to the reader. Now I've been taught what essays are meant to look and feel like, I can take my world of ideas and pull the different parts into the right place to make it make sense sequentially, so that whoever is marking my ideas can read the picture off the page.
>
> Third year undergraduate

Tutors can also ensure that assignment deadlines do not create a bottleneck of work, and allow some flexibility over deadlines.

> The Professor announced that she didn't like the timetable, brought forward the submission date for the proposal, completely scrapped the presentation (which is the only thing I am any good at!) and brought the deadline for the summative written work forward.
>
> It was the straw that finally broke me, as I was already ridiculously tired and just couldn't stop crying (not normal!). I've had to take a few days off to protect my sanity, as I couldn't pull myself together and get my head round it all. It feels quite hard; as it is such a big change, it throws my workload planning out of the window.
>
> Postgraduate, mature student

Making sure that procedures are fully understood is critical. One Russell Group university (a UK grouping of institutions which claim superior academic reputations) relied on all the procedures being published somewhere on their web site, and compounded the difficulties by simply assuming that all students were familiar with them. Inflicting unreasonable procedures can lead to litigation.

Staff can play a significant role in advising students to seek out a diagnostic assessment. A good diagnostic report facilitates inclusive learning by helping students to reframe their understanding of themselves, their learning history and how to begin building on their strengths while recognizing their difficulties. This can be a life-changing process.

Academic assessment

Academic assessment should assess the essential elements being learned, without combining these with unnecessary barriers to achievement.

> I was fortunate in undertaking my doctorate in the mid-70s, when academics were more concerned with the quality of ideas than the consistency of spelling.
>
> RC

One lecturer said 'the ideas are all really good'. I expressed relief that I could just polish it up and get on with my other essays. He laughed and said 'you're not planning to hand it in like this are you?!'

'Well.' I said sheepishly.

'The grammar, and structure – it makes no sense!'

My heart dropped and my stomach turned; I was so dismayed and so ashamed, I felt humiliated and incapable. I was stressed for weeks trying to restructure and change that essay round to 'make sense', not really knowing what I was trying to achieve. It has just struck me though: if it really made no sense, how did he understand the ideas in it in the first place?

Sociology undergraduate

Different discourses of dyslexia (Pollak, 2005) can have a dramatic impact on personal and academic development. Sometimes, dyslexics can feel angry about how they have been misjudged and humiliated. It is important that this is not misinterpreted, but allowed a voice. Counsellors can also have an important role to play.

Strategies

Those diagnosed as dyslexic in the United Kingdom are entitled to a wide range of assistive technology that can revolutionize their learning and achievement.

I have fallen in love with the reading software – it has allowed me to read a whole academic book for the first time ever! This has been an utter revelation. I SO had no idea that books could actually make so much sense!!

Mature postgraduate student

Using screen readers can be time-consuming. Reading lists need to be reduced by focusing on the most relevant books, chapters or paragraphs. Instigating opportunities to talk about the concepts in the reading may prove far more valuable than reading them.

> I passed my degree by getting discussions going in seminars about the concepts; I could never manage the reading, so I just discussed the ideas and implications implicit in the concepts that others introduced. It was really effective; all my seminar feedback says I was an asset to the class and I got a 1st.
>
> Social science undergraduate

Unfortunately, it appears that in many cases, the technology given to dyslexic learners remains largely unused (Litterick, 2006). The training individuals receive on how to use it is often entirely a technical affair: a crash course in technical capability that takes little account of their course, or learning needs and strengths. The impact can be extraordinary if the assistive technology is recognized as built around our senses and capable of forming a powerful individualized learning styles environment (DfES and NIACE, 2004).

> Getting voice recognition was like being given wings!
>
> Access student

Technical expertise needs to service the learning priorities and be integrated into the learning support.

> I never realised how much fun learning could be! I had been predicted a third, but within a few weeks I managed a 2:1.
>
> Third year undergraduate using concept-mapping and voice recognition

If the Assessment of Need does not specify what is required, it can be changed by approaching the original assessor and explaining what is needed.

Managing problems of sequence

Time

Learners are expected to organize a great deal more of their own time at university than prior to it. For many dyslexic students, this is extremely challenging (Herrington, 2001). Errors are constantly made and then meetings are avoided through sheer embarrassment. It can be very difficult for nondyslexics to recognize the extent of the difficulty.

Even now I have to be constantly vigilant to avoid muddling up Tuesdays and Thursdays (they not only have similar letters, but I perceive them in similar colours). At least once a year, I discover I am using the wrong day's timetable. At least once a year, I find myself coming home an hour early, or an hour late due to misreading an analogue watch. These events remain intensely embarrassing for me. How would they feel to a new undergraduate who is trying to be taken seriously by their peers and tutors? Dyslexics often avoid disclosing any difficulties with tutors to avoid such embarrassment. My own view is that a dyslexic mentoring system would prove invaluable.

RC

Many students find that setting alarms and reminders is very useful, and handheld computers or mobile phones can serve this function well (if you remember to set the alarm). Some colleges have installed automatic texting services (to remind learners to be on time at events) with a great deal of success. This can help all learners, and is apparently easy and cheap to install on computer systems.

I have to keep a diary of events; without it I couldn't tell you whether I had last done something two days ago, two months ago or two years ago. This is even the case for very important or emotional events. Similarly I have to save and file all my emails. Without being able to check, I couldn't tell you for certain if I had spent 5 hours dealing with a request yesterday or if I hadn't seen the email at all, or when I had done something and sometimes whether I had done it at all. This is also true of physical things – unfortunately I haven't figured out a way of saving those yet.

Postgraduate student

I find that being able to keep my emails is an invaluable tool for keeping track of time-based information and events. When emails are deleted, so is my work life and I feel lost. When any work event is challenged, I feel vulnerable unless I can track back through emails and see what happened when. A random-access electronic trail is far more useful than a paper-trail, which I can't usually find. It is essential that I keep all my emails, and not have my inbox restricted.

RC

Organizing writing

The moment of cognition when everything suddenly makes sense is paramount for holistic thinkers. Consequently, it is pointless starting to write before that moment of inspiration. Unfortunately, learners are rarely taught how to do this. They are taught to read the texts and make notes. This in itself is unlikely to lead to the required moment of inspiration (which involves standing back from the information and allowing it to reconfigure in your mind). Without it, the holistic learner tends to put off writing. This can lose valuable time. An alternative is to over-study, taking many times the time taken by nondyslexic learners to go over and over the information. Some students literally map out several possible essays, before having the onerous task of reducing this to one. Allowing flexibility over deadlines can therefore be an essential feature of inclusive learning.

In other words, accumulating information does not in itself lead to inspiration; it is coming to the information from an angle that allows you to 'see' it in a new and meaningful way. The earlier this is achieved, the easier it is to make sense of all the bits of information. Without it, the learner is forced to decide to write something before it is too late to write anything. Getting this timing right is almost impossible. It is always much easier if the learner is passionately interested in the subject, since they are more likely to start with a viewpoint that enables them to organize the information meaningfully, and engage in the 'recursive activity' of academic writing (Price and Skinner, 2007).

Academic Subject

I wanted to be an actor, but I found it difficult to memorize lines. So I thought I could avoid this by doing media studies. But I'm hopeless at it and find that I have loads I can't remember anyway!

Media studies undergraduate

Diversity can play an important role in whether a course, or employment, is appropriate or not. We might be tempted to assume that a course, or profession, that required good memory for detail and personal organization would not suit most dyslexics. However, this also depends on the passionate interest and motivation of the individual (i.e. diversity) as well as the learning, or work, environment, strategies and barriers. Making assumptions about the 'inevitable limitations' of an individual is disabling; examples can always be found of individuals who have surmounted extreme difficulties in achieving their aims (usually associated with passionate interest). Nevertheless, it remains important to recognize the nature of the gap between an individual's profile of strengths/difficulties and the expectations of the course, or employment, so that informed choices can be made (and, where appropriate, expectations challenged). This can lead to meaningful concepts of learner (or employee) entitlement and responsibilities.

Course analysis is the process through which realistic expectations can be developed and the learning journey made transparent. From the perspective of the course tutor, this begins by mapping their expectations, which then allows learners to question their validity. If the expectations are not made explicit, learners cannot make informed choices and ought not then to bear all the responsibility for failure. Different subjects make different demands on learners and these need to be explicit.

Work placements can create additional barriers for dyslexic students. The environment may be perceived as even less dyslexia-friendly than university and generate the imperative to hide difficulties, rather than disclose them. McCandless and Sanderson-Mann (2006) found that 50% of dyslexic nurses never disclosed dyslexia to their colleagues, and 30% never disclosed to their practice mentor. This means that their vulnerability and dangers increase in the workplace. It is a fear of inappropriate repercussions that drives this secrecy. Some UK universities, in response to the DDA, have taken responsibility for organizing dyslexia awareness for nurse practitioners. Safe medical practice depends on the development of better understanding and more dyslexia-friendly work placements.

We can identify the elements of course and work placement success as:

1. Passionate interest in the subject
2. Good understanding of own strengths and weaknesses
3. Inclusive ethos in the workplace
4. Good understanding of the demands of the subject, or work

5. Finding a match of needed skills to assessment (or how work will be judged).
6. Availability of appropriate support.

The legitimate, essential elements of the subject need to inform the design of fair and rigorous assessment. For example, a working sociologist would not normally be expected to write essays under timed conditions, or rely on memory for relevant quotations. The timed element and memory burden introduce spurious, unnecessary aspects to the assessment process for the convenience of the tutor marking the work. Different subjects and professions have different appropriate requirements. Spurious elements need to be eliminated, or individual arrangements made for assessment.

> My academic success is largely due to avoiding courses with unseen exams!
> Dyslexic learner with PhD

Strategies for Inclusion

Exemplification of how these five elements interact is provided in the following table. The questions on the top/right are mainly appropriate for course coordinators. The questions on the bottom/left are mainly appropriate for tutors (Table 4.1).

The questions are premised on the belief that universities need to develop open and supportive systems, rather than defensive strategies intended to protect them from litigation. The best defence is a transparent system. Universities would benefit from encouraging dyslexics to challenge their systems, since we all stand to benefit from transparency and inclusive learning.

Conclusion

> *Ultimately, only when 'learning difference' is perceived as 'normal' and literacy practices accessible for all, can we be confident about effective learning for all. (Herrington and Hunter-Carsch, 2001, p. 130)*

The social-interactive model of dyslexia enables us to shift our attention from the difficulties experienced by dyslexic learners towards the difficulties

Table 4.1 Questions about inclusion

	Diversity	Subject	Learning environment	Strategies	Barriers
					Issues for course coordinators
Diversity		What are the demands that the subject will make on learners in relation to diversity? Have these been made explicit to applicants?	Has a course analysis ensured that expectations are reasonable?	Is 'learning to learn' with 'feedback for learning' built into the course design? How far does 'learning support' influence course design?	Do course directors receive diversity training to raise awareness about the unnecessary barriers that courses can create?
Subject	Is good self-awareness/awareness of students re strengths, difficulties and motivation used to facilitate a good match with a course?		Are the learning activities (and assessment methods in particular) consistent with, and justified by, the demands of the subject?	To what extent do the demands of the subject require specific outcomes? And what is in place to help learners to achieve them?	Do the demands of the subject underpin barriers, or to what extent are they the result of taken-for-granted expectations?
Learning environment	Is the accepted/expected range of teaching and learning strategies insufficient to support dyslexic learners? How can this be diversified?	Is appropriate assessment in place to ensure fair access to achievement? Does learning support meet the demands of the subject?		To what extent can 'alternative' strategies be built into normal expectations and processes?	What unnecessary barriers can be eliminated? What is the justification for the barriers that remain?
Strategies	What opportunities are there to develop strategies that suit dyslexic learners? Does feedback lead to self-awareness for dyslexics?	To what extent are the demands of the subject made transparent? And to what extent are strategies taught to enable all learners to meet them?	How do all learners gain access to successful strategies? Do they get 'feedback for learning' to improve their strategies?		How far has the elimination of unnecessary barriers reduced the need for the development of 'compensatory' strategies?
Barriers	Do all staff have access to diversity training to raise awareness about the unnecessary barriers that their practice can create?	What individualized support is in place to challenge or overcome subject barriers?	Is individual support merely maintaining the existence of unnecessary barriers to learning and the dependence of the learner?	Do all staff value and support individualized strategies for overcoming barriers? Are diagnostic reports an entitlement?	

Issues for tutors

that universities experience in removing unnecessary barriers to learning. The current challenge is not how dyslexic learners can be supported, but how a whole-organizational approach to university systems can enable all learners to learn. As the UK's Inclusive Learning Report (Tomlinson, 1996), intended for the further education sector, maintained:

> There is a world of difference between, on the one hand, offering courses and training and then giving some students who have learning difficulties additional human or physical aids to gain access to those courses and, on the other hand, redesigning the very processes of learning, assessment and organisation so as to fit the objectives and learning styles of the students. But only the second philosophy can claim to be inclusive, to have as its central purpose the opening of opportunity to those whose disability means that they learn differently from others. (Tomlinson, 1996, p. 4)

Universities are struggling to rise to this challenge and often displace their responsibilities onto learning support tutors and the Disabled Students' Allowance. There remain significant barriers to achievement which leave universities vulnerable to litigation, since the DDA requires organizations to be proactive (DDA, 2005). Nevertheless, this is an historic opportunity to redesign the very processes of learning, assessment and organization to benefit all learners and substantially support the aspirations of widening participation.

References

Black, P. and Wiliam, D. (1998) *Inside the Black Box: Raising Standards through Classroom Assessment*, Kings College, London.
Black, P. and Wiliam, D. (2002) *Standards in Public Examinations*, Kings College, London.
Bourdieu, P. and Passeron, J.-C. (1977) (translated by Richard Nice) *Reproduction in Education, Society and Culture*, Sage, London.
Cooper, R. (1997) *The Learning Styles Diagnostic Screening Handbook*, www.outsider.co-uk.com/docs/ls_handbook.pdf (accessed 20 March 2008).
Cooper, R. (2006a) *A Social Model of Dyslexia*, South Bank University, London.
Cooper, R. (2006b) Making learning styles meaningful. *PATOSS Bulletin*, **19** (1), 58–63.
Cooper, R. (2007) The point of reframing 'learning styles' is to make a difference. *PATOSS Bulletin*, **20** (1), 50–55.

Cooper, R. and Miles, T. (2006) *Revised Adult Dyslexia Screening*, ADO www.outsider.co-uk.com (accessed 20 March 2008).

Cottrell, S. (2001) Developing positive learning environments for dyslexic students in higher education, in *Dyslexia & Effective Learning in Secondary & Tertiary Education* (eds M. Hunter-Carsh and M. Herrington), Whurr, London.

DfES (2004) *Pedagogy and Practice: Teaching and Learning in Secondary Schools, Unit 1: Structuring Learning*, www.standards.dfes.gov.uk/secondary/keystage3/downloads/sec_pptl042404u1structure.pdf (accessed 20 March 2008).

DfES and NIACE (2004) *A Framework for Understanding Dyslexia*, www.dfes.gov.uk/readwriteplus/understandingdyslexia/ (accessed 20 March 2008).

Disability Discrimination Act (DDA) (2005) Her Majesty's Stationery Office, London, www.opsi.gov.uk/Acts/acts2005/ukpga_20050013_en_1 (accessed 20 March 2008).

Evans, B.J.W. (2001) *Dyslexia and Vision*, Whurr, London.

Fawcett, A.J. and Nicolson, R.I. (2001) Dyslexia: the role of the cerebellum, in *Dyslexia – Theory and Good Practice* (ed. A.J. Fawcett), Whurr, London.

Fraser, V. (2006) What is the point of learning styles? *PATOSS Bulletin*, **19** (2), 19–25.

Griffiths, C. (2007) Pragmatic abilities in adults with and without dyslexia: a pilot study. *Dyslexia*, **13** (4), 276–96.

Hattie, J.A. (1999) *Influences on Student Learning*, www.arts.auckland.ac.nz/staff/index.cfm?P=5049 (accessed 20 March 2008).

Herrington, M. (2001) An approach to specialist learning support in higher education, in *Dyslexia & Effective Learning in Secondary & Tertiary Education* (eds M. Hunter-Carsh and M. Herrington), Whurr, London.

Herrington, M. and Hunter-Carsch, M. (2001) A social-interactive model of specific learning difficulties e.g. dyslexia, in *Dyslexia: A Psychosocial Perspective* (ed. M. Hunter-Carsch), Whurr, London.

James, A. (2004) *An Investigation and Comparison of Computer-Based Screening Tests for Dyslexia for Use in FE and HE institutions*. 6th BDA international conference, www.bdainternationalconference.org/2004/presentations/sun_p1_c_1.shtml (accessed 20 March 2008).

Klein, C. (2003) *Diagnosing Dyslexia*, Basic Skills Agency, London.

Krupska, M. and Klein, C. (1995) *Demystifying Dyslexia*, London Language and Literacy Unit.

Litterick, I. (2006) *Speech Recognition, Dyslexia and Disabilities*, www.dyslexic.com/dictcomp (accessed 21 May 2008).

McCandless, F. and Sanderson-Mann, J. (2006) *Dyslexia and Practice Environment Learning in Nursing*, www.nottingham.ac.uk/teaching/resources/methods/practicals/dyspelst681/ (accessed 20 March 2008).

Miles, T.R. and Varma, V. (eds) (1995) *Dyslexia and Stress*, Whurr, London.

Morgan, E. and Klein, C. (2000) *The Adult Dyslexic in a Non-dyslexic World*, Whurr, London.

Oliver, M. (1990) *The Politics of Disablement*, Palgrave Macmillan, Basingstoke.

Orton, S.T. (1925) Word-blindness in school children. *Archives of Neurology and Psychiatry*, **14**, 581–613.

Pollak, D. (2005) *Dyslexia, the Self and Higher Education*, Trentham Books, Stoke-on-Trent.

Price, G. and Skinner, J. (2007) *Support for Learning Differences in Higher Education, the Essential Practitioners' Guide*, Trentham Books, Stoke-on-Trent.

Rice, M. and Brooks, G. (2004) *Developmental Dyslexia in Adults: A Research Review*. London, National Research and Development Centre for adult literacy and numeracy (NRDC).

Riddick, B. (2001) Dyslexia and inclusion: time for a social model of disability perspective? *International Studies in Sociology of Education*, **11** (3), 223–36.

Smith-Sparke, J., Fawcett, A.J., Nicholson, R.I. and Fisk, J.E. (2001) *Everyday Memory and Dyslexia*. Paper presented at BDA 5th International Conference, University of York.

Snowling, M.J. (2000) *Dyslexia: A Cognitive Developmental Perspective*, Blackwell, Oxford.

Specific Learning Difficulties Working Group (2005) *DfES Guidelines*, www.patoss_dyslekia.org/DSA2.html (accessed 20 May 2008).

Stein, J. (2001) The magnocellular theory of developmental dyslexia. *Dyslexia*, **7**, 12–36.

Thomas, J.A. (1995) *Meaning in Interaction: An Introduction to Pragmatics*. Longman, London.

Thomson, M. (1990) *Developmental Dyslexia*, John Wiley, Chichester.

Tomlinson, J. (1996) *Inclusive Learning* (The Tomlinson Report), FEFC, Coventry.

West, T. (1991) *In the Mind's Eye: Visual Thinkers, Gifted People with Learning Difficulties, Computer Imaging and the Ironies of Creativity*, Prometheus Books, New York.

Williams, L.V. (1983) *Teaching for the Two-Sided Mind*, Simon & Schuster, New York.

Wolf, M. and O'Brien, B. (2001) On issues of time, fluency and intervention, in *Dyslexia: Theory and Good Practice* (ed. A. Fawcett), Whurr, London.

Useful Web Sites

www.dyslexia-college.com
www.dyslexic.com
www.nottingham.ac.uk/dyslexia
www.brainhe.com/resources/Dyslexiainadultsweblinks.html

Chapter 5

Dyspraxia

Sharon Drew

What's in a Name?

Dyspraxia, or Developmental Coordination Disorder (DCD), has only received concentrated attention from researchers in the past 20 years or so. Much of the literature has centred on children, and longitudinal investigations are only just beginning to be published. There is therefore very little in the public domain regarding the long-term implications for motor coordination difficulties. For this reason it is necessary to draw upon studies of children in order to provide a framework for this chapter.

The presenting features of motor incoordination have been described in the literature for some time, although only relatively recently gaining acceptance as a discrete type of neurodiversity. Over the years, numerous terms have been ascribed to children presenting with clumsiness that was not as a result of any obvious neurological impairment or cognitive deficits. These have included: clumsy, awkward and maladroit (Missiuna and Polatajko, 1995), developmental dyspraxia (Gubbay, 1975), perceptual motor dysfunction and motor delay (Henderson and Barnett, 1998), with some terms being subsequently discarded as they have unfavourable connotations (Johnston, Short and Crawford, 1987). However, the research that has investigated developmental movement problems has generally been plagued by a lack of consensus on two fundamental issues: its name and its definition (Dewey and Wilson, 2001).

The Diagnostic and Statistical Manual of Mental Disorders (DSM) III-R (American Psychiatric Association, 1987) first allowed for motor incoordination within its coding in the 1980s. Following this, in London, Ontario, 1994, internationally recognized experts agreed that the term DCD should be used as the nomenclature to describe this condition, together with a descriptive definition, and minimal desiderata for assessment (Fox and Polatajko, 1994).

The consensus described DCD as:

A chronic and usually permanent condition characterised by impairment of both functional performance and quality of movement that is not explicable in terms of age or intellect, or by any other diagnosable neurological or psychiatric features. Individuals with DCD display a qualitative difference in movement which differentiates them from those of the same age without the disability. The nature of these qualitative differences, whilst considered to change over time, tends to persist through the life span. (Fox and Polatajko, 1994)

Although the term DCD is now internationally recognized, the term 'developmental dyspraxia' remains frequently used by a variety of professional disciplines and the general public in the United Kingdom. This term has derived from adult neurology and is used by neurologists, occupational therapists and neuropsychologists (Denckla, 1984; Cermak, 1985; Denckla and Roeltgen, 1992; Dewey, 1995; Missiuna and Polatajko, 1995). In the context of neurodiversity in higher education, the important aspect is that developmental dyspraxia denotes a combination of motor learning and planning problems.

The UK Dyspraxia Foundation offers the following simple definition which dyspraxic people themselves often find acceptable:

Developmental dyspraxia is an impairment or immaturity of the organisation of movement. It is an immaturity in the way that the brain processes information, which results in messages not being properly or fully transmitted. The term dyspraxia comes from the word praxis, which means 'doing, acting'. Dyspraxia affects the planning of what to do and how to do it. It is associated with problems of perception, language and thought. (Dyspraxia Foundation, 2008)

The UK Developmental Adult Neurodiversity Association (DANDA) (an organization of, rather than for, neurodiverse people) puts it like this:

Dyspraxia literally comes from two Greek Words 'dys' meaning ill or abnormal and 'praxis', which means doing. This is a negative and self-fulfilling label that implies that we are not capable of taking action. There are two types of dyspraxia, which are quite different:

developmental dyspraxia and acquired dyspraxia. Developmental dyspraxia is when someone is born with dyspraxia, and acquired dyspraxia can be caused by a stroke or head injury and produces much more severe disabilities. The former type of dyspraxia includes difficulties with coordination, spatial awareness, perception, language and short term memory.   (DANDA, 2008)

Despite a revision of the coding in the fourth edition of the DSM (American Psychiatric Association, 2000), and consensus description of DCD (Fox and Polatajko, 1994; Leeds Consensus Statement, 2006), there still remains ambiguity and inconsistency in the different terms used, with professionals from diverse backgrounds using the terms differently (Henderson and Barnett, 1998; Polatajko, 1999; Peters, Barnett and Henderson, 2001, Lívia *et al.*, 2006). What this does indicate is an important issue, in that the frequent name changes imply that the underlying cause for motor coordination difficulties is still not fully understood. Furthermore, the term DCD unfortunately infers that the characteristics relate solely to childhood (and thus the assumption that 'you grow out of it'). It is important therefore that the term 'developmental' is not misconstrued where it actually implies that it 'develops', that is, changes over the lifespan.

The debates aside, for the purposes of this chapter, the term dyspraxia will be used, partly due to the greater public awareness of the term, but principally because its definition includes cognitive aspects.

What Causes Dyspraxia?

Research suggests that there is no single causative factor. Various hypotheses have been investigated at different levels and a wide range of approaches have been taken to identify the source of the difficulties experienced (Barnett, Kooistra and Henderson, 1998). The factors considered centre on brain damage or dysfunction, genetic predisposition, impairment in information processing or an impoverished environment. What is known is that dyspraxia is the result of the interaction of the individual's make-up (genetics) and the environment. It is not a disease and it cannot be transmitted. Neither is it life-threatening. There are no blood tests for it like those for arthritis, heart disease and diabetes. It is not something that can be 'cured'; neither surgery nor drugs have anything to offer (Fox, 1998).

I had a dyspraxic daughter and spent a lot of time looking at dyspraxia, so yes I suppose it was nice to know that I was a dyspraxic not a dyslexic, because I always thought I was. There were so many things that I can't do with my hands. Also there is a link going back to the 1890s. My great aunt actually had the reading and writing difficulties but she also, I don't have them particularly but fingers that stick backwards the wrong way. When I was little people used to say 'your Aunty Phil's horrible stick-back bendy fingers'. My daughter can put her hand up vertical, you know real hyper-flexibility. Aunty Phil tripped and dropped and spilt everything and everybody thought that she was you know goofy and clumsy.

There were all the endless stories about the muck-ups this poor woman made and how clumsy and stupid she was. But of course it was obviously her dyspraxia. My mother didn't have the literacy difficulties, but she has massive difficulty with numeracy and is completely disorganised and as cack-handed as they come. She only has to look at a camera and she has jammed it. She can't use a tin opener. And when we were kids we often thought she was very lazy because she refused to iron and hoover because she said that she was too intelligent and it was demeaning. Actually I think she found it so difficult she couldn't do it and still to this day she actually has someone come into the house specially to hoover.

Sophie

Whom Does It Affect?

It is necessary here to draw from the statistics found in the childhood literature, where studies undertaken suggest that the incidence ranges from 3% to 22% of the population. The varying percentages are related to an inconsistency in definition, screening and assessment tools (Keogh *et al.*, 1979; Losse *et al.*, 1991; Maeland, 1992; Geuze and Berger, 1993; Revie and Larkin, 1993; Cermak and Larkin, 2002). However, the figure widely quoted is 5–6% of the population. As with some other types of neurodiversity and disability, a higher prevalence is currently found in males than in females. With growing research, this opinion may alter in the future. The incidence of dyspraxia is found not to be related to level of education or socio-economic status (Blondis, 1999).

Is Dyspraxia Just a Movement Problem?

Evidence from recent research strongly indicates that dyspraxia co-occurs with other specific learning differences such as dyslexia, attention deficit hyperactivity disorder and Asperger's Syndrome. However, the defining characteristic of dyspraxia is motor incoordination, which may or may not be accompanied by any number of additional indicators and overlapping neurodiversity. As Grant points out in Chapter 3, indicators of dyspraxia include relative weaknesses in working memory and processing speed.

What Are the Long-Term Implications?

Although there remains comparatively little in the research domain with regard to this, initial studies suggest that for individuals with mild-to-moderate dyspraxia, the outcome into adulthood is good, as many individuals learn successful strategies. However, studies indicate that at least 50% of more significantly motor-impaired children will continue to experience motor difficulties as adults. Many of them will also develop secondary difficulties in the areas of physical health, fitness, mental health, social well-being, and educational performance and achievements (Shaffer *et al.*, 1985; Gillberg, I.C. and Gillberg, C., 1989; Gillberg, I.C., Gillberg, C. and Groth, 1989; Losse *et al.*, 1991; Geuze and Berger, 1993; Hellgren *et al.*, 1993; Cantell, Smyth and Ahonen, 1994; Schoemaker and Kalverboer, 1994; Bouffard *et al.*, 1996).

Assessment and Identification

Sometimes students wonder whether their experience indicates a specific learning difference, and sometimes staff ask themselves the same question about a student. Below is a simple neurodiversity indicator list, which can be used as a signpost for students who may feel they are having some difficulty accessing course work and feel they need help:

Ten Indicators of Possible Neurodiversity for Students in Higher Education

1. Are you often late for appointments?
2. Do you spend longer studying than others?
3. Are your files in a mess?
4. Do you have difficulty handing your work in on time?
5. Do you find it difficult to concentrate?
6. Is your handwriting difficult to read?
7. Do you find typing or computer mouse control difficult?
8. Have you ever been described as 'clumsy'?
9. Are you easily distracted?
10. Do you get lost around the campus?

In terms of dyspraxia, while it would appear that adults continue to experience problems with motor coordination, there is no specific indication in the literature regarding which areas in adults may be impaired, that is, whether or not they show the same spectrum of impairments as dyspraxic children (Cousins and Smyth, 2003). Most individuals who are dyspraxic will have developed a variety of compensatory techniques to manage their problems before reaching university. Some will have had their difficulties 'officially' recognized and they may have been helped to develop such strategies. However, others will have been compensating unconsciously and masking their difficulties. Consequently, it is not unusual for the problems to go unrecognized until an individual has to live away from home, and they may become more apparent when the individual is under stress.

Unfortunately, there is no one, or battery of assessments, to identify dyspraxia in adulthood. Dyspraxia is a 'collection of indicators', and information needs to be gathered from a variety of tasks and over a period of time. Using a background interview, as Grant points out in Chapter 3, can offer a reflection of the everyday life and the self-understanding of an individual. This can reveal important information not found through questionnaires or formal testing. The interview should consider the student's education and social background. It will also be important as part of the information-gathering process that a developmental history is elicited, which may likely reveal evidence of delay in acquiring a number of skills through childhood, such as the ability to dress independently, using cutlery, personal care skills, pre-writing, use of tools, kicking and catching a ball, running or pedalling a bicycle. Clumsiness may be generalized, restricted to groups of somewhat similar tasks or highly task-specific, rather than due to a delay. It is the extreme difficulty and distress experienced in trying to master one of more of these skills that distinguishes dyspraxic people from their peers. Even if the task is learnt, it tends to be performed very slowly and inconsistently. It is important to listen to the student to elicit the clues, for example, hours spent daily unsuccessfully trying to learn simple tasks, tearful opposition to teaching/learning skills, emotional outbursts evoked by simple activities that others would find easy, the bright, articulate individual failing to complete work or being totally disorganized (Fox, 1998).

I had no problems getting a place at university and was really excited to be starting a degree in modern languages. But as soon as I got on campus everything started to go wrong. It was the practical things that challenged me: close to tears I would spend up to an hour trying to get the key in the door to my student digs. I could not find my way around the campus and it was a nightmare trying to work out how to use the washing machine or change the duvet on my bed. All of these things were a massive challenge to me so I tried to hide my problems from the other students. I could not even open a bottle of wine or make someone a cup of tea as it would take me so long. After three weeks I suffered a nervous breakdown and had to return home. I felt incredibly bleak and wanted to hide away from the world.

Jane

(Jane returned to university later; not only did she obtain learning support and achieve a first class degree, she also met the man who became her husband.)

In terms of screening and assessment, knowledge and understanding of typical development, and the range of other neurodiversity, are important skills of the interviewing professional involved. It is highly probable that the student will present with issues surrounding learning. An Educational Psychology assessment is therefore useful in determining the profile of strengths and weaknesses. Usually in the case of dyspraxia, performance skills tend to be out of alignment with the student's verbal skills. Should any significant concerns regarding motor coordination be apparent, the student may need to be referred to his/her medical practitioner for a medical examination to eliminate any underlying neurological problems.

> When I was assessed, they said I was quite severely dyslexic and that I had mild dyspraxia and they kind of explained why some of the things that I do makes me come under that label. For example, the dyspraxia: I've always known I'm clumsy and I bump into things but I didn't – I just thought I was the same as everybody else and I didn't realise that that was – that there was a reason behind these things.
>
> Jemima

Characteristics of Dyspraxia which Can Impact on Learning and Teaching

Students may experience difficulties in some, or all, of the following areas:

- Gross motor skills: poor performance in sport especially team and ball games, general clumsiness and poor balance, difficulties in learning skills involving coordination of body parts. Fatigue may also be a feature.
- Manual and practical work: problems using computer keyboards and mice, frequent spills in the laboratory and elsewhere, difficulty measuring accurately, difficulty using tools and apparatus, slow, poor or illegible handwriting, messy presentation/work and problems with craftwork or cookery.
- Personal presentation and spatial skills: untidy and rumpled appearance, clumsy gait, poor posture, frequent bumping into things and tripping over.
- Memory and attention span: poor attention span, poor short-term memory, easily distracted in learning/work environments (especially by noise and bright lights), difficulty following group discussions, slow retrieval of information, especially when under stress; may become disorientated, for example, getting lost in buildings and in new environments.
- Written expression: erratic spelling and punctuation, awkward and confused sentence structure, poor proof-reading, inclusion of irrelevant material in essays. Maintaining productivity of written work, that is, keeping up in lectures, being slow to finish or illegible written work. Written work not commensurate with verbal skills.
- Visual and oral skills: trouble keeping place while reading and writing (tracking problems), poor relocating – cannot easily look from screen/overhead to notes, difficulty in word-finding, and wrong pronunciation of newly introduced words, speaking indistinctly, loudly, fast or slowly, interrupting inappropriately.

- Numerical and mathematical skills: tendency to reverse and mistype numbers, signs or decimal points, frequent and apparently careless mistakes, particular difficulty with geometry – both drawing and using equipment such as a compass or protractor and difficulty with spatial awareness, for example, drawing shapes, graphs and tables.
- Social, communication and emotional difficulties: problems with oral interaction and communication, low self-esteem and lack of confidence; frustration, defensiveness or aggression, over-talkative and excitable behaviour; withdrawn and reserved or may experience anxiety, stress and depression.
- Executive functions: these are central processes that are most intimately involved in providing organization and order to our actions and behaviour. They tap into skills such as: setting a goal – knowing what to do (what is to be achieved), planning the steps or procedure appropriate to the task, holding the plan in working memory while executing it, actioning the steps and shifting between them, for example, if distracted, can return to the task and pick up where it was left off; monitoring the progress of the task for both pace and quality, making flexible changes in the plan as needed, and finally, evaluating the outcome for use of the plan in a subsequent similar activity. This area can be the most significant in educational settings.

I always fell over a lot as a child and I'm incredibly clumsy, I knock everything over even now still, drinks, everything like that. I always bang the side of my hip against doorframes too. I'm not great at walking in straight lines – yeah oh my god I never realised any of that had anything to do with it. My handwriting's illegible. I can make it, of course I can make it legible and I do write my exams. I do have the choice of using a computer in my exams but I chose not to, because partly back to the planning part of it and when I do things on computer I would go back over things and I just don't think I could do it in the time available, I don't know I could do and write an essay in the time available in an exam. So that's why the extra time for me in exams is incredibly important, in terms of going very slowly over it.

Amethyst

The following is a checklist, which can be used by relevant education staff as a framework for discussion; it also serves as a summary of the key indicators of dyspraxia.

Table 5.1 Dyspraxia Student Screening Checklist

FUNCTIONAL AREA	YES	NO	COMMENTS

Planning and Movement (gross motor skills)

- Clumsy gait and movement in general, difficulty changing direction, stopping and starting. Poor quality of movement and control of movement.
- Poor posture – weak muscle tone and strength, reduced stamina. Difficulty standing for long periods.
- Lack of body awareness in space.
- Lack of rhythm.
- Possibly late reaching infant motor milestones – walking, talking, sitting and standing.
- Tendency to bump into other people, bump into things and trip over.
- Difficulty in mastering childhood functional skills – riding a bike, learning to dress – managing buttons.
- Difficulty learning to drive a car.
- Difficulty with sports, ball games and team games.
- Lack of rhythm – dancing, playing instruments, aerobics.

Eye/Hand Coordination

- Manual dexterity – difficulties with unscrewing things, sewing, managing locks with keys, craftwork, mechanical things, domestic chores, DIY.
- Handwriting – problems with pen grip, pressing too hard or too soft, may not always finish work.
- Personal care – difficulty with make-up, doing hair, shaving and a tendency to look untidy.

Table 5.1 Dyspraxia Student Screening Checklist (cont'd)

FUNCTIONAL AREA	YES	NO	COMMENTS

Perception
- Difficulty translating messages into actions.
- Following instructions – not instinctive, needs to be taught step by step.
- Little sense of time, direction, speed, weight – poor map-reading, confusion over hand preference, left/right discrimination.
- Difficulty distinguishing sounds/screening them from background noise.
- Oversensitive to noise, light or touch.

Language
Difficulties with:
- Continuous talking.
- Understanding and using complex verbal and written language.
- Understanding and using paralinguistic features (volume, intonation, pitch, rate, fluency, nasality, vocal quality).
- Understanding and using nonverbal communication (posture, facial expression).
- Eye contact, gesture, touch, proximity, sounds – groans, sighs, 'tuts'.
- Pragmatic social communication (initiation, turn-taking).
- Perspective taking, topic selection and maintenance, clarification and repair, compromise, negotiation, accepting and giving criticism (appropriate style to situation).

Table 5.1 Dyspraxia Student Screening Checklist (cont'd)

FUNCTIONAL AREA	YES	NO	COMMENTS

Thought and Memory
- Difficulty planning and organizing thoughts.
- Unfocused, messy, cluttered, erratic.
- Poor memory (especially short-term) and may keep forgetting and losing.
- May find it hard to do more than one thing at once.
- Slow to finish tasks if finished at all.
- May daydream and wander about aimlessly.
- May have literacy and numeracy difficulties.

Social and Emotional Problems
- Tendency to be easily frustrated – have emotional outbursts and be impulsive.
- Difficulties with listening – especially in large groups.
- May find it difficult picking up on nonverbal signals and judging the tone or pitch of voice in themselves and others. Wants immediate satisfaction.
- Can play the clown.
- Can be slow to adapt to new situations and learn new skills.
- Can have problems with teamwork and have a tendency to take evasive action when they face a difficult situation.
- May be insomniac, stressed, depressed, anxious and indecisive.
- May have phobias, fears and obsessions.
- May have lack of self-esteem and difficulties being assertive.
- Tendency to opt out of things that may be too difficult.
- Prone to emotional outbursts.

Issues in Higher Education

Success at college or university relies heavily on independent learning skills and demands the ability to deal with many different things at one time. Many students who are dyspraxic will have had a poor experience of learning during school years. Throughout this time, the individual's unique styles of learning will not have been compatible with the traditional teaching styles used in mainstream schools. The mismatch between the delivery and absorption of information can often be the main contributing factor when these individuals do not achieve their potential in the learning environment. In higher education, it is important for the tutor to gain an understanding of the student's strengths and abilities, in order to enable the student to learn through appropriate teaching strategies and accommodations where necessary.

Students with dyspraxia already recognize that others will not understand the nature of their difficulty. It is rarely a lack of ability that causes a dyspraxic adult to fail at Higher or Further Education; it is more often due on the student's part to a lack of understanding of the task demands, difficulties with organization and working with their tutors and peers, and on the part of the institution to a lack of awareness and inclusive practice.

General support for students might include: an assessment of individual need, advice on suitable courses, an institutional policy on assisting students with dyspraxia, grants to help with purchase of equipment and support where necessary, informing tutors and setting up support groups. However, it should be remembered that each individual has different needs.

Most dyspraxic students will need help and advice, not only regarding ways of successfully completing a particular course of study, but also on course selection. Below are some examples of how dyspraxia can impact on the ability to access a selection of courses.

Table 5.2 Impact of dyspraxia an selected courses

Potential challenges to learning and achievement	Subjects
Anxiety/Stress	**Computing** May experience difficulty with mouse control and keyboard

Potential challenges to learning and achievement	Subjects
Language/ Comprehension Difficulties	**Dance, Drama and Performance** May experience difficulties with their gross motor skills which can affect their ability to balance and learn skills of co-ordination. They may also display a clumsy gait, poor posture and a tendency to bump into or trip over things.
Memory/Recall Difficulties Motor/Manual Dexterity Difficulties	**English** May experience difficulties with memory and attention span and be easily distracted in the learning environment. They may also experience some difficulties similar to characteristics of dyslexia such as erratic spelling and punctuation, awkward and confused sentence structure, poor proof-reading, inclusion of irrelevant material in essays and they may be slow to complete work.
Organizational Difficulties	**Geography** They may also experience gross and fine motor difficulties which may impact on written, practical and field work sessions.
Speech Difficulties	**Hospitality, Leisure, Sport and Tourism** May experience difficulties with gross and fine motor skills leading to poor performance in sport, general clumsiness, poor balance, and difficulties learning skills involving coordination of body parts, Also this may impact on manual, practical work and written work.
Visual Difficulties	**Mathematics, Statistics and Operational Research** May experience difficulties with memory and attention span and be easily distracted in the learning environment. They may also experience some difficulties similar to characteristics of dyslexia or dyscalculia such as a tendency to reverse or mistype numbers, signs or decimal points; frequent and apparently careless mistakes, particular difficulty with geometry – both drawing and using equipment such as a compass or protractor and difficulty with spatial awareness, e.g. drawing shapes, graphs, tables, etc.

Potential challenges to learning and achievement	Subjects

Music

May also experience some difficulties similar to characteristics of dyslexia. Problems with gross and fine motor skills may lead to difficulties learning skills which involve co-ordination of body parts, timing and rhythm. Difficulties with writing may affect ability to write musical scores and problems with short-term memory or attention span leading to stress and anxiety associated with memorising pieces of music for presentation purposes.

Nursing

May also experience characteristics of dyslexia, affecting the quality and quantity of written work.

Specific difficulties with gross and fine motor skills may impact on the manual and practical work, including frequent spillages, difficulty with using hoists and administering drips, difficulty measuring, and possible disorientation, especially in unfamiliar surroundings.

Physiotherapy

Difficulties with gross and fine motor skills may impact on manual, practical work and written work.

Adapted from www.scips.worc.ac.uk/disabilities/dyspraxia.html

Work Placements and Careers

I studied to be a dyslexia teacher and part of the work I had to do was to make games and exercises for the children I had to teach. This was really difficult; using sticky-back plastic and cutting up things in a straight line, or drawing a straight line, was really difficult. I had some good ideas, but often produced really messy untidy work and was once told to start again.

Mary

Many students who are dyspraxic are able to achieve well academically and go on to have very good careers without issue, as they often choose employment which utilizes their strengths rather than their weaknesses. Much literature focuses on the deficits of dyspraxia rather than the positives, but these are important when considering courses and/or careers.

The following are strengths which have been identified in many dyspraxic adults:

- Are able to learn with determination and plenty of practice.
- Can be creative and original thinkers.
- Have a good sense of humour which they use at times to get them through adversity.
- Are fond of and good at caring for animals.
- Have empathy for others and are often successful in professions such as caring or teaching.
- Are hard-working and determined to succeed.
- Are honest, genuine and sincere, because they do not put on a false act to impress others.

They are also described as:

- Being creative problem-solvers, as the individual needs to work around their neurodiversity. This allows them to 'think outside the box', often leading to more creative solutions and imaginative answers to problems.
- Being outgoing personalities.
- Having strong compensatory skills.
- Highly motivated.
- Being persistent – despite frustrations, many keep trying until they meet with success.

Teaching and Learning – What Can the Tutor Do?

Not all educators understand or are responsive to the needs of individuals with neurodiversities such as dyspraxia. When teaching methods are not appropriate, students who are dyspraxic may become frustrated and experience failure. This may cause them to drop out of educational programmes or make them afraid to enter educational programmes in the first place.

Higher education requires active participation and a high level of personal organization and drive. It is also an increasingly social activity, involving complex academic interactions with peers and tutors. Traditionally, it relies heavily on reading, hearing and producing the written word. It often involves working in buildings that were not designed with access in mind. It can be a difficult environment for many students, and it is still strewn with barriers for those with any type of disability.

The barriers to learning faced by dyspraxic students can be many and complex, and differ from student to student and often from day to day. Knowledge of the existence of such barriers and their disabling impact can help the tutor to appreciate their implications for learning. It will also help to set the legal concept of 'reasonable adjustments' into context. A flexible and student-centred approach and a willingness to adapt existing teaching strategies are key to inclusive teaching in lectures, seminars and tutorials. Sadly for the tutors, there is no single answer to the difficulties faced by dyspraxic students, so a creative trial-and-error approach is necessary.

Preparing the Teaching Session

Creating a more accessible learning environment for students who are dyspraxic should start with the planning of the teaching sessions:

- Look at the learning outcomes, to ensure that they are as inclusive as possible and that they do not unnecessarily or unintentionally disadvantage some students.
- Consider the teaching strategies planned. Identify the practical learning activities taking place and consider the skills and abilities the students are required to employ.
- Consider whether there are any aspects of the practical activities that may present difficulties for students with particular impairments. For each activity, identify possible issues.
- Does the practical activity present insurmountable barriers to students who are dyspraxic?
- Students are able to respond better when they have sufficient time to read an article and absorb information, consider ideas and points for a discussion, or develop a presentation. Let students know well in advance what they should read or prepare.
- Provide outline notes in advance or put them online so students can familiarize themselves with new subject matter and terminology. They will then understand what is expected of them and which activities they will be undertaking.

The Teaching Environment

Consideration should be given to the location for teaching a group of students, and whether it is likely to lead to difficulties for those who are dyspraxic. For example:

- Is there space to manoeuvre around the room?
- Are boards, videos and screens positioned where they can be viewed in comfort?
- Is mains power available for specialist equipment?
- Arrange the furniture where possible for maximum effect.

Structuring Teaching Time

Many students with dyspraxia experience fatigue and are unable to study effectively for long periods. Modification in the way the teaching occurs can help to reduce the impact of these difficulties:

- Have regular breaks.
- Permit the use of recording devices, but do not draw attention to their use.
- Accept that the student might need to leave a teaching session early or go for a break.
- Long sessions can also be too much for students whose concentration is poor. Break the lecture up with an activity.
- Outline the structure of the session, then recap by going over key points using multi-sensory methods – show pictures rather than text, or run a short video.

Facilitating Participation

A tutor or lecturer's role in encouraging and facilitating participation is vital, and may be all the more important where a student finds it hard to participate:

- When dividing groups of students into teams for project work or presentations, check that the individual is placed within a supportive group.
- Avoid talking to the students while writing on the board (back turned).
- Eliminate background noise as far as possible and speak clearly.
- Any text or diagrams written on the board, on overhead projections or given in PowerPoint presentations should also be read aloud.

- Talk through any calculations and describe graphs and charts. Make sure this information is also available to the student in their preferred accessible format (or electronically).
- New or unusual vocabulary should be spelled out.
- Say things more than once, and (in one-to-one meetings) ask for instructions to be repeated to ensure the student has understood. This is also a good indicator of how much information can be retained at once by the student.
- When using visual aids, allow extra (silent) time for students to look at or read what is being presented before talking about it.
- Place lecture notes on the Virtual Learning Environment to allow students to access them in their own time.
- Use structural indicators in lectures to assist with the sequence and flow, for example, use concepts such as 'firstly' and 'lastly' to conclude.
- When beginning a lecture, summarize what went on in previous lectures and give an overview for the topic in that session.
- If a teaching session introduces a large amount of new terminology, provision of a glossary of key terms can be very useful.
- The use of timetables, flowcharts, mind-maps and handouts will all support poor memory and organization skills.
- If practical work is involved in a session, ensure the student can handle the equipment safely.
- Use clear, bold headings and present materials in bullet points.
- Repeat and rephrase questions posed by others, and if appropriate, contextualize.
- Videoing lectures can be very helpful.
- Allow sufficient time for students to settle down and demonstrate their skills to the full.
- Plan flexible programmes of study to respond to variations in capacity to learn.
- Use a frame or ruler to identify the line of text and to help move the eye to the next line.
- Use colour and imagery to highlight key points or important details.
- Encourage other students to give assistance.

For some students who are dyspraxic, certain learning situations can be difficult or uncomfortable. Examples include:

- Difficulties participating in discussions, leading to an apparent unwillingness to join in, or making contributions that do not seem relevant;
- Difficulties making presentations;
- Problems with group activities and interacting with peers; and
- Behaviours that interfere with learning or participation, or which affect the learning of others.

Try some of the following strategies to help them to feel more comfortable in participating in these learning activities:

- If appropriate, it may be helpful to discuss these aspects directly with the student during personal tutorials and together attempt to work out strategies that both student and tutor are comfortable with.
- Avoid the need for students to read aloud.
- Avoid asking for presentations without due warning.
- Do not expect the student to read an article at speed in order to discuss it.
- Do not expect the student to participate in a discussion without some preparation.
- Deal sensitively with personal information and focus on what is needed to help the student to learn.
- If students are avoiding certain situations because of anxiety, consider exposing them to the situation in small but increasing steps.
- Encourage problem-solving attitudes that will help students dismantle the larger problems into lots of smaller ones and then to resolve them by practical steps. Small steps to deal with anxiety over presentations could include: discussion of the anxiety with the student; observation of others; preparing the subject; rehearsing in private; recording the presentation; practising before a friend; getting as relaxed as possible on the day.
- Be sensitive to the fact that some people will find it very difficult to work in a group. Do not force participation.
- Encourage a supportive environment and activities that can accommodate individuals when they find social interaction problematic.
- Some students may experience changes in behaviour that may create an uncomfortable situation in the learning environment. It is better to allow students to withdraw, if they wish to, rather than feel obliged to *manage* the behaviour, which could lead to confrontation. This behaviour is more likely to be caused by external circumstances rather than the current learning situation.

Writing and Recording – Assignments, Essays and Reports

Recording is generally one of the key issues for a student with dyspraxia. Often they can struggle to take notes in lectures. Assignments can be poorly organized, with spelling and grammar errors evident. It may be helpful therefore to:

- Provide extra time for coursework.
- Provide one-to-one tuition at least once a week from a specialist support tutor.

- Provide help with planning, organization, writing and paragraphing.
- Offer existing essays and reports as examples to the student.
- Provide help with proof-reading.
- Provide written directions and checklists for assignments.
- Visually highlight important information and instructions.
- Explore the potential for a scribe.
- Explore the potential to use assistive technology, for example, for recording.
- Explore whether another student would take the role of scribe for the dyspraxic person during lectures.
- Provide handouts of lecture notes.

Other Strategies for Teaching and Learning

- Provide opportunities for over-learning.
- Provide clear work/assignment guidelines.
- Provide formal tutorials to assist with planning and organization of work – help to break assignments into steps. Provide opportunities for feedback and checking understanding.
- Give example reports/essays/projects.
- Provide indirect support – e-mails or phone calls to check on progress.
- Encourage students to seek general stress management and relaxation training as they may increase confidence and well-being, and therefore the ability to cope more easily.
- Encourage students to seek support for their anxieties, for example, study skills and exam strategies training, or speaking to a counsellor about personal anxiety.
- Extensions of deadlines should be available, but some discussion of how this will impact on future work should take place.
- Provide students with plenty of information regarding assignments and examinations.
- Provide practice, reassurance and possibly extra time for formal assessments, and consider providing alternative assessment approaches when appropriate.

The best compromise for people such as myself would probably be the automatic dispensation of deadline extensions.

Joanna

I don't know where the dyslexia ends and dyspraxia begins. It's just like untidiness, forgetfulness – it's like organisational. Finding papers and where I've put things. Once, you would come into my office it was like 'whoa!', but I have got better at it recently and I'm trying to put in strategies so I suppose in a way would be good to look at my dyspraxia more to identify what it is that I do, so that I can have strategies.

I have students who struggle to do that too, so we do like Gantt charts and spider maps and things like that, because I think generally a lot of students don't know how to organise their time. So I say 'let's make a target for next week' and then I'll say 'you have you do it' and things like that. I'll always say 'have you been to student support?' as well, because I've got very limited knowledge of stuff like that – having organisers where you can put things in and stuff like that.

Leah, dyslexic and dyspraxic lecturer

Technology and Dyspraxia

The use of technology for dyspraxic students within a learning environment can be extremely helpful; this is covered in detail in Chapter 10. It will be important to bear in mind that any equipment provided needs to fit the requirements of the course and most importantly, be relevant to the needs of the individual. It is also important not to forget 'low tech' devices, selection of which is given in Appendix 5.A to this chapter.

Special Arrangements

Dyspraxic students are likely to be eligible for special arrangements for examinations. The arrangement will depend on the degree of functional difficulty and the examining board. These could be:

- additional reading time;
- additional working time;
- enlarged print on the exam paper;
- coloured exam paper;
- use of a computer;
- a reader;
- a scribe;
- provision of a separate room in which to take the exam.

Social Aspects of Higher Education

> Most students with dyspraxia suffer at some stage with anxiety, stress, low self-esteem and depression because of the multiple difficulties they experience. I did not suffer academically, as I gained a degree without too much difficulty. But I have lived very much in my head with little faith or confidence in my body. I always played up to this uselessness – pointing out my shortcomings before others could – and this led others to view me as severely as myself.
>
> Ceri

For some students, the transition into higher education can be difficult. In addition to managing their workload, they may experience difficulties settling into university life from a social perspective and organizing their independent living either on or off campus. Such students may therefore also need help in this area:

- Encourage the student to use visual schedules and calendars.
- Help students to use *to-do* lists and checklists.
- Have a clearly identifiable person whom students can go to for support with organizational issues.
- Support for the organization of clothes, laundry, keeping track of meals, tickets, nutrition and other personal aspects may be required in certain cases.
- Organize orientation sessions for students to assist with navigation around the building(s), materials and learning resources.

> At university, most people think you are at least by name, the typical uni student – much partying, drinking, working too, keen to get on in life, living in a student house, etc. I'm not. I'm in my second year, living in halls of residence (most 2nd years are in houses), and finding it stressful keeping on top of the workload. Fortunately I've got used to explaining my 'problem' – the frequent question, 'why are you still in halls?' kind of leads you instantly into the answer 'well I'm dyspraxic, which is why I have big shoes, and have to carry a laptop all the time, and often drop things – that's what the coffee stains are on the floor, sorry!'
>
> Melanie

The above example shows how fitting in from a social perspective can be key factor for an adult who is dyspraxic. Numerous studies have examined the social, emotional and behavioural problems associated with motor difficulties, which has led to a growing body of evidence that the lack of movement skill may have damaging consequences for social and psychological development (Losse *et al.*, 1991; Cantell *et al.*, 1994; Schoemaker and Kalverboer, 1994). In addition to receiving support for the academic aspect of university life, students with dyspraxia may also need help with the social aspect.

> I speak too loudly but at other times speak too softly. I am bad at making eye contact. I think more quickly than my brain can process the thoughts and end up blurting things out inappropriately. I frequently interrupt others without realising it, but resist all the appropriate signs and go on talking. In company people are too polite to point this out but it's interesting that people do not seek me out for second and subsequent conversations. It is not uncommon for me to fail to dress properly and leave zips and buttons undone or misaligned.
>
> Adrian

> Looking ahead to the rest of my life, I might have to get a few broken bones mended but no I can really see it affecting me, well I hope it won't anyway. Yes, I pick things up and don't pick them up and drop them, I do. Yes more expensive for drinks, yes the general – I am weary of knocking things over. It's actually when I get run down, when I'm tired that's when my dyspraxia and dyslexia start coming out and my mother will say if I'm incredibly tired, 'Oh you're very tired, aren't you?' Because I do knock things.
>
> Amethyst

Summary

Research suggests that individuals with poor coordination have been around for a long time; the incidence ranges from 3% to 22% of the population, with more males being affected than females. The evidence from recent research strongly supports the view that dyspraxia coexists with other neurodiversities. There is no single factor that causes dyspraxia. It is diverse in nature and its aetiology uncertain. There also remains an inconsistency in the term being used to define the nature of the movement incoordination, despite an international consensus. The frequent changes in the name reflect the fact that the underlying cause for dyspraxia is still not yet fully understood.

Those entering higher or further education whose dyspraxia has been recognized can often obtain practical and financial support from the outset. In some incidences, entering university or college is the first time that difficulties or issues with learning have been acknowledged or identified. In this case, the impact on the individual can have the effect of being able to make sense of a turbulent educational past. Disability legislation has opened doors to further education opportunities (Clark, 2003). This, together with a growing awareness of the differing neurodiversities such as dyspraxia, insofar that they are not solely related to childhood, has meant that the needs of those individuals who learn differently can be accommodated and supported, leading to successful achievements in their studies.

Appendix: Practical Resources for Dyspraxic Students

There are a number of resources that can be purchased to support dyspraxic students during the course of their studies. Here are a few examples from the United Kingdom:

Figure 5.A.1 Penagain

Available from www.penagain.co.uk. These pens are ergonomically designed to adapt to the contour of the hand, thus alleviating stresses frequently observed with a standard pen.

Figure 5.A.2 Stabilo pen

These pens have an integral grip moulded into the barrel of the pen. They can be purchased from high street retailers. The pen is available for both left- and right-handed people.

Figure 5.A.3 Yoro pen

This is an ergonomically designed pen aimed to promote comfort in the hand when writing over longer periods. They are available for both right- and left-handed people and are commercially available from several high street stores.

Figure 5.A.4 Soft pen/pencil grips

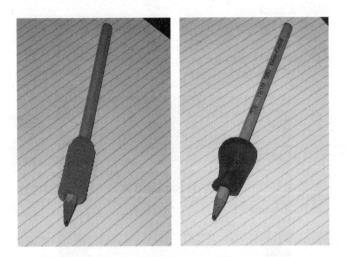

These soft grips can be added to pens or pencils and are particularly useful for those who tend to grip too tightly. A variety of grips can be found at: www.taskmasteronline.co.uk

Grips for left-handed students can be found at www.leftshoponline.co.uk and www.anythingleft-handed.co.uk A selection of other items for home and study can also be found at these sites.

Figure 5.A.5 Angled writing surface (and integral file)

This portable writing surface is available from www.backinaction.co.uk. An accompanying seating wedge to promote good posture is also available and fits inside the pack.

Figure 5.A.6 Ruler clipboard

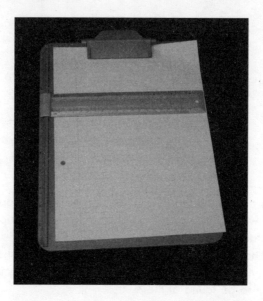

These clipboards are commercially available from stationers and have an integral ruler. The clipboard helps to keep papers together and the ruler helps with keeping writing even, as well as with reading text.

Figure 5.A.7 Rulers

Rulers with integral handles can help when needing to manipulate for lines and diagrams. These can be found at high street stationers.

Figure 5.A.8 Scissors

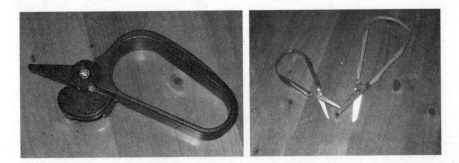

For students who struggle with manipulating regular looped scissors, a variety of more specialized scissors can be found at www.peta-uk.com.

Figure 5.A.9 Voice recording pens

Recording pens are useful tools to help recall short pieces of information or instructions during or after a lecture. These pens can be found on the internet. Here is an example of a useful website: http://kjglobal.co.uk/acatalog/Pen_Recording_Device_.html

Other useful equipment suppliers in the UK

- **Home Craft Ability One Ltd** Shelly Close, Lowmoor Road Industrial Estate, Kirkby-in-Ashfield, Nottinghamshire NG17 7ET Tel: 01623 720005
- **Nottingham Rehab Supplies (NRS)** Norvara House, Excelsior Road, Ashby de la Zouch, Leicestershire LE65 1NG Tel: 0845 120 4522 www.nrs-uk.co.uk

- **Lakeland Limited** www.lakelandlimited.co.uk
- www.sensorycomfort.com (USA)
- www.gadgets.co.uk
- www.betterware.co.uk
- www.watchminder.com

References

American Psychiatric Association (1987) *DSM III-R Diagnostic and Statistical Manual of Mental Disorders*, 3rd edn, APA, Washington, DC.

American Psychiatric Association (2000) *DSM-IV-TR Diagnostic and Statistical Manual of Mental Disorders*, 4th edn, APA, Washington, DC.

Barnett, A.L., Kooistra, L. and Henderson, S.E. (1998) 'Clumsiness' as a syndrome and symptom. *Human Movement Science*, **17**, 435–47.

Blondis, T.A. (1999) Motor disorders and attention-deficit/hyperactivity disorder. *Pediatric Clinical North America*, **46**, 899–913.

Bouffard, M., Watkinson, E.J., Thompson, L.P. *et al.* (1996) A test of the activity deficit hypothesis with children with movement difficulties. *Adapted Physical Activity Quarterly*, **13**, 61–73.

Cantell, M.H., Smyth, M.M. and Ahonen, T.P. (1994) Clumsiness in adolescence: educational, motor, and social outcomes of motor delay detected at 5 years. *Adapted Physical Activity Quarterly*, **11**, 115–29.

Cermak, S.A. (1985). Developmental dyspraxia, in *Neuropsychological Studies of Apraxia and Related Disorders* (ed. E.A. Roy), Elsevier (North Holland), Amsterdam, Netherlands, pp. 115–248.

Cermak, S.A. and Larkin, D. (2002) *Developmental Co-ordination Disorder*, Delmar, Canada.

Clark, T. (2003) Post 16 provision for those with autistic spectrum conditions: some implications of the Special Educational Needs and Disability Act 2001 and the Special Needs Code of Practice for Schools. *Support for Learning*, **18** (4), 184–89.

Cousins, M. and Smyth, M.M. (2003) Developmental co-ordination impairments in adulthood. *Human Movement Science*, **22**, 433–59.

Denckla, M.B. (1984) Developmental dyspraxia: the clumsy child, in *Middle Childhood: Development and Dysfunction* (eds M.D. Levine and P. Satz), University Park Press, Baltimore, MD.

Denckla, M.B. and Roeltgen, D.P. (1992) Disorders of motor function and control, in *Handbook of Neuropsychology* (eds I. Rapin and S.J. Segalowitz), Elsevier Science, Amsterdam.

Developmental Adult Neuro-Diversity Association (DANDA) (2008) *Definition of Dyspraxia*, www.danda.org.uk (accessed 23 February 2008).

Dewey, D. (1995) What is developmental dyspraxia? *Brain and Cognition*, **29**, 254–74.

Dewey, D. and Wilson, B.N. (2001) Developmental co-ordination disorder: what is it? in *Children with Developmental Co-ordination Disorder: Strategies for Success* (ed. C. Missiun), Hawthorn Press, New York.

Dyspraxia Foundation (2008) *Definition of Dyspraxia*, www.dyspraxiafoundation. org.uk (accessed 23 February 2008).

Fox, A.M. (1998) *Clumsiness in Children*, webmaster@orcn.ahs.ca (accessed 23 February 2008).

Fox, A.M. and Polatajko, H.J. (1994) 'The London Consensus' – From *Children and Clumsiness: An International Consensus Meeting*. London, Ontario, Canada, 11–14 October 1994.

Geuze, R.H. and Berger, H. (1993) Children who are clumsy: five years later. *Adapted Physical Activity Quarterly*, **10**, 10–21.

Gillberg, I.C. and Gillberg, C. (1989) Children with pre-school minor neurodevelopmental disorders. IV: Behaviour and school achievement at age 13. *Developmental Medicine and Child Neurology*, **31**, 3–13.

Gillberg, I.C., Gillberg, C. and Groth, J. (1989) Children with preschool minor neurodevelopmental disorders. V: Neurodevelopmental profiles at age 13. *Developmental Medicine And Child Neurology*, **31**, 14–24.

Gubbay, S.S. (1975) *The Clumsy Child*, W.B. Saunders, New York.

Hellgren, L., Gillberg, I.C., Bagenholm, A. and Gillberg, C. (1994) Children with deficits in attention, motor control and perception (DAMP) almost grown up: psychiatric and personality disorders at age 16 years. *Journal of Child Psychology and Psychiatry*, **35**, 1255–71.

Hellgren, L., Gillberg, C., Gillberg, I.C. and Ennerskog, I. (1993) Children with deficits in attention, motor control and perception (DAMP) almost grown up: general health at 16 years. *Developmental Medicine and Child Neurology*, **35**, 881–92.

Henderson, S.E. and Barnett, A.L. (1998) The classification of specific motor co-ordination disorders in children: some problems to be solved. *Human Movement Science*, **17**, 449–70.

Johnston, O., Short, H. and Crawford, J. (1987) Poorly co-ordinated children: a survey of 95 cases. *Child: Care, Health and Development*, **13**, 361–67.

Keogh, J.F., Sugden, D., Reynard, C.L. and Calkins, J. (1979) Identification of clumsy children: comparisons and comments. *Journal of Human Movement Studies*, **5**, 32–41.

Leeds Consensus Statement (2006) *Developmental Co-ordination Disorder as a Specific Learning Difficulty*. Economic & Social Research Seminar Series 2004–2005, UK.

Lívia, C., Magalhães, L.C., Missiuna, C. and Wong, S. (2006) Terminology used in research reports of developmental coordination disorder. *Developmental Medicine & Child Neurology*, **48**, 937–41.

Losse, A., Henderson, S.E., Elliman, D. *et al.* (1991) Clumsiness in children – do they grow out of it? A 10-year follow-up study. *Developmental Medicine and Child Neurology*, **33**, 55–68.

Maeland, A.F. (1992) Handwriting and perceptual-motor skills in clumsy, dysgraphic, and normal children. *Perceptual and Motor Skills*, **75**, 1207–17.

Missiuna, C. and Polatajko, H.J. (1995) Developmental dyspraxia by any other name. *American Journal of Occupational Therapy*, **49**, 619–28.

Peters, J.M., Barnett, A.L. and Henderson, S.E. (2001) Clumsiness, dyspraxia and developmental co-ordination disorder: how do health and educational professionals in the UK define the terms? *Child: Care, Health and Development*, **27** (5), 399–412.

Polatajko, H.J. (1999) Developmental Co-ordination Disorder DCD: Alias the Clumsy Child Syndrome, in *A Neurodevelopmental Approach to Specific Learning Disorders* (eds K. Whitmore, H. Hart & G. Willems) MacKeith Press, London.

Revie, G. and Larkin, D. (1993) Task specific intervention with children reduces movement problems. *Adapted Physical Activity*, **10**, 29–41.

Schoemaker, M.M. and Kalverboer, A.F. (1994) Social and affective problems of children who are clumsy: how early do they begin? *Adapted Physical Activity Quarterly*, **11**, 130–40.

Shaffer, D., Schonfield, I., O'Connor, P.A. *et al.* (1985) Neurological soft signs and their relationship to psychiatric disorder and intelligence in childhood and adolescence. *Archives of General Psychiatry*, **42**, 343–51.

Further Reading

Biggs, V. (2005) *Caged in Chaos – A Dyspraxic Guide to Breaking Free*, Jessica Kingsley, London.

Colley, M. (2005) Learning support for dyspraxic students, in *Neurodiversity in FE and HE: Positive Initiatives for Specific Learning Differences* (ed. D. Pollak). Conference proceedings, Leicester, De Montfort University, www.brainhe.com (accessed 28 May 2008).

Colley, M. (2006) *Living with Dyspraxia: A Guide for Adults with Developmental Dyspraxia*, Jessica Kingsley, London.

Drew, S. (2005) *Developmental Co-ordination Disorder*, Whurr, London.

Grant, D. (2005) *That's the Way I Think: Dyslexia and Dyspraxia Explained*, David Fulton, London.

Kirby, A. and Drew, S. (2003) *Guide to Dyspraxia and Developmental Co-ordination Disorder*, Fulton, London.

Portwood, M. (1999) *Developmental Dyspraxia Identification and Intervention: A Manual for Parents and Professionals*, 2nd edn, David Fulton, London.

Weronowska, N. (ed.) (2003) *Dyspraxic Voices – Adult Experiences of Dyspraxia and Related Conditions*, DANDA, London.

Web Sites

www.open.ac.uk/inclusiveteaching/pages/inclusive-teaching/
   barriers-to-learning.php
www.rdg.ac.uk/studyskills/dyslexia_dyspraxia/dyspraxia_info.htm
www.scips.worc.ac.uk/disabilities/dyspraxia.html
www.brainhe.com
www.dyspraxiafoundation.org.uk

Chapter 6

Dyscalculia

Clare Trott

Definitions

There is currently no widely accepted definition of dyscalculia. While a number of definitions exist, many rely on the deficit model. Dyscalculia can be traced back as far as Kosc (1974, p. 165), who defined developmental dyscalculia as 'a structural disorder of mathematical abilities which has its origin in a genetic or congenital disorder in those parts of the brain that are the anatomical-physiological substrate of the maturation of the mathematical abilities adequate to age, without a simultaneous disorder of general mental functions'.

In attempting to define dyscalculia, much of the focus has been on the discrepancy between intelligence and mathematical ability. The Diagnostic and Statistical Manual of Mental Disorders Fourth Edition (DSM-IV; American Psychiatric Association, 2000, section 315.1), used by educational psychologists, defines mathematics disorder in terms of test scores: '(A)s measured by a standardised test that is given individually, the person's mathematical ability is substantially less than would be expected from the person's age, intelligence and education. This deficiency materially impedes academic achievement or daily living.' There are two key features of this definition, firstly, the mathematical level compared to expectation and, secondly, the impedance of academic achievement and daily living. In support of the first key feature, Butterworth (2001) says, 'most dyscalculic learners will have cognitive and language abilities in the normal range, and may excel in non-mathematical subjects.' In terms of the second key feature, The American National Center for Learning Disabilities (NCLD, no date) says: 'Dyscalculia is a term referring to a wide range of life long learning disabilities involving math ... the difficulties vary from person to person and affect people differently in school and throughout life.'

The United Kingdom's National Numeracy Strategy (DfES, 2001, p. 2) concludes that: 'Dyscalculia is a condition that affects the ability to acquire arithmetical skills. Dyscalculic learners may have difficulty understanding simple number concepts, lack an intuitive grasp of numbers, and have problems learning number facts and procedures. Even if they produce a correct answer or use a correct method, they may do so mechanically and without confidence.' This would appear to be more applicable to education in the early years. In higher education (HE), the emphasis is less on basic computation and more on the application and understanding of skills and techniques. A more precise specification comes from Sharma (1997): 'Dyscalculia is an inability to conceptualise numbers, number relationships (arithmetical facts) and the outcomes of numerical operations (estimating the answer to numerical problems before actually calculating).' The emphasis here moves away from numerical operations and more towards conceptualizing and estimating, which would appear to be a more appropriate view for HE, since the understanding of numerical concepts and relationships is central to many studies in HE. It is essential that the students' lack of understanding of mathematical concepts should be at the heart of dyscalculia: 'A lack of a true comprehension or understanding of maths will be a key characteristic of dyscalculic people' (Chinn, 2006, p. 16).

Thus, the key features of any definition of dyscalculia should include the mathematical ability being substantially less than expectation, the 'impedance of academic achievement or daily living' and the fact that students have an inability to conceptualize with a failure to understand number concepts and relationships.

Prevalence

Current estimates for the prevalence of dyscalculia vary from 3% to 8% of the population. However, all available estimates are based on data for children, and no figures relating specifically to HE, or indeed for the adult population, exist. Butterworth (2002b) contends that about 40% of dyslexic children have some degree of difficulty with learning mathematics and additionally 5–6% of children of average to superior intelligence having a specific learning deficit in mathematics. Earlier estimates by Kosc (1974) and Gross-Tsur, Manor and Shalev (1996) give the figure as 6.4% and 6.5%, respectively, while more recent estimates from Geary (2004) give the figure as 5 to 8%.

Why Do Students Struggle?

One of the things that distinguishes people who are good at maths, have effective 'mathematical brains', is an ability to see a problem in different ways. This is because they understand it. This, in turn, allows the use of a range of different procedures to solve it and to select the one that will be most effective in this particular task.   (Butterworth, 2002a)

Butterworth (1999) believes that infants are born with a single 'number module' that is used for number representations and situated in the parietal lobe. Landerl *et al.* (2004, p. 106) claim that 'the underlying cause of dyscalculia is likely to be related to dysfunction of this system'. Dehaene and Cohen (1998) state: 'An elementary number system is present very early in life in both humans and animals, and constitutes the start-up tool for the development of symbolic numerical thinking that permeates our western technological societies' (cited in Piazza and Dehaene, 2004, p. 3).

Recent research by Piazza *et al.* (2007) has shown that this region is activated in response to numbers, presented as either a pattern of dots or as Arabic numerals, and further, that this region processes numerical information. Their findings demonstrated that the two hemispheres of the parietal lobe act differently in processing numbers. It is the left lobe that contains abstract numerical representations, but the right lobe shows a dependence on the notation used, either as Arabic numerals or as words. Similarly, Cohen Kadosh *et al.* (2007) found numerical representations, which are notation-dependent, in the right parietal lobe. Following publication of their findings, Cohen Kadosh *et al.* (2007) point out that: 'Most people process numbers very easily – almost automatically – but people with dyscalculia do not.'

Difficulties Experienced

Mathematical difficulties

Students in HE may experience mathematical difficulties due to their neurodiversity and this is often coupled with severe mathematical anxiety. The mathematical difficulties students may face include understanding and using mathematical concepts and relations. They may struggle with mathematical symbols or digits or have difficulty in performing specific mathematical operations.

Desoete, Roeyers and De Clercq (2004) use a deficit-based model to identify the weaknesses that children with dyscalculia may display. This includes difficulties with: multi-step routines and mathematical or arithmetical strategies, recalling number facts, relating visuo-spatially to number lines, ordering by size, symbol recognition, understanding numerosity (the number of items in a collection (Butterworth, 1999)) and transcoding between the modalities of Arabic digit, written word and the numerical quantity implied.

More specifically, Beacham and Trott (2005) identify a range of characteristics presented by dyscalculic students in HE. Such characteristics include difficulties in recognizing, reading, writing or conceptualizing numbers, understanding numerical or mathematical concepts and their interrelationships. Students with dyscalculia may struggle with numerical operations, both in terms of understanding the process of the operation and in carrying out the procedure. Further difficulties may arise in understanding the systems that rely on this fundamental understanding, such as time, money, direction and more abstract mathematical, symbolic and graphical representations.

A case study will serve to illustrate the nature of the problems highlighted in relation to dyscalculia.

Steven was a mature student. He was very practical and literate, but, at the same time, very quiet and reflective. He was identified as dyscalculic during his first year of higher education. Difficulties were identified with his working memory and with the processing of visual symbolic information, as well as struggling with basic arithmetical skills. He had previously encountered difficulty with GCSE mathematics, achieving only a grade F. For Steven, placing numbers correctly on a number line and reading scales were difficult, so that affected his ability to read and understand information presented graphically. Further difficulties arose with the interpretation of tables of data, thereby rendering as meaningless the many tables of output he met during the statistical elements of his course. His lack of understanding of basic number concepts also meant that he inevitably continued to struggle with his course.

Mathematical anxiety

In the above case study, Steven was very anxious about the statistical elements of his course. For some students in HE, mathematics anxiety often overrides everything else and is born out of the fear of numerical, mathematical or statistical material. It is commonplace among many students, but particularly among those students with dyscalculia or mathematical difficulties. Mathematics anxiety is characterized by low mathematical confidence, leading to a negative, disempowering position. It can result from a lack of understanding of the mathematics itself or from knowledge gaps. Prior experiences play a vital role, if there exists a poor mathematical history, then the student is likely to experience anxiety when faced with mathematics or statistics. Arem (2003) equates mathematics anxiety to a wall, a barrier that hinders efforts to succeed mathematically.

Mathematics anxiety is defined by Ashcraft and Faust (1994, p. 98) as: 'Feelings of tension, apprehension, or even dread that interfere with the ordinary manipulation of number and the solving of mathematical problems.' An alternative definition from Tobias and Weissbrod (1980, p. 65) states that mathematics anxiety is: 'The panic, helplessness, paralysis, and mental disorganization that arise among some people when they are required to solve a mathematical problem.'

Very often, mathematical anxieties are rooted in childhood. Early experiences can shape the way we feel about mathematics. These early impressions are often formative and are very difficult to alter later in life. One student, Kate, who is dyslexic and experiences mathematical difficulties, describes her early experiences. She describes her lack of understanding of basic mathematical concepts and the lack of progress together with the problems of being placed in a low set. Kate clearly identifies the very early roots of her problems, citing her dyslexia, describing a downward spiral that led to her leaving school with no qualification in mathematics:

It all started out, I suppose, from a young girl, suffering with dyslexia. Going to school and not understanding the concept of number – and not really getting the correct tuition and I think that's when my anxiety started – because I was in the classroom, the maths was progressing but I wasn't, and I was getting further and further behind and then when I eventually got to high school, it got even worse – because the syllabus obviously got more difficult. And basically, I was put into a classroom of people which were a bit disruptive and I wasn't getting proper tuition, so therefore I didn't learn the syllabus and I left school without any maths qualification.

Kate

In 'Damn the Three Times Table' (Blackburn, 2003, p. 1), the author also describes her early experiences, which paint a vivid picture of her feelings and the onset of mathematics anxiety:

From the age of 6 when I stood stuttering and red-faced, yet again unable to recite my 3 times table and the class genius was invited to smugly recite his 13 times tables immediately after to show how easy it was, I thought something wasn't right. Not only was it not right, it wasn't ruddy fair. Hot tears would run down my cheeks and I'd creep away feeling stupid, angry, miserable and very, very alone.

Siobhan, a second year Social Science student, had a similar experience:

It started with tables and learning numbers, I couldn't do that. And they made you stand up in front of the class and say it and of course, I couldn't do it. I got into trouble and the teacher always picked on me.

Many students believe that they are alone in their lack of understanding, that the others in the class find it easy and this in turn may induce anxieties. This is reflected in Kate's account of her early experiences.

I couldn't understand the concept of the number between nought and one, I couldn't understand the fractions, it may seem very simple to people who are looking at this now and thinking 'that's so simple' but for me, that was very difficult and it caused me a lot of anxiety.   (Kate)

Ashcraft and Kirk (2001, p. 235) describe mathematics anxiety as 'an on-line reduction in the available working-memory capacity'. For Kate, this is highly relevant, since she has working memory difficulties associated with dyslexia. Taken together with her mathematics anxiety, her working memory is likely to be severely at risk.

And the thing is about the anxiety, it sort of crossed over in my learning, really, because I was trying to learn about the maths. The anxiety got involved ... It hampered my learning of something I found quite difficult. I had to try and control the anxiety as well as learn the maths.   (Kate)

Ashcraft and Kirk (2001) also found that students, who perform poorly in an examination recall becoming confused and experience an inability to concentrate, often focusing on their poor mathematical ability. 'The anxiety reaction involves attention to or preoccupation with intrusive thoughts or worry' (Ashcraft and Kirk, 2001. p. 235).

This is entirely consistent with Kate's experience. She describes the confusion and panic she felt in an examination and its consequent effects:

I sat an exam in statistical analysis and I was doing really well for the first part of the exam and I came across something I could not understand. The ability to not understand something in maths – that's when the anxiety takes over. I just felt so panicky that I wanted to run out of the exam – I just basically sat in the exam and I cried, and I was so frustrated. (Kate)

These characteristics may be coupled with physiological signs such as increase heart rate, sweating or nausea. Cindy is a dyscalculic student, and her difficulties with mathematics began in early childhood although she was not identified as dyscalculic until her first year at university. Cindy's difficulties with mathematics are deep-rooted and have a very real physical effect. She says that when she has to do any maths, she feels nauseous and gets an itchy red rash.

Abeel (2003, p. 14) describes her long battle with dyscalculia. She suffers panic attacks and develops an eating disorder as well as depression. Of one experience in her early years of school, she writes:

As each wave of kids finishes their papers, I begin to feel more weight and pressure. My stomach tightens and I begin to anticipate the sickening feeling of being the last one to finish.

Mathematics anxiety will often be a major obstacle to seeking help. It is very daunting to make the initial approach and students feel embarrassed and believe everyone else finds the mathematics easy.

... so it can be quite intimidating because you think that everyone in there knows so much more than you do and that's the worry ... it's often very difficult to ask for help. Very difficult, ... pride and embarrassment get in the way of seeking help. (Kate)

Steven, a student with dyscalculia, who also experiences mathematics anxiety, expresses similar feelings:

The hardest thing when you have some sort of problem is actually asking someone for some help because you often feel that they may think you are stupid or you're too shy, and you don't want to feel stupid in front of your peer group, for example, or your friends.

Many students will always retain the underlying fears and anxieties but increasing mathematical confidence will help students to succeed. It is also important to establish strategies to help them cope with the anxiety. If the anxiety can be reduced, then some of the working memory can be freed up to enable more effective learning with greater engagement and a growth in confidence. After seeking help, Steven showed that he made an important journey to a more empowering position:

I think I will be able to go forward with some confidence which is the most important thing. Breaking down the barrier, getting over that wall is really important and I don't see it being as restrictive as I did when I was younger.

Screening for Specialist Tutors to Use

There is currently no screening tool for dyscalculia that is appropriate to HE.

Any test consisting of a series of arithmetical computations focuses on the mastery of learned skills and does not provide a detailed picture of a student's understanding. 'Tests which focus on performance do not provide any basis understanding the underlying cause of the observed phenomena' (Gregoire, Noel and Nieuwenhoven, 2003, p. 7). Furthermore, such a measure is unlikely to yield useful information as a sound foundation for subsequent support.

The Dyscalculia Screener (Butterworth, 2003) is suitable for children up to the age of 14. The screener emphasizes the difference between number processing and arithmetic. The screener is 'built primarily upon early mechanisms for processing small numerosities' (Landerl, Bevan and Butterworth, 2004, p. 105). Central to the tool is the notion of subitizing, that is the ability to recognize the numerosity of a number of dots without having to count them. Butterworth believes that we have the facility for subitizing small numbers. However, children with dyscalculia will struggle with this level of subitizing.

DysCalculiUM

The DysCalculiUM first-line screening tool is being developed at Loughborough University by Beacham and Trott (2005). The tool has grown out of an urgent need to identify students who may be at risk of dyscalculia. One student in particular highlighted this urgent need. The student had very basic difficulties with understanding fundamental number concepts and relationships. Following a negative result from dyslexia screening, an educational psychologist confirmed a neurodiverse profile of dyscalculia with no sign of dyslexia. Thus, the need for a suitable screening tool became apparent.

From the outset, it was important that the tool was developed to focus on the understanding of the concepts and interrelationships which underpin the more advanced mathematics and statistics that are an essential part of many courses in HE.

> Another prerequisite of the tool was that it was as user-friendly as possible, thus not causing additional stress to those whose mathematical confidence may already be low and who may well have anxieties deeply rooted in the early years of their mathematical histories. It is important to establish what is understood, not what can be achieved under pressure.   (Trott, 2007, p. 9).

Alongside the screening tool, a model was developed that relies on this core understanding. This model is based on six key areas, some of which are further subdivided into component parts:

- conceptual understanding of number
- number comparison
  - verbal
  - symbolic
  - visual-spatial
- number operations
  - conceptual, focusing on the ability to conceive the correct operation to achieve the required outcome or to reverse a process
  - inferential, focusing on the ability to, given an operational definition, make comparative inferences about an outcome, without realizing the outcome or to infer an operational relationship
- abstract symbolic
- graphical understanding
- spatial-temporal, incorporating both direction and time

Beacham and Trott (2005, 2006) reported very encouraging results from early trials of DysCalculiUM, particularly in relation to the ability of the screener to distinguish the dyscalculic student from the dyslexic student, a key requirement. Trials on a larger scale were then conducted, which allowed for the collection of more general data for the further education and HE population so that thresholds could be determined to establish participants who would be 'at risk of dyscalculia'. Data have also been gathered from students who had already been identified as dyscalculic. Very promising measures of sensitivity and specificity are reported by Trott (2007).

Analysis was conducted to compare the scores of dyscalculic students with dyslexic students in terms of the areas of the model defined previously. A control group of students not known to be neurodiverse was also included. It was found that there was a clear difference between the dyscalculic group and the other two groups. However, as required, there was little or no difference between the dyslexic and control groups, as is necessary in the screening tool.

There is some evidence to suggest that a very small number of high-achieving dyscalculic students may not be seen as 'at risk' by the screening tool. These students were taking strong science-based courses. A case study by Robertson (2004) reported that a postgraduate engineering student, who had been identified as possibly dyscalculic, had a full understanding of algebraic thinking and the higher-level techniques and processes, although he struggled at the basic computational level. The DysCalculiUM screening tool focuses on understanding rather than on numerical computation, therefore, caution needs to be aired when interpreting the results for students studying science or engineering courses.

The overall picture of results emerging gives substantial evidence in support of the effectiveness of the DysCalculiUM screening tool, not least in the substantial agreement between the appropriate indicators of 'at risk' performance on the screener and those individual students who have already been identified as dyscalculic through recognized assessments.

Issues in HE

Course selection and transition

Before I left college I was studying business and finance. The business side – most of it was quite interesting and I could do that. The accounting aspect was hopeless so I didn't think I was going to pass the course. ... The job I was doing wasn't too applied in terms of mathematics so I was able to struggle through, but clearly I couldn't really be too sharp on the deals I could do because obviously the maths wasn't there. ... So coming back to education I was fortunate to choose a course where the maths was only GCSE and C Grade requirement and I thought that at least I can attempt that ...   (Robert, Mature student with dyscalculia)

This vivid description serves to highlight one student's difficulty in the transition to HE. There are, of course, many issues that can arise. A student with dyscalculia can experience difficulties with numbers in many contexts and, since numerical information is at the heart of many everyday situations, there is a clear potential for problems to arise. Some courses are often seen as essentially not mathematical, but do have a large statistical content. This is often the starting point of difficulties for many dyscalculic students. The course choice needs to be carefully considered in terms of the mathematical and statistical content. Robert focused on the entry requirements and not on the course content. He very quickly found that his course contained two years of statistics. Another difficulty was that it had been several years since Robert took his General Certificate of Secondary Education examinations (GCSEs) and for many students the time gap between GCSE Mathematics and entry to HE is particularly a problem.

The transition to HE can often be traumatic. The basic essentials such as arriving on time and finding the way can be a daily problem for the dyscalculic student:

I cannot tell the time on a 24-hour clock ... If I look at a 24-hour clock, I don't see the time. I only see the time it isn't. I'll be waiting for it to say '15:25' (collect children from school time) and unless it says that, then it is irrelevant. Even if I have a clock in front of me where I can count each minute, time on the right side of the clock is 'now' and on the other it's 'non-time'. Any time on the left side is impossible to understand and even counting each minute, I can't put the hands to say '17:47'. That whole 'forty-something' area is a black hole of confusion no matter how many times it is explained to me. Time is for other people.   (Blackburn, 2003, p. 2)

Difficulties with telling the time clearly have implications for arriving to lectures and appointments at the correct time and even mealtimes. Nicky is a second year student with dyscalculia, who has great difficulty telling the time. She described her life as 'run by a lot of alarms'. The alarms, set by a friend, indicate the lectures and appointments she needs to attend. Nicky said that she often wakes up during the night and has no idea if it is time to get up or even for how long she has been asleep. Coupled with the difficulty of telling the time is the fact that many dyscalculic students have problems with directions and with travel. Blackburn (2003, p. 3) continues:

> *I've missed countless trains and buses or got on the wrong train on the wrong platform at the wrong time. Travel directions have to be written in minute detail as I have no understanding of the motorway network and anything more than 'take the next left' goes in one ear and out the other. I can get lost in a box.*

For Helen, a first year student, arriving at university involved having to find her way around a large campus. Helen's dyscalculia, together with her dyspraxia, meant that she found this an almost impossible task. The difficulties associated with orientation resulted in her getting lost everywhere, including inside a lecture theatre. It was helpful for Helen to have straightforward written directions and to be aware of landmarks to look out for. Her difficulties were also helped by the use of friendly guides and by repeatedly walking the route. Like Jess, Helen has problems with time and time management, including confusion over the passage of time. She also experiences difficulty reading tables and consequently timetables and calendars are of little use to her. Some helpful strategies are the use of a customized timetable with spacing, colour and highlighting; use of a specially developed university calendar with a large moveable blob to count semesters and week numbers; the use of a personal data assistant which enables Helen to structure her days/weeks more effectively (Szumko, Trott and Trigg, 2006).

Parallel with the problem of time management is that of financial management. Budgeting with a student loan can be a delicate balancing operation for many students. If the student is dyscalculic, then this can be very problematic and can have serious consequences with mounting debts and ensuing stress. Financial literacy is a basic premise to living on a student budget with a student loan. This financial literacy stems from a fundamental understanding of money and its value, together with the ability to plan ahead and allocate amounts to varying and competing demands. If a student is struggling at this basic level, then debts are likely to escalate and this will increase their anxiety.

Blackburn (2003, p. 3) describes her daily battle with understanding money:

Yesterday I had to add £36 to £5 and dutifully wrote a cheque to pay for some school trips. Later, after a bemused conversation with the school secretary who wondered why I had sent them far too much and a page showing how to add 36 to 5 being sent home from school, my other half asked me 'what genius of calculatory confection have you come up with today, dear?

In a response to Blackburn (2003), Farmer (2004, p. 3) says:

But oh, the humiliation if anyone queried the amount of coins that I had given them, or expected me to count the change!

Alex is a first year student with dyscalculia, and for her there is a daily anxiety associated with shopping for even basic provisions. Her strategy is always to shop with a large bank note (usually £20) so that she is assured of having enough to pay for the items. This results in her having to carry around a large amount of change, which has no meaningful value to her. Every few days, a friend counts out the change, goes to the bank and exchanges it for notes that enable Alex to go to the shops again. Alex would never consider entering a bank herself, it is too anxiety-provoking.

Learning and teaching

Very often in HE there is a discrepancy between the teaching style and the learner perspective. For a dyscalculic student in a lecture, there are likely to be issues around the pace of the mathematical sections of the lecture, with the lack of understanding and consequent cognitive processing at the heart of the issue. As the student struggles with the conceptual understanding, the lecture will have moved on considerably. There are also likely to be some gaps in the mathematical arguments or calculation and reasoning processes. Many students are comfortable to fill in the required steps for themselves, however, the dyscalculic student or a student with mathematical difficulties is unlikely to be able to do this, thus compounding the lack of understanding and the attendant anxiety. Lectures with high mathematical or statistical content will therefore be a source of high anxiety for the dyscalculic student. Many avoid attending these lectures. They will therefore fall even further behind, generating further anxiety, leading to more avoidance and creating a cycle of failure. Steven, a mature student with dyscalculia, commented:

I think the problem escalated in me ... a fear of maths to the extent where you probably go out of your way to avoid issues of maths ... because you just have the fear, and maybe you can do the maths but you feel that you can't.

It is imperative to raise awareness of the problems faced by students with dyscalculia and mathematical difficulties, particularly among academic staff throughout HE. Partly, this can be done through professional development within and between institutions. It is also important to consider the needs of students with dyscalculia or mathematical difficulties in terms of the design, delivery and assessment of a course, in order to make it more accessible. In these terms it is useful to compare two statistically-based courses, both of which relied heavily on analysing and interpreting data through a statistical package. Both courses included an enrolled student who had been identified as dyscalculic. One of the courses was delivered through traditional lectures. From the perspective of the dyscalculic student, these were delivered too quickly and without the intervening steps of the mathematical processes given. The student felt confused and anxious. The other course had no formal lectures, but relied on tutorials with pre-reading essential to these tutorials. At the outset this seemed to be less anxiety-provoking, but the pre-reading requirement gave rise to considerable anxiety, as the student did not understand the statistical material set. Tutorial discussions involving statistical analysis and interpretation proved intimidating. Both courses involved computer-based laboratory sessions. These involved working with data that sometimes had to be entered by hand. One of the dyscalculic students became very confused with the data and frequently made errors. The rows and columns of figures were overwhelming and caused the student to become very anxious and reluctant to attend the sessions. One course was assessed by an examination and a multiple-choice test. In contrast, the other course was assessed entirely through coursework projects. Both the examination and class test proved to be very difficult for the dyscalculic student. In summary, a course could be constructed that drew on the positive aspects of both courses and also allowed a more private space for a student with high mathematical anxiety who feels intimidated in laboratory sessions. Extra support sessions would also benefit students who struggle.

Work placements and careers

Tobias (1993) contends that: 'millions of adults are blocked from professional and personal opportunities because they fear or perform poorly in mathematics.' Numerical understanding is key to many work placements and careers, even those work areas that appear to be nonnumerical. A promotion may mean that the employee has to take on budgets and financially related work. Many employers consider numerical reasoning an essential skill and one that is useful in the selection process for both work placements and graduate employment. Clearly, a student with dyscalculia is likely to struggle at this stage of the selection process and is likely to be excluded from the further selection stages. Increasingly, the application process requires that candidates submit an application and complete tests online. These very often include a test of numerical reasoning. If the candidate is struggling with this element, they are unlikely to be called for interview. For students with dyscalculia, appropriate support and practice are not often available in HE. They are likely to face further barriers in terms of their mathematical confidence and anxieties. Many dyscalculic students simply do not apply for positions that require numerical reasoning tests. Lucy, a student with dyslexia and mathematical difficulties, undertook a placement for which she was not required to take a numerical reasoning test. Lucy believes that she will not be successful with such tests and, for one of her placement applications, was required to go to an assessment day. She did not attend:

It's something I will try to avoid but that will restrict the jobs I can apply for.

Sarah is also a student with dyslexia and mathematical difficulties. Her experience was similar to Lucy's. The selection process for her placement involved numerical and verbal reasoning tests. Sarah described the numerical testing as 'gruelling' and 'by far the worst part of the interview process'. However, unlike Lucy, Sarah did complete the tests and subsequent interviews. It allowed her strengths in other areas to shine through and she was offered the placement. Sarah also benefited from extra time in the tests, which the company organized after she disclosed her neurodiversity.

During her placement, Sarah's strengths continued to impress the company and she was given increasing responsibilities. However, her greatest challenge remained the numerical work that the job routinely required.

The figure work was with big numbers, checking for errors when copying the figures into spreadsheets. It was a real challenge for me and my boss commented on the errors in my work. I reminded him that I had difficulties and he was okay about it. I asked him to continue to check my work and point out any mistakes. I was happy for him to do this.

Sarah took a very forthright approach to her placement. She is clearly aware of both her strengths and weaknesses and is entirely at ease with her neurodiversity. Sarah embraces the social model (Oliver, 1990). However, students like Sarah are the exception and many, like Lucy, feel the need to avoid numerically based tasks in the workplace.

Nursing is an area that has generated much interest recently, particularly in terms of the numerical skills required. Clearly, there are severe consequences of inaccurate drug dose calculations:

Competence in mathematical calculation skills required for clinical nursing practice has been presented as a pre-requisite to nurse registration.   (Sabin, 2003, p. 4)

For a nursing student with dyscalculia, the implications are clear, and since the student needs to be able to understand the calculation, be competent in carrying out the calculation procedure and then be able to apply these in clinical practice, the process is likely to break down at each stage. The student may also experience considerable anxiety, which may become even greater in the practical clinical situation and when under pressure. Self-efficacy is a key component here, with students lacking confidence in their own mathematical skills. Sabin (2003) suggests that further anxiety may be 'generated by the perceived consequences of error' (Sabin, 2003, p. 8). Allen and Papas (1999), as cited by Sabin (2003, p. 31), conclude:

Transferring skills from an academic exercise to a real-life scenario introduces additional aspects of problem-solving, including time pressure, physical environment, and anxiety about the math problem and the mechanics of actually preparing and administering the medication.

The workplace can be a source of anxiety for the dyscalculic. To be asked: 'Can you just check these figures for me?' is a task that would clearly send panic waves through the dyscalculic employee. Blackburn

(2003, p. 3) equates the inability of an employee to conduct financial calculations with a lack of trust on behalf of the employer:

Work is incredibly difficult as I've lost jobs because I can't count properly. It somehow implies untrustworthiness if someone doesn't want to handle money or avoids using figures.

Farmer (2004, p. 4) describes being expected to undertake financial checks:

I temped for a very large telecommunications company for quite a long while, just before giving up work to have my first son. They must have been desperately short of staff, as they put me, a temp at that time, in charge of a seven hundred and fifty thousand pound budget (and no, I couldn't write that in figures with any degree of certainty). I confess to being terrified – until I found that all I was actually expected to do was run my fingers along the two different computer printouts (ours and the Customs and Excise) and check that what they had charged my division for, was actually on our sheet. No calculations required! Why didn't you say so?

Comparisons, I can do. Symbol matching, I can do, just don't ask me to say what's written there. Most of the time the amounts I was looking for were so big they weren't money to me, they were just chunks of numbers, and abstracted like that, reduced to shapes, they lost their power to terrify. 2003.00 on my sheet, and 2003.00 on their page – matched up. Sorted!

Ruth, a student with dyscalculia, described her experience, as a 16-year-old, working in a bakery on a Saturday. Ruth was excited about her first job but on the first morning she was expected to serve customers in the bakery and, of course, this involved adding up the prices of the items purchased, handling the money and giving correct change. She could not do any of these requirements, particularly when there was a queue of customers. Her stress level reached such a height that, by mid-morning, she was no longer able to remain in the bakery and went home in tears. Ruth has not entered the workplace since. She remains very anxious about her prospects on graduation.

Social issues

One of the major social issues facing a student with dyscalculia is the sense of isolation that can result from this learning difference. It is important for students in HE to enjoy the benefits of peer interaction, both academically and socially. In the academic sense, it is usual for students to discuss and learn in cooperation. In the social sense, students engage in sports and other social activities that generate friendships.

Martin is a dyscalculic student who was identified in his final year of his degree. He is a keen rugby player. Martin described the difficulties he experienced on the rugby pitch, due to his dyscalculia. He is unable to keep track of the scores and cannot tell how far ahead or behind his team is, relative to the opposing team. He often asks one of his teammates about the current score. However, Martin enjoys his sport and engages well with his teammates. His dyscalculia does not isolate him.

However, some dyscalculic students may avoid engaging in social activities such as going shopping at the weekend with their peers or having to buy a round of drinks in a student bar. For most students, these are part of the general student life and a major source of peer interaction. For the dyscalculic student who has difficulties with money, these activities are likely to be avoided, thus isolating them from their peers. Even arranging to meet a friend for a coffee may, for some dyscalculics, be too difficult as they may experience problems with the arranged time of meeting.

As well as being at risk of social isolation, a student with dyscalculia may find an increasing academic isolation. Pollak (2005) focused on the self-images of students with dyslexia in HE. Pollak (2005, p 51) says: 'Beliefs about dyslexia have a profound effect upon their sense of identity.' He believes that both the view that the individual has regarding a specific learning difference and the label itself can significantly determine the identity and self-esteem of the individual. Therefore, a positive view of dyslexia is likely to result in higher self-esteem and a more positive identity. This is also true for dyscalculia. Moreover, the dyscalculic student will often be faced with a further issue: that of their self-image as a mathematics learner. According to Boaler, William and Zevenbergen (2000), for students with a substantial mathematical or statistical content in their course, it is important that they develop a sense of who they are in relation to mathematics. Further, Boaler, William and Zevenbergen state that identity is seen in relation to a social or cultural group and feelings of security are gained from group membership. They cite Roberts *et al.* (1999), who found that those individuals with a positive view of their group tend to have high self-esteem, while a negative view of the group leads to low self-esteem.

A student who struggles with the mathematics or statistics in their course is not likely to feel part of the effective learner group, seeing themselves as isolated outsiders with a poor mathematical self-image. This will have an accompanying low mathematical self-esteem that results in a lack of mathematical confidence and heightened mathematical anxiety. If the student is dyscalculic and has a negative view of their neurodiversity, their self-esteem and confidence will be lower still. They are likely to avoid interactions with their peers, whom they may see as more successful and socially included within the class.

Pollak (2005, p. 65) says: 'Identity is partly shaped by the pronouncements which reach us via abstract expert systems.' The influence of the 'expert', the nature of the difficulty and the age at identification are all influential factors in respect of self-esteem. For a dyscalculic student with a poor mathematical history, who has consistently struggled and failed and perhaps been labelled as a failure, the effect on their identity is clear.

Thus, the dyscalculic student does not feel part of the effective learner group and can become an isolated outsider with a poor mathematical self-image, low mathematical self-esteem, lacking in mathematical confidence and experiencing high mathematical anxiety. In relation to their understanding of the mathematics and statistics in their course, students repeatedly use phrases such as: 'I am the only one' and 'others think it simple'. This comparison of themselves in relation to the others in the group shows that they do not see themselves as part of the effective learner group but as an outsider. It is a lonely place to be. The social isolation is apparent. Abeel (2003, p. 23) describes a moment from one of her early mathematics classes from which the reader glimpses that feeling of isolation:

> I dart a look at the clearly comprehending faces of the rest of the class. I feel far away from everyone, removed, alone in my ignorance.

What Can Be Done to Help?

It is clear that students with dyscalculia or mathematical difficulties derive great benefit from specialist help and support. Several institutions now have Mathematics Support Centres where students can receive help. A few of these centres now provide specialist one-to-one support for students with dyscalculia, which can be tailored to their individual needs. It is important to create time and a private space for such students, so that they can go through the work at their own pace and in a way that aids understanding. If the specialist support has good communication links to the other student services, it provides a more joined-up support package for the student. This makes the initial approach easier for the student, although this is still a very difficult step for many because the anxiety and embarrassment are often insurmountable. It is, however, essential that early identification is made, so that appropriate support can be offered.

The support approach should be multi-sensory, allowing the student to understand the concepts and relationships. The multi-sensory approach will also provide a framework to support the working memory. Furthermore, the student needs to be reassured and put at ease as they are very likely to be anxious about the sessions. Well-structured, student-centred support will increase confidence, reduce anxiety and thereby free up the working memory. Increased confidence in their mathematics should also create an improved identity, both in terms of their neurodiversity and their mathematics.

Steven, a mature student with dyscalculia, received one-to-one specialist support directed towards his immediate need for statistics help related to his course, including the understanding and interpretation of graphs and tables. More specifically, this involved the identification and colour-coding of key cells in tables of statistical output, removing those not relevant so that the output was more manageable. He describes the positive impact of the intervention:

> Well, really to take a forward approach and get some applied help, and specifically regarding the course that I am doing, which probably gives you a bit more confidence and to help you perhaps with more everyday aspects like basic numeracy. I think that as you get one-to-one support you are able to look forward and to attack the course without feeling scared by it.

References

Abeel, S. (2003) *My Thirteenth Winter*, Scholastic, New York.
Allen, S. and Papas, A. (1999) Enhancing math competency of baccalaureate students, *Journal of Professional Nursing* **15** (2), 123–29.
American Psychiatric Association (2000) *DSM-IV Diagnostic and Statistical Manual of Mental Disorders*, 4th edn, APA, Arlington, VA.
Arem, C. (2003) *Conquering Math Anxiety*, 2nd edn, Brooks Cole, Florence, KY.
Ashcraft, M. and Faust, M. (1994) Mathematics anxiety and mental arithmetic performance: an exploratory investigation. *Cognition and Emotion*, **8**, 97–125.
Ashcraft, M. and Kirk, E. (2001) The relationships among working memory, mathematics anxiety and performance. *Journal of Experimental Psychology: General*, **130** (2), 224–37.

Beacham, N. and Trott, C. (2005) Development of a first-line screener for dyscalculia in higher education. *SKILL Journal*, **81**, 13–19.

Beacham, N. and Trott, C. (2006) Project report: wider use of dyscalculium, an electronic tool for dyscalculia in H.E. *MSOR Connections*, **6** (2), 12–19.

Blackburn, J. (2003) *Damn the Three Times Table*, http://ddig.lboro.ac.uk/personal_perspective.html (accessed 5 October 2008).

Boaler, J., William, D. and Zevenbergen, R. (2000) The construction of identity in secondary mathematics education. In Matos, J. and Matos, M. (eds) *Proceedings of the Second International Mathematics Education and Society Conference*. Universidade de Lisboa http://nonio.fc.ul.pt/mes2/dylanboro.doc (accessed 5 October 2008)

Butterworth, B. (1999) *The Mathematical Brain*, Macmillan, London.

Butterworth, B. (2001) *Educational Leadership Interview*, http://www.mathematicalbrain.com/int06.html (accessed 26 November 2007).

Butterworth, B. (2002a) *From Fear of Fractions to the Joy of Maths*, www.mathematicalbrain.com/test.html (accessed 26 November 2007).

Butterworth, B. (2002b) *Mathematics and the Brain*. Opening address to The Mathematical Association, conference, Reading, UK. http://www.mathematicalbrain.com/pdf/malecture.pdf (accessed 5 October 2008).

Butterworth, B. (2003) *Dyscalculia Screener*, NFER Nelson, London.

Chinn, S. (2006) What dyslexia can tell us about dyscalculia. *Dyslexia Review*, **18** (1), 15–17.

Cohen Kadosh, R. (2007) *The Root of Dyscalculia Found*, www.ucl.ac.uk/media/library/dyscalculia (accessed 26 November 2007).

Cohen Kadosh, R., Cohen Kadosh, K., Kaas, A. *et al.* (2007) Notation dependent and independent representations of numbers in the parietal lobes. *Neuron*, **53** (2), 307–14.

Desoete, A., Roeyers, H. and De Clercq, A. (2004) Children with mathematics learning disabilities in Belgium. *Journal of Learning Disabilities*, **37** (1), 50–61.

DfES (2001) The National Numeracy Strategy. *Guidance to Support Pupils with Dyslexia and Dyscalculia*, DfES 0512/2001, http://publications.teachernet.gov.uk/eOrderingDownload/DfES-0512-2001.pdf (accessed 26 November 2007).

Farmer, K. (2004) *Response to 'Damn the Three Times Table'*. http://ddig.lboro.ac.uk/personal_perspective.html (accessed 5 October 2008).

Geary, D.C. (2004) Mathematics and learning disabilities. *Journal of Learning Disabilities*, **37** (1), 4–15.

Gregoire, J., Noel, M.P. and Nieuwenhoven, C. (2003) *Tedi-Math: A Test for Diagnostic Assessment of Mathematical Disabilities*, Harcourt Test Publishers, Belgium.

Gross-Tsur, V., Manor, O. and Shalev, R.S. (1996) Developmental dyscalculia: prevalence and demographic feature. *Developmental Medicine and Child Neurology*, **38**, 25–33.

Kosc, L. (1974) Developmental dyscalculia. *Journal of Learning Disabilities,* **7** (3), 164–77.

Landerl, K., Bevan, A. and Butterworth, B. (2004) Developmental dyscalculia and basic numerical capacities: a study of 8–9-year-old students. *Cognition,* **93**, 99–125.

National Center for Learning Disabilities (NCLD) (no date) Dyscalculia, www.ncld. org/content/view/463/456174 (accessed 26 November 2007).

Oliver, M. (1990) *The Politics of Disablement,* Macmillan, Basingstoke.

Piazza, M. and Dehaene, S. (2004) From number neurons to mental arithmetic: the cognitive neuroscience of number sense, in *The Cognitive Neurosciences,* 3rd edn (ed. Michael Gazzaniga), www.unicog.org/publications/ PiazzaDehaene_ChapGazzaniga.pdf (accessed 04 January 2008).

Piazza, M., Pinel, P., Le Bihan, D. and Dehaene, S. (2007) A magnitude code common to numerosities and number symbols in human intraparietal cortex. *Neuron,* **53** (2), 293–305.

Pollak, D. (2005) *Dyslexia, the Self and Higher Education – Learning Life Histories of Students Identified as Dyslexic,* Trentham, Stoke-on-Trent.

Roberts, R.E., Phinney, J.S., Masse, L.C. and Chen, R. (1999) The structure of ethnic identity of your adolescents from diverse ethnocultural groups, *Journal of Early Adolescence* **19** (3), 301–22.

Robertson, J. (2004) *Dyslexia, Dyscalculia and Engineering – a case study.* Notes from a presentation given to The Dyscalculia and Dyslexia Interest Group conference, Loughborough University http://ddig.lboro.ac.uk/ 2004_conference/documents/jan_robertson_presentation.doc (accessed 26 November 2007).

Sabin, M. (2003) *Competence in Practice-Based Calculation: Issues for Nursing Education. A critical review of the literature.* Learning and Teaching Support Network (LTSN), www.health.heacademy.ac.uk/publications/occasionalpaper (accessed 4 January 2008).

Sharma, M. (1997) Dyscalculia, www.dyscalculia.org/BerkshireMath.html (accessed 2 May 2007).

Szumko, J., Trott, C. and Trigg, E. (2006) *A Model of a Joined-Up Support Service.* Dyscalculia and Dyslexia Interest Group conference, Loughborough University http://ddig.lboro.ac.uk/2006_conference/documents/ Clare_jacqueline_Eleanor.ppt (accessed 7 October 2008).

Tobias, S. (1993) *Overcoming Math Anxiety,* W.W. Norton, New York.

Tobias, S. and Weissbrod, C. (1980) Anxiety and mathematics: an update. *Harvard Educational Review,* **50** (1), 63–70.

Trott, C. (2007) Identifying dyscalculia in HE. *Dyslexia Review,* **18** (2), 9–14.

Further Reading

Beacham, N. and Trott, C. (2005) Screening for Dyscalculia within HE. *MSOR Connections,* **5** (1), 40–43.

Berch, D. and Mazzocco, M. (2007) *Why Is Math so Hard for Some Children? The Nature and Origins of Mathematical Learning Difficulties and Disabilities*, Paul H. Brookes, Maryland.

Buxton, L. (1981) *Do You Panic about Maths?: Coping with Maths Anxiety*, Heinemann Educational, London.

Chinn, S. (2007) *Dealing with Dyscalculia: Sum Hope*, 2nd edn, Souvenir Press, London.

Chinn, S. (2004) *The Trouble with Maths*, Routledge Falmer, London.

Dehaene, S. (1997) *The Number Sense*, Oxford University Press, New York.

Dehaene, S. and Cohen, L. (1997) Cerebral pathways for calculation: double dissociation between rote verbal and quantitative knowledge of arithmetic. *Cortex*, **33**, 219–50.

Desoete, A. and Grégoire, J. (2006) Numerical competence in young children and in children with mathematics learning disabilities. *Learning and Individual Differences*, **16** (4), 351–67.

Desoete, A. (2006) *Dyscalculia in Belgium: Definition, Prevalence, Subtypes, Comorbidity, and Assessment*, http://ddig.lboro.ac.uk/pages/research.html (accessed 4 January 2008).

Gifford, S. (2005) *Young Children's Difficulties in Learning Mathematics*. Review of research in relation to dyscalculia. London, Qualifications and Curriculum Authority (QCA/05/1545), www.qca.org.uk/libraryAssets/media/mathematics_report.pdf (accessed 12 January 2008).

Hannell, G. (2005) *Dyscalculia: Action Plans for Successful Learning in Mathematics*, David Fulton Publishers Ltd., London.

Hembree, R. (1990) The nature and relief of mathematics anxiety. *Journal for Research in Mathematics Education*, **21**, 3–46.

Henderson, A., Came, F. and Brough, M. (2003) *Working with Dyscalculia*, Learning Works, Marlborough, Wiltshire.

Johnson, D. (2003) *Math Anxiety, Literature Review*. Humboldt State University, Arcata, California, www.humboldt.edu/~dlj1/mathLitRev.doc (accessed 12 January 2008).

Robertson, J. and Wright, F. (2005) Learning support for students with mathematical difficulties, in *Neurodiversity in FE and HE: Positive Initiatives for Specific Learning Differences* (ed. D. Pollak), Conference proceedings, De Montfort University, Leicester, www.brainhe.com (accessed 28 May 2008).

Robertson, J. (2005) Does dyscalculia affect the learning of mathematical concepts? in *Neurodiversity in FE and HE: Positive Initiatives for Specific Learning Differences* (ed. D. Pollak). Conference proceedings, De Montfort University, Leicester, www.brainhe.com (accessed 28 May 2008).

Sheffield, D. (2006) *How does Anxiety Influence Maths Performance and What Can We Do About It?* Dyscalculia and Dyslexia Interest Group conference, Loughborough University http://ddig.lboro.ac.uk/2006_conference/2006_prestentations_conference.html (accessed 7 October 2008).

Trott, C. and Beacham, N. (2007) *DyscalculiUM: A First-Line Screener for Dyscalculia in Higher Education*, www.brainhe.com/staff/types/documents/ DMU06.ppt (accessed 12 January 2008).

Useful Web Sites

www.dyscalculia.org/
www.dyscalculiainfo.org/
http://personal.cis.strath.ac.uk/~jnw/dig/
www.unicog.org/main/pages.php?page=Home
www.mathematicalbrain.com/
http://ddig.lboro.ac.uk
www.coe.fau.edu/mathitudes/
www.ldonline.org/indepth/math

Chapter 7

Asperger Syndrome: Empathy Is a Two-Way Street

Nicola Martin

Empathy is a two-way street. Colleagues who have read anything about Asperger syndrome (AS) will be familiar with the view that people who have AS lack empathy, and therefore have difficulty understanding the world view of others (Frith, 1989; Baron-Cohen and Bolton, 1993; Frith and Happe, 1999; Howlin, Baron-Cohen and Hadwin, 2000; Tantum, 2000; Attwood, 2007). Beardon and Edmonds (2007), Bogdashina (2006) and others argue that practitioners need to flex their empathy muscles in order understand people who have AS. In this chapter I aim to enable colleagues to begin to do so.

'Individual' is an important word. If you have met one person with AS – you have met one person with AS. *The Curious Incident of The Dog in The Night-time* (Haddon, 2003) is a stereotype about a little boy, not someone old enough to attend university. The film 'Rain Man' is a stereotype too. Asperger himself (1944, p. 63) described 'wide individual differences' among those he first identified.

People with AS are increasingly providing insights into their experiences which challenge misconceptions (Blackburn, 1991; Sinclair, 1993; Grandin, 1996; Walker Sperry, 1998; Arnold, 2003; Edmonds and Warton, 2005; Grandin and Johnson, 2005; Lawson, 2006; Tammet, 2006; Hughes, 2007). Drawing upon the views of 'disabled' people (if this is a term which can be applied to those with AS) in order to inform service development is entirely congruent with the emancipatory ethos, which underpins the UK Disability Equality Duty (HMSO, 2006).

Exploring what people with AS understand by neurodiversity is an interesting starting point. The term was coined initially by individuals with AS who began communicating mainly via the Internet towards the close of the last millennium. As online communities developed, their discussions increasingly enabled participants with AS to explore common characteristics and develop a shared cultural identity as part of neurodiversity, rather than as neurotypical (NT) (aspiesforfreedom.com; autistics.org; nas.org.uk/aspergerunited; Ventura33; wrongplanet.net). The disability versus difference debate gathered pace among people with AS as well as among practitioners (Baron-Cohen, 2000; Bogdashina, 2003). A shared identity and a forum for highlighting positive characteristics associated with AS, and the idea of an 'autism culture', began to develop (aspiesforfreedom.com). Neurodiversity gained an association with 'being different in a good way', while NTs were described, sometimes tongue-in-cheek, as rather strange, mainly because of their 'obsessive interest' in social interaction (Lawson, 2001; Beardon and Edmonds, 2007). The dawn of the World Wide Web provided people who may have found face-to-face communication challenging with a platform for the first time (e.g. outsiders.org.uk). As practitioners, even if NTs form the majority of our number, we need to consider our practice with the neurodiverse nature of AS in mind (Bogdashina, 2003; Beardon and Edmonds, 2007; Jordan, 2007). People with AS who describe NTs in terms of a stereotype may also need to think about the diversity within the NT population. The term neurodiverse does not embody one type and NTs are not all the same either.

The story of Stuart (not his real name) in the United Kingdom illustrates the difference versus disability argument:

Stuart has four science A levels and thirteen GCSEs, all of which are A or A* grades. He is studying physics at a Russell Group university and has consistently gained top marks – i.e. 90+% in the first two years. Ninety per cent is not good enough for Stuart; his concern is about what happened to the other 10%, and he still worries about his failure to get A* in two of his GCSEs. Stuart sets the highest possible standards for himself, and those around him have difficulty understanding his 'perfectionism'. He is happiest when he is immersed in coursework but does have a lively social network, mainly via Facebook, where he mostly talks physics. He is really good at chess and plays weekly at the university chess society, and daily on the Internet. Stuart feels anxious about his marks and is starting to be concerned about his future as he approaches his final year. People really like him. He has a sharp sense of humour and an unusual way of looking at things. When Stuart went to university, his parents were worried. He had been bullied at school and they were convinced he 'didn't know how to look after himself'. Stuart is not bullied at university and has built a series of sensible practical daily living routines. He has divided his student loan into a weekly budget and eats regular meals, mainly involving vegetables, rice and tomatoes sauce, taking great delight in sourcing the cheapest ingredients from the Saturday market. He isn't interested in nightclubbing. Stuart received a diagnosis of AS when he was seven from a communication therapist. He was playing in parallel with other children, that is, doing his own thing on the periphery, and, at the time, his only topic of conversation was the solar system. Throughout his childhood and teenage years, Stuart was on the edge of the crowd. Between 13 and 16 he was bullied and called a weirdo. This stopped when he changed schools, but caused Stuart a lot of unhappiness at the time. He is self-conscious about his diagnosis.

Stuart's situation is not atypical (although the idea that everyone with AS is a genius is erroneous). Average intelligence or above is specified in diagnostic criteria (Gillberg, 1992; Leekam *et al.*, 2000). A study of 117 students with AS from 17 UK universities (Martin, 2005) found the majority to be young males, usually starting science-based courses around the age of 20 with good A levels. Many had been bullied and began university, still living in the family home, with anxious parents in the background. Arguably science, maths, engineering and computer-based courses are often more suited to the logical learning style of people with AS.

Is Stuart a disabled person? He is the most able student on his course and is liked and respected by others. He is managing his money. Socially, Stuart does what he enjoys. Negative previous experiences and the extremely high academic standards he sets himself cause him anxiety, and when he is very anxious he finds it hard to function. Stuart does not like that his peers might see him as different and is resentful of his parents' perception that he can't cope. He puts quite a lot of energy into proving people wrong.

Women with AS, older students, part-timers, distance learners, postgraduates, researchers, those with family responsibilities or working to pay their own way through university also form part of the population of students with AS (Martin, 2005). I have never met a student who reminded me of Rain Man and would describe the learners I have had the privilege to work with as determined, charming, funny, dedicated and diverse. In my view, gender differences are often marked. (This view is echoed by Lawson, 2003, Ensum, 2007 and others.)

Genius pressure can be part of the experience of a student with AS, and *The Curious Incident of the Dog in the Night-time* (Haddon, 2003) might contribute to this problem. Staff sometimes cites this as a reference which has informed their understanding (Martin, 2005). Alternatively, parents and others may view individuals with AS as incapable of performing some simple tasks (while being brilliant at other things). The student may have exceeded everyone's expectations by 'making it' to university (Madriaga, 2006), and might have better A-level grades than his or her peers (Martin, 2005).

'Perfectionism' can manifest itself for a range of reasons, but 'proving everyone who bullied me at school and all the people who thought I was a useless weirdo wrong' is often a major motivation (Martin, 2005).

Screening for the Specialist Tutor to Use

Is screening for AS at university necessary, or possible? Arguably an inclusive environment is flexible and supportive and able to nurture individualistic ways of approaching learning (Tomlinson, 1996). Universities offer a range of services, open to all students and designed to develop social inclusion as well as academic engagement. First year students in particular often feel isolated, get into difficulties with their student loan and miss their families. With excellent support for all students, a label as a passport to specialist services perhaps becomes less critical. On the other hand, universities are impersonal places and resources may need to be targeted. Baron-Cohen (2000) suggests that the word 'disability' attracts services whereas the term 'difference' does not, and a post-16 diagnostic label is necessary in order to access Disabled Students' Allowance (DSA), which is currently the most reliable mechanism in the United Kingdom for providing bespoke one-to-one support.

Blending in is very often on the agenda for a person with AS (Beardon and Edmonds, 2007). Being singled out for support badged as being for disabled students could well run counter to this goal and be detrimental to self-esteem. Riddell, Tinkling and Wilson (2005) found that only 25% of UK students who declared impairment accessed DSA, which is another reason why it is important not to rely exclusively on this system.

On the other hand, people diagnosed in adulthood sometimes describe a sense of relief (Beardon and Edmonds, 2007; Hughes, 2007) and resources follow the label (Baron-Cohen, 2000). Reflection on the potential impact of labelling on self-esteem must be careful, and dynamic, as reactions may change over time. Diagnosis is a process, not an event. Initial relief may, or may not, give way some time later to less positive feelings (Beardon and Edmonds, 2007).

Lisa (not her real name) received a diagnosis as a postgraduate, and explained that she felt relief initially. The feeling lasted for four days. After this Lisa became very anxious, because she felt that she did not have control of the information. Having been accompanied to the diagnostic interview by a lecturer, Lisa described feeling very self-conscious every time she saw this person and was increasingly agitated because she did not know who knew and who did not. The confidential nature of the diagnosis had not been made explicit and was not obvious to Lisa.

Characteristics such as aloofness, arrogance, anxiety and 'being a loner' are sometimes seen as evidence of AS by staff (Martin, 2005). Suggesting this to students is ill-advised, as some may have received a diagnosis earlier and have chosen to reinvent themselves at university (Madriaga *et al.*, 2008). A tactless approach could unintentionally undermine the student. It is necessary to employ some empathy – how would you like it if you were trying to seem like everyone else and someone came up to you and said, 'I can't help noticing that there is something different, odd, peculiar about you'?

Arguably in an environment where there are numerous opportunities to 'disclose' and alternative sources of assistance are in place for those who choose not to, diagnosis is less of an issue. Holding out the possibility of diagnostic assessment when no such service is available is another potential pitfall. Proceed with caution, and/or practise being supportive in an inclusive style, that is, offer assistance relevant to individuals without necessarily going down the diagnostic route, an avenue which should only be pursued if the student has chosen to proceed in that direction. The UK National Autistic Society web site (www.nas.org.uk) provides information about where a diagnosis can be obtained, and the picture is at best patchy (Beardon and Edmonds, 2007; Woolsey, 2007).

The process of screening for dyslexia is a well understood and usual practice. Adult screening for AS is more unusual than the fairly scarce adult screening for learning differences such as dyspraxia, so it is difficult to know how to advise a student who may be seeking a diagnosis. It is possible that, at the point at which the approach is made, the Internet has guided the seeker in the direction of Baron-Cohen *et al.*'s (2001) Autism Quotient (AQ) test, or some similar self-assessment tool. The Internet is alive with sources, some more reliable than others. Carefully gauging the reaction to the outcome of any self-assessment process is an essential precursor to offering advice about what to do next. Questions like 'how do you feel about the outcome of the screening?' may be less than helpful, as it is often hard for someone with AS to describe their feelings, and body language may be a sharper indicator. If a student decides never to come near disability services again post-diagnosis, they might find themselves going through anguish alone.

If a student wants a diagnosis, questions such as 'who can provide a service locally?' and 'who is going to pay for it?' need to be resolved in order to avoid suggesting an unfeasible course of action. Universities will also have to work out how to meet the cost (likely to be around £600 in 2008). Arguably, it is discriminatory not to do so, when funds for diagnostic assessment of dyslexia are often available.

There is no blood test; diagnosis is carried out by a clinician such as a clinical psychologist and based on observable criteria. Ideally, a detailed developmental history, possibly involving parental recollections, consideration of characteristics in a range of contexts, and motivation underpinning behaviours, will form part of the process, making it unlikely that full process can occur in a single visit. In practice, the procedure usually happens all in one day. When a range of practitioners are involved, this can enhance the quality of the outcome (Baron-Cohen, 2000; Ensum, 2007).

Diagnostic assessment instruments have been developed for use with children and adults. (See Lovecky, 2004 for a critical evaluation, and Baron-Cohen *et al.*, 2005 for a detailed description of the Adult Asperger Assessment (AAA), which combines screening instruments and a clinical interview diagnostic approach.) Protocols are usually derived from Diagnostic and Statistical Manual of Mental Disorders Fourth Edition (DSM-IV; American Psychiatric Association, 1994) or ICD10 (World Health Organization, 1992). A précis of Gillberg's (1992) criteria developed from DSM-IV is presented here:

A. Qualitative impairment in social interaction evidenced by at least two of the following:

1. Marked impairment in nonverbal communication including eye contact, facial expression, and body postures and gestures to regulate social interaction
2. Peer relationships not appropriate to developmental level
3. Lack of spontaneous sharing of enjoyment, interests, or achievement, with others
4. Deficit in social or emotional reciprocity

B. Restricted, repetitive, stereotyped behaviour, interests or activities, indicated by at least one of the following:

1. Abnormally intense or focused preoccupation with stereotyped pattern(s) of interest
2. Rigid adherence to nonfunctional rituals or routines
3. Stereotypical or repetitive gross or fine body movements
4. Persistent preoccupation with parts of objects

C. Symptoms described in A and B occur to an extent which impairs functioning
D. Early language delay is not noted
E. Lack of other significant developmental delays
F. Criteria for schizophrenia or other specific pervasive developmental disorders are ruled out

The DSM-IV criteria are AS-specific and there is much debate around the interrelatedness of, and boundaries between, AS and autism (Bishop, 1989). A difference is the requirement to be of at least average intelligence, without having experienced significant language delay prior to the age of five, in order to be diagnosed with AS (Bishop, 1989). Blackburn (2008) has autism, not AS, and sees a clear distinction between her experience of other people and that of individuals with AS. The desire to go ice-skating, for example, motivates Blackburn to interact with other people because she requires their help. People with AS, in contrast, want friends for companionship and a sense of belonging. Kanner's (1943, p. 242) original description of autism notes 'self-sufficiency' and 'lack of affective tie to people'. Asperger (1944) refers to his observations of interactions with others, very much focused on special interests. Multiple negative encounters, particularly during adolescence, can leave someone with AS with damaged self-esteem because of a perceived failure to fit in (Arnold, 2003; Lawson, 2003; Hughes, 2007). Blackburn (2008), in contrast, says she does not care what other people think. While avoiding stereotyping, remembering the differences Blackburn describes may be helpful.

The term 'triad of autistic impairments' (Wing, 1996) is common in medical model literature. 'Triad' refers to three characteristics: communication, social interaction and flexibility, all of which are evident in diagnostic criteria along with additional factors such as sensory sensitivity and issues with executive functioning and central coherence (which impact on planning and organization) and theory of mind or empathy (Frith, 1989; Happé, 1994; Baron-Cohen and Swettenham, 1997; Bogdashina, 2003, 2005; Beaumont and Newcombe, 2006; Happe *et al.*, 2006; South, Ozanoff and McMahon, 2007). Clearly the word 'impairment' is ideologically loaded (Hughes, 2007). Diagnostic reports can describe characteristics associated with AS in very negative ways, and the argument for doing so is often resource-led (Baron-Cohen, 2000). Similarly, assessments for the DSA (in the United Kingdom) are often peppered with words like 'can't', 'difficulty', 'problem' and 'deficit'; the justification for doing so is to influence gatekeepers of the money. Care with language is essential. The recipient of a report written in purely negative terms, and received often at a time of transition and therefore vulnerability, is not going to feel good. On the other hand, the system requires impairment to be specified if disability funding is to be allocated (and reasonable adjustments made).

Useful information about the individual's preferred learning style is often missed from reports. Many people with AS are visual thinkers (Lawson, 1999b; Arnold, 2003; Grandin, 2006), and display characteristics such as being single-channelled, ordered and literal (Lawson, 1999a). Positive words like 'focus' and 'application' are better than 'obsession' and 'rigidity'. It is necessary to try to understand how a person is thinking, in order to offer effective services (Beardon and Edmonds, 2007). Asperger (1944, p. 47) cautioned that 'all educational transactions have to be done with the affect turned off'. Use of loaded language in assessment reports will not promote a sense of calm. Grandin and Johnson (2005), Lawson (1999a) and others echo Asperger's (1944, p. 58) observation that 'they have to learn everything via the intellect', suggesting that a logical approach to teaching and learning would make sense. The aim of assessment for support is to minimize barriers in order to foster success, so a long list of perceived failings and deviations from neurotypicality has no useful place.

Overcoming Barriers in Higher Education

If an individual has difficulty with communication, then other people need to communicate as clearly as possible (Madriaga *et al.*, 2008). The impact of past experiences of social isolation and possibly bullying needs to be considered, with a view to creating more positive social contexts (Martin, 2005). Clarity and predictability (warning in advance of changes in routine) create a more inclusive environment for those who find the unpredictable difficult (Lawson, 2001). Sensory overload can occur in busy loud places, so creating quiet spaces and ensuring that individuals know how to access them makes sense (Bogdashina, 2005). Challenges with executive function and central coherence can impact on the ability to prioritize, see connections between events or areas of learning which may appear to be isolated from each other, and to be personally and academically 'organized' (Lawson, 2001; Attwood, 2007). Assisting the student with time management, seeing the interrelatedness of things and planning and executing day-to-day life as well as academic work would be helpful (Jamieson and Jamieson, 2004; Harper *et al.*, 2004; Howley, 2005; Martin, 2005). Understanding that high levels of anxiety can result from a chaotic environment in which the boundaries are unclear, rules are not explicit, and people do not always say what they mean, can help practitioners to behave in a chaos-reducing rather than anxiety-provoking fashion (Beardon and Edmonds, 2007). It would be useful if people could be empathic towards individuals who may find it hard to see things from another person's point of view.

The student who took a message that a class was cancelled and did not pass it on to her classmates was not being rude. She had not considered that the implied, rather than stated, expectation was that she should pass it on, not having the theory of mind to realize that what was in her head was not in the heads of her flatmates. The staff member lacked the theory of mind to work out that the student might not make the necessary empathic mental leap. Had he realized, he would have added 'and please let your flatmates know because I have not told them' (Martin, 2005).

Lack of flexibility, in deficit model language, could be reinterpreted positively as 'application' (Grandin, 1996; Arnold, 2003; Tammet, 2006). A student may well have an intense interest in a particular area of study. The word 'obsession' could be applied here, with all its negative connotations, or expressions like 'fascination', 'intense interest', 'wealth of knowledge' or 'expertise' may be employed. Asperger (1944, p. 88) had already reached the conclusion that the degree of focus an individual with AS could employ had the potential to enable a fantastic level of achievement: 'Able autistic individuals can rise to eminent positions and perform with such outstanding success that one may conclude that only such people are capable of certain achievements'. Understanding something about how a person with AS may see the world could help staff to nurture talent and motivation (Lawson, 2001, Bogdashina, 2005; Beardon and Edmonds, 2007).

Abdul (not his real name) had a thorough understanding and passionate interest in a very narrow aspect of computer programming. Luckily he was taking a computer studies BSc degree. Unfortunately, the course demanded that he looked at wider applications of ICT beyond his area of special interest. Abdul's tutor, Ian, understood that Abdul would spend most of his time on the aspect of the course that interested him most. He also realized that Abdul really wanted his degree. The approach he took was to be absolutely clear and unambiguous in his communication and very practical in the way he helped Abdul to organize his time. Abdul was successful and his success was facilitated by his tutor helping him to plan how he should approach his course work. Ian told Abdul quite simply: 'If you don't complete x module you will fail your course'. He even went so far as to say: 'You don't have to enjoy that module; you just have to do it and pass it in order to get your degree'. Ian learned empathy and Abdul got a first and went on to study a PhD, where he was able to narrow and deepen his focus.

The Triad of Impairment

Institutions and individuals in power relationships towards students may be empathic, clear communicators with the mental flexibility to create effective environments. They may adopt a holistic approach, considering the whole student in the social as well as the academic context. Valuing neurodiversity and embracing inclusion, they may go out of their way to ensure that all students feel nurtured and receive the backup they require, whether or not they come with a diagnostic label. Conversely, the university may exhibit a triad of impairment in their ability to deliver good communication, flexibility and socially appropriate experiences. Failure usually occurs as a result of lack of empathy with the worldview of individuals with AS. However, with appropriate motivation, attention and development work, institutions and their staff can improve over time.

An irresistible urge to locate the deficit somewhere other than with people who have AS (in this case within the institution) may be prompted by the writings of Lawson (2006). Learning from the widely available insights of those with AS, universities can achieve improvements in communication, flexibility and the user-friendliness of social environments (Martin, 2005; Beardon and Edmonds, 2007; Madriaga *et al.*, 2008).

Communication: the need for order and clarity

Anxiety about change is common among people with AS (Lawson, 1999b, 2001; South, Ozanoff and McMahon, 2007). Working towards smoother transitions into, through and beyond university will inevitably reduce the anxiety which occurs when moving from one phase to another is a haphazard and chaotic process (Lawson, 1999, 2003; Jordan, 2007).

Goode (2007) laments the extent to which disabled students are in the position of having to start university without appropriate backup. In the United Kingdom the Sheffield universities, together with the further education college and the DSA Assessment Centre, work together to address this issue via an annual event held in March involving prospective students and their supporters. The necessary steps are clearly explained in order to enable the students to navigate the complex road to accessing the DSA in a timely fashion (Jackson and Martin, 2007).

Consideration of each aspect of the student journey and effective communication at every point is necessary. Institutions fail when individuals within them demonstrate value judgements, which place the responsibility to understand the message solely with the recipient. Like empathy, communication is a two-way street, and it is the responsibility of the giver of information to be as clear as possible and check that it has been received with understanding.

Specificity regarding assignments may need to include detailed instruction about the process, as well as the desired outcome. Lack of clarity can cause anxiety. When assignment briefs are unclear, time can be wasted because of misunderstanding what is required. Comments like 'I should be in my office sometime next week if you want to come along for a chat' do not make sense (Martin, 2005). 'Go to the library, find five references and spend about two hours on the (very clear) question which is worth a specified number of marks' will make a lot more sense than 'go away and do some research'. The student may well build on their skills, but this is more likely when firm foundations are laid initially by an empathic tutor, and ongoing attempts to assist with finding links between what may seem to be discreet and distinct areas are built into the learning experience. Clearly the benefit will be felt by other students too. 'Just beef this section up a bit' roughly translated into AS-friendly speak might be re-worded as: 'You have gone into enough depth about x and y but you need to spend some more time thinking about z. Add in two or three paragraphs explaining clearly the relationship between x, y and z. Please come and talk to me if what I have written here is not really clear'. 'Bring your draft assignment to my office at 2 p.m. on Monday, 2 February with a list of up to three points you would like to discuss with me about your draft; the meeting will last half an hour'.

Flexibility

Inherent in being flexible is the understanding that people need to be treated as individuals. AS may be the only thing two students with the label have in common. Asperger (1944, p. 67) cautioned against 'letting the child's unique personality vanish behind the type'. (The reference is relevant across the age range, and the age of the student is important. One student lamented the fact that he, at 18, had been put in touch with a middle-aged woman with AS on another course, with a view to friendship. He did not connect with her because, in his eyes, she was too old.)

Students may be at different stages in relation to their reaction to their diagnosis, and not everyone is willing to disclose or make use of services badged as being for disabled students (Martin, 2005; Madriaga *et al.*, 2008). Counselling may benefit some students who are experiencing depression and anxiety, but this cannot be viewed as a panacea. If depression is the result of social exclusion, assisting the student to join clubs and societies may be more appropriate. When anxiety occurs as a direct result of trying to cope in an unclear and unpredictable environment, addressing the environmental factors may well alleviate the anxiety over time. It is necessary to empathize in order to work this out of course. It is also a very good idea to talk to students, who may well say something like 'I am very depressed because my group go off for coffee and don't invite me and I want to go with them' or 'I feel really worried when the lecturer says we have to hand in our work on a particular date and then says we don't have to give it in until two weeks later.' Empathy does not have to involve the employment of psychic powers. Listening is usually a good start.

A level of flexibility around the way services are delivered is important. The UK DSA regulations are fairly strict about what is and is not fundable. Anxiety about unreliable public transports, or being preoccupied by having very noisy flatmates, or feeling tired, or hungry, can overwhelm a student. The DSA does not cover dealing with misery and the acquisition of independent living skills, but students are not going to engage with learning if they are overwhelmed by practical and emotional concerns. Maslow (1970) makes clear that lower-order requirements for sustenance and nurture/belonging have to be met before engagement with higher-order thinking, that is, learning, is possible. If someone feels worried, left out, hungry, tired, thirsty, unloved and unwelcome, throwing DSA-funded note-takers at them, or assistance with planning assignments and so on might be missing the point, and a waste of money. Assuming that there is an army of social services personnel ready to deal with nonacademic issues is unrealistic, so finding a way forward is necessary (Martin, 2005).

Some students with AS engage in behaviour which serves a purpose for them but which other people might fail to understand. NTs do things which people with AS find unusual all the time (Beardon and Edmonds, 2007). An individual who slowly lines up his pens on his desk before his lecture may well be doing so because the order this creates, in a confusing environment, gives him a sense of control. The activity may be puzzling to others but is not disruptive to anyone else. Blackburn (2008) gives the example of a conversation about television between two NTs, which she viewed as odd and mildly ridiculous. X said to Y: 'Did you see East Enders last night?' Y said 'yes' and then X preceded to go over what had happened in East Enders despite the fact that Y had confirmed that she had in fact seen that episode too. Even more confusing to Blackburn was that both parties seemed to be enjoying this activity which was totally pointless in her eyes. Blackburn was able to display the mental flexibility to ignore the NTs because what they were doing was not really impinging on her to any great extent. Ignoring the lining up of the pens, rather than labelling the behaviour as a ritual and placing some value judgement on its appropriateness, seems like a sensible, empathic approach.

The social environment

First year students often experience real nervousness about what other people are going to think of them. For students with AS, prior negative experiences can exacerbate feelings of anxiety about new people and new situations (Beardon and Edmonds, 2007). Organizing Freshers' week activities based on the assumption that all the potential participants like a lot of noise may be missing the point for the majority of students who have AS (and for others among the diverse student population). In one student union building there is a design on the floor, which is like a meandering bright red stream surrounded by vivid yellow circles. The sensory environment was so unpleasant for a student with AS that she did not intend to enter the space again. Bright lights, crowds, noise, confusion and lack of predictability are characteristics of a typical Freshers' fair. Amazingly enough, not everyone likes it. Freshers' week is marketed as the time to join in with clubs and societies, the one big opportunity to have a social life. People who have often experienced social isolation and bullying in the past may have high hopes of Freshers' week as the gateway to a new life. Mustering every ounce of courage to enter the bear garden that is Freshers' fair may therefore be a really big deal. They screw up all their courage to take what may feel like a descent into hell as people shout, lights flash and someone in a gorilla costume thrusts a carrier bag of condoms and vodka shots at them.

Prior experience of social isolation and bullying is common (Attwood, 1998; Beardon and Edmonds, 2007). Therefore, inexperience in peer relationships, or wariness because of previous negative interactions and the fear that peers could be plain nasty, may follow (Martin, 2005; Hughes, 2007). A degree of vulnerability is also possible because of the interrelationship between limited social experience, a desire to make friends, and difficulty with working out other people's motivation (Beardon and Edmonds, 2007). One student with AS got into trouble for growing cannabis on his windowsill for a friend. Another spent a great deal of money in the bar in the first week buying drinks for people who did not reciprocate. Someone else was called upon to do all the driving all the time for 'friends' (Martin, 2005; Madriaga *et al.*, 2008).

In an inclusive university, academic engagement is only one component of the experience; consideration of how to assist students (many of whom have left home for the first time) to make friends is also important. With an increasing trend towards studying close to the family home, the social requirements of those who live with their parents (whether the individual has AS or not) merit careful thought.

Prejudices

Try to empathize with students who are confronted by other people's prejudices and erroneous expectations on a daily basis. Parents have probably gone through the whole range of human emotions during their child's journey and had little support in understanding that their son or daughter has moved into adulthood. Students with AS have often massively exceeded parental expectations, and parents can be rather confused, as well as delighted, about how their son or daughter succeeded against all odds (Madriaga *et al.*, 2008). Teachers may not have mentioned university as an option or provided the encouragement necessary to build confidence (Madriaga, 2006). Parents are likely to find it hard to trust university staff, and it is very easy to communicate this insecurity to their offspring. The message 'my mum and dad, teacher, careers advisor ... don't think I can do it' could contribute to a heightened level of anxiety and a lowered sense of self-worth (Martin, 2005).

Madriaga *et al.* (2008) cite the example of Rachel who was keen to live in halls of residence but put off by her mother, who convinced her that she would not cope. Rachel resented this and felt that she was missing out. There is a big difference between 'can't do it' and 'haven't done it before'. Parental nervousness is understandable and perhaps could be alleviated with better information about support in HE, and wider publication of success stories (Jackson and Martin, 2007). Another student in Madriaga *et al.*'s (2008) study talks about reinventing himself at university and the sense of euphoria he experienced because he found that he was able to cope well. Being absolutely determined to 'show them all' (Arnold, 2003) can be extremely positive, unless of course it tips over into the sort of perfectionism which means that getting a mark of 99% feels like failure (Martin, 2005).

Good Quality Services

Reliability is the cornerstone of effective services. A holistic approach which considers all aspects of interaction between the individual and the institution is recommended. The following quality indicator questions, which are organized as a timeline of the student journey, may be useful:

1. Is the culture inclusive and is diversity valued, not problematized?
2. Are staff AS-aware, empathic and reliable?
3. Is pre-entry support planned?
4. Are communications clear?
5. Is the sensory environment calm in places?
6. Is not tolerating bullying the norm?
7. Are services available for all students who struggle with loneliness and anxiety?
8. Are social opportunities diverse and easy to access?
9. Is there help available for students to develop independent living skills?
10. Are all aspects of the student journey considered, from pre-entry to post-exit? Does this include help with finding a job? (In the United Kingdom, the National Autistic Society runs a service called Prospects, which helps people on the autism spectrum to find work and employers to recruit, train and retain them.)

There is a growing body of personal accounts of students with AS who have had successful university experiences (Arnold, 2005; Beardon and Edmonds, 2007; Madriaga *et al.*, 2008). These are testament to determination and commitment. Grandin (1996) is firmly of the view that without AS the world would be short of a wide range of necessary inventions. Asperger (1944, p. 74) was alive to this possibility, suggesting that he knew of 'numerous autistic individuals among distinguished scientists'. We ignore the opportunity to nurture the talent of people who have AS at our peril!

References

American Psychiatric Association (1994) *DSM-IV-TR Diagnostic and Statistical Manual of Mental Disorders*, 4th edn, APA, Washington, DC.

Arnold, L. (2003) *Neurological Difference Page*, www.larry-arnold.info/Neurodiversity/index.htm (accessed 12 December 2007).

Asperger, H. (1944) *Autistic Psychopathy in Childhood.* A translation of the paper by U. Frith, in *Autism and Asperger Syndrome* (1991) (ed. U. Frith), Cambridge University Press, Cambridge.

Aspergerunited, www.nas.org.uk/aspergerunited (accessed 10 November 2007).

Aspies for freedom, www.Aspiesforfreedom/com (accessed 10 November 2007).

Attwood, T. (1998) *Asperger Syndrome: A Guide for Parents and Professionals*, Jessica Kingsley, London.

Attwood, T. (2007) *The Complete Guide to Asperger's Syndrome*, Jessica Kingsley, London.

Autistics.org, http://autistics.org (accessed 12 November 2007).

Baron-Cohen, S. (2000) Is Asperger's Syndrome/high functioning autism necessarily a disability? *Development and Psychopathology Millennium Edition*, **12**, 489–500.

Baron-Cohen, S. and Bolton, P. (1993) *Autism: The Facts*, Oxford University Press, Oxford.

Baron-Cohen, S. and Swettenham, J. (1997) Theory of mind in autism: its relationship to central coherence, in *Handbook of Autism and Pervasive Developmental Disorders*, 2nd edn (eds D. Cohen and F. Volkmar), Wiley, Chichester.

Baron-Cohen, S., Wheelwright, S., Skinner, R. and Martin, J. (2001) *The Autism Spectrum Quotient (AQ): A Self-Administered Test for High Functioning Autism (HFA)*, Autism Research Centre, Cambridge.

Beardon, L. and Edmonds, G. (2007) *ASPECT Consultancy Report: A National Report on the Needs of Adults with Asperger Syndrome*, www.shu.ac.uk/theautismcentre (accessed 24 October 2007).

Beaumont, R. and Newcombe, P. (2006) Theory of mind and central coherence theory in adults with high functioning autism and Asperger syndrome. *Autism: The International Journal of Research and Practice*, **10** (4), 365–82.

Bishop, A. (1989) Autism, Asperger syndrome and semantic pragmatic disorders: where are the boundaries? *British Journal of Disorders in Communication*, **24**, 107–21.

Blackburn, R. (1991) *Finding My Way. Being Me*, www.autism.net (accessed 20 January 2008).

Blackburn, R. (2008) *Logical Illogical*. Lecture at Sheffield Hallam University Autism Centre. March 2008.

Bogdashina, O. (2003) *Sensory Perceptual Issues in Autism and Asperger Syndrome: Different Sensory Experiences, Different Perceptual Worlds*, Jessica Kingsley, London.

Bogdashina, O. (2005) *Communication Issues in Autism and Asperger Syndrome. Do We Speak the Same Language?* Jessica Kingsley, London.

Bogdashina, O. (2006) *Theory of Mind and the Triad of Perspectives on Autism and Asperger Syndrome: A View from the Bridge*, Jessica Kingsley, London.

Edmonds, G. and Warton, D. (2005) *The Asperger Syndrome Love Guide: A Practical Guide for Adults with Asperger's Syndrome to Seeking, Establishing and Maintaining Successful Relationships*, Paul Chapman, London.

Ensum, I. (2007) *Developing Services Locally for Young People and Adults with AS and HFA*, www.autism-support-somerset.org (accessed 20 March 2008).

Frith, U. (1989) *Autism: Explaining the Enigma*, Blackwell, Oxford.

Frith, U. and Happe, F. (1999) Theory of mind and self-consciousness. What is it like to be autistic? *Mind and Language*, **14**, 1–22.

Gillberg, C. (1992) Diagnosis and treatment of autism, in *The Autism Spectrum* (ed. L. Wing), Ulysses Press, Berkeley, CA.

Goode, J. (2007) Managing disability: early experiences of university students with disabilities. *Disability and Society*, **22** (1), 35–49.

Grandin, T. (1996) *Thinking in Pictures, and Other Reports on My Life*, Vintage, New York.

Grandin, T. (2006) *Seeing in Beautiful Precise Pictures*, www.npr.org (accessed 23 February 2008).

Grandin, T. and Johnson, C. (2005) *Animals in Translation*, Simon & Schuster, New York.

Haddon, M. (2003) *The Curious Incident of The Dog in the Night-Time*, Vintage, New York.

Happé, F. (1994) *Autism: An Introduction to Psychological Theory*, UCL Press/ Psychology Press, London.

Happe, F., Booth, R., Charlton, R. and Hughes, C. (2006) Executive function deficits in ASD and AD/HD: examining profiles across domains and ages. *Brain and Cognition*, **6** (11), 25–39.

Harper, J., Lawlor, M. and Fitzgerald, M. (2004) *Succeeding in College with Asperger Syndrome: A Student Guide*, Jessica Kingsley, London.

Her Majesty's Stationery Office (HMSO) (2006) *Disability Equality Duty*, www. direct.gov.uk/ded (accessed 10 July 2007).

Howley, M. (2005) Students with Asperger's Syndrome in further and higher education, *in Neurodiversity in FE and HE: Positive Initiatives for Specific Learning Differences* (ed. D. Pollak). Conference proceedings, Leicester, De Montfort University, www.brainhe.com (accessed 28 May 2008).

Howlin, P., Baron-Cohen, S. and Hadwin, J. (2000) *Teaching Children with Autism to Mind Read*, John Wiley & Sons, Chichester.

Hughes, P.J. (2007) *Reflections: Me and Planet Weirdo*, Chipmunk, London.

Jackson, V. and Martin, N. (2007) Towards a smooth transition into higher education for disabled students in South Yorkshire. *NADP News*, **13**, 23–25.

Jamieson, J. and Jamieson, C. (2004) *Managing Asperger Syndrome at College and University*, David Fulton, London.

Jordan, R. (2007) Address at Autism Centre for Education and Research launch event, University of Birmingham, 4 October 2007.

Kanner, L. (1943) Autistic disturbances of affective contact. *Nervous Child*, **2**, 217–50.

Lawson, W. (1999a) *Adolescents, Autism Spectrum Disorder and Secondary School*, www.mugsy.org/assschool.htm (accessed 12 September 2007).

Lawson, W. (1999b) *Asperger's Syndrome and Promoting a Healthy Self Esteem*, www.mugsy.org/esteem.htm (accessed 12 July 2007).

Lawson, W. (2001) *Understanding and Working with the Spectrum of Autism. An Insider's View*, Jessica Kingsley, London.

Lawson, W. (2003) *As a Woman with Asperger Syndrome*. Autism Asperger Publishing Company Newsletter, May/June 2003, www.asperger.net/newsletter_mayjune03lawson.htm (accessed 06 October 2007).

Lawson, W. (2006) Typical development, learning styles, single attention and associated cognition in autism (SAACA). *Good Autism Practice*, **7** (2), 61–71.

Leekam, S., Libby, S., Wing, L. *et al.* (2000) Comparison of ICD10 and Gillberg's criteria for Asperger's Syndrome. *Autism: The International Journal of Research and Practice* **4** (1), 11–28.

Lovecky, D. (2004) *Gifted Minds: Gifted Children with ADHD, Asperger's Syndrome and Other Learning Deficits*, Jessica Kingsley, London.

Madriaga, M. (2006) Research report on transition of disabled learners from further to higher education. European Access Network Newsletter 3, February 2006, www.ean-edu.org/news (accessed 11 April 2007).

Madriaga, M., Goodley, D., Hodge, N. and Martin, N. (2008) *Experiences and Identities of UK Students with Asperger Syndrome*, www.heacademy.ac.uk/events/detail.researchseminar/08feb (accessed 20 March 2008).

Martin, N. (2005) *Towards a Better Understanding of Effective Strategies to Support University Students with Asperger's Syndrome*, www.nadp-uk.org (accessed 10 October 2007).

Maslow, A.J. (1970) *Motivation and Personality*, 2nd edn, Harper & Row, New York.

NAS (2007) *PJ Hughes Biography*, www.nas.org.uk/nas/jsp/polopoly.jsp (accessed 10 November 2007).

Outsiders.org.uk www.Outsiders.org.uk (accessed 10 May 2007).

Riddell, S., Tinkling, T. and Wilson, A. (2005) *Disabled Students in Higher Education: Perspectives on Widening Access and Changing Policy*, Routledge, London.

Sinclair, J. (1993) *Don't Mourn for Us*, http://ani.autistics.org/don't_mourn.html (accessed 6 July 2007).

South, M., Ozanoff, S. and McMahon (2007) The relationship between executive function, central coherence and repetitive behaviours in high functioning autism spectrum. *Autism: The International Journal of Research and Practice*, **11** (5), 437–53.

Tammet, D. (2006) *Born on a Blue Day*, Hodder & Stoughton, London.

Tantum, D. (2000) Psychological disorders in adults and adolescents with Asperger's Syndrome. *Autism: The International Journal of Research and Practice*, **4** (1), 47–63.

Tomlinson, J. (1996) *Inclusive Learning*, Further Education Funding Council, HMSO, London.

University Students with Autism and Asperger's Syndrome. www.users.dircon.co.uk/~cns/ (accessed 29 May 2008).

Ventura33 https://ventura33.com (accessed 26 June 2007).

Walker Sperry, V. (1998) From the inside looking out – a view of the world as seen by one with Asperger Syndrome. *Autism: The International Journal of Research and Practice*, **2** (1), 81–87.

Wing, L. (1996) *The Autistic Spectrum: A Guide for Parents and Professionals*, Constable, London.

Woolsey, I. (2007) *Patterns of Social and Educational Support for Students with Asperger Syndrome/High Functioning Autism in Further and Higher Education in the United Kingdom*, www.shu.ac.uk/autismcentre (accessed 12 December 2008).

World Health Organization (1992) *International Classification of Diseases (ICD-10)*, 10th edn, bjp.rcpsych.org/cgi/content/full/176/6/576 (accessed 20 March 2008).

Further Reading

Murray, D. (2006) *Coming Out Asperger: Diagnosis, Disclosure and Self-Confidence*, Jessica Kingsley, London.

Chapter 8

Attention Deficit (Hyperactivity) Disorder – AD(H)D

Mary Colley

Introduction

The abbreviation AD(H)D stands for Attention Deficit (Hyperactivity) Disorder. The 'H' is usually placed in brackets because not everyone experiences hyperactivity. Until fairly recently, it was believed AD(H)D affected only children, but it is now understood that it persists into adulthood in up to 70% of cases (Hallowell and Ratey, 2006, p. 8). This means there will be a significant number of students with AD(H)D at university – recognized or unrecognized. Educators and student support staff therefore need to learn how to recognize and understand AD(H)D, and how to support students.

This chapter will begin by defining AD(H)D and the theories and models concerning its cause. It will then describe how AD(H)D manifests itself at university, how it can be identified and how to support such students. The term 'ADDer' will be used, rather than 'student with AD(H)D', mainly because it is shorter, but partly because it is a term chosen by some ADDers themselves.

What AD(H)D Is and How to Recognize It

Definition and types of AD(H)D

The most prominent definition of AD(H)D is given in the American manual DSM-IV (American Psychiatric Association, 1994). This presents AD(H)D as a unitary condition with three subtypes:

- mainly hyperactive/impulsive;
- mainly inattentive; and
- the combined type.

The DSM-IV also includes a useful checklist of indicators of AD(H)D, of which more below.

Roughly 5–8% of the American population have AD(H)D (Hallowell and Ratey, 2006, p. 8). Other countries such as New Zealand and Canada have comparable figures. It is probably less prevalent in the United Kingdom, but there are no studies to back this up. The indicators were once thought to dissipate during adolescence, but numerous studies have now shown that this is by no means always the case. According to Barkley (1997, p. 65) studies have shown that AD(H)D 'persists into adolescence in 50–80% of cases clinically diagnosed and into adulthood in 30–50%'. Hallowell and Ratey (2006, p. 8) cite up to 70% of cases as continuing. AD(H)D is known to be hereditary in up to 90% of cases (Young and Bramham, 2007, p. 5).

Barkley and Murphy (1998, p. 1) define AD(H)D as 'a specific developmental disorder … that comprises deficits in behavioural inhibition, sustained attention and resistance to distraction, and the regulation of one's activity to the demands of a situation (hyperactivity or restlessness)'. Barkley (1997) views poor behavioural inhibition and self-regulation as the central impairment in AD(H)D.

History

AD(H)D was first described by George Still in 1902 as a 'defect in moral control' (Barkley, 2006, p. 4). It was often seen as minimal brain damage, particularly between the 1930s and 1970s (Barkley, 2006, pp. 5–8). Until the late 1970s, AD(H)D was seen as a childhood disorder characterized by chronic restlessness and impulsivity and known as hyperkinetic disorder (Brown, 2005, p. 9). At about this time, it was recognized that these children also had significant problems paying attention to tasks; in 1980 the name was changed to Attention Deficit Disorder (ADD) (ibid.). In 1994 these two strands were merged and became Attention Deficit (Hyperactivity) Disorder – AD(H)D (DSM-IV). As a neurobiological impairment, this is now covered by disability legislation in some countries, among them the United Kingdom (DDA, 1995, 2005).

The UK's Developmental Adult Neurodiversity Association (DANDA) sees AD(H)D as part of the spectrum of neurodiversity, overlapping in particular with dyslexia, dyspraxia and Asperger's Syndrome. It, along with the other conditions, is seen as a specific information-processing difference, or as part of a cognitive profile which shows many peaks and troughs in processing information.

AD(H)D and executive functions

AD(H)D is also increasingly seen as linked to an impairment of the brain's 'executive functions' or cognitive management functions (Barkley, 1997; Brown, 2005, p. 10). These functions include the ability to prioritize, integrate and regulate other cognitive functions.

Barkley (1997) lists a number of severe difficulties in respect of impaired inhibition that affect every aspect of a person's life. These include poor academic performance; above-average risk of delinquency; poor family and social relationships; anxiety and depression; a greater likelihood of substance abuse; driving accidents; and problems in employment.

Barkley (2006, pp. 316, 321) also suggests that behavioural self-control depends on four executive functions: nonverbal working memory (including foresight, hindsight, sense of time and concentration); verbal working memory or internalization of speech; self-regulation of emotions and motivation; and reconstitution (being able to use what has been learned before). These impairments, he states, strongly lead to associated motor control and execution deficits, both gross and fine; he cites poor handwriting as one of the main examples of a motor deficit.

Brown (2006) sees behavioural inhibition as only one of six executive functions/cognitive problems in AD(H)D. These include difficulties with organization and prioritization; focusing, sustaining and shifting attention; regulating alertness and determining speed; managing frustration and regulating emotions; utilizing working memory; and problems with regulating and monitoring actions.

Imagine a student starts an essay having done some preparation. The deadline is the next day. She has collected all the necessary equipment, but cannot find some necessary books when she needs them. Agitated, she rushes and starts to write the essay regardless. After a bit, she finds them at the bottom of a disorganised pile, and has to start again. She then finds she can't find some vital notes but continues nevertheless – without any planning or system because she thinks it will be quicker this way! She gets interrupted by a phone call and becomes very distracted. She finally settles down again, and after an hour of frenzied writing, realises she has not tackled the essay topic at all, and has to start yet again. That student is very unlikely to get that essay in on time.

(adapted from *The Disorganised Cook* (Denckla, 1996, cited in Brown, 2006, p. 11)

Whatever the theory, it is crucial that educators fully accept the fact that AD(H)D is a real impairment, not just a lack of willpower or a behavioural problem. Students can often only motivate themselves when a subject truly interests them. In this case they often hyper-focus or obsess – which is one of the reasons why some people are so sceptical that AD(H)D truly exists.

Brown (2006) states that AD(H)D can look like a 'lack of willpower' but in fact it is not. It is a chemical problem that undermines the management system of the brain. The two chemicals concerned are dopamine and norepinephrine. Without the effective release and reuptake of these, the neural pathways cannot effectively carry messages.

Overlap with other types of neurodiversity

Although AD(H)D does occur on its own, this is relatively rare. Mostly, it occurs with other specific learning/processing differences and for this reason it is sometimes not recognized during assessment (Young and Bramham, 2007, p. 8). For example:

- Dyslexia has been shown to overlap with AD(H)D in over 50% of cases (Adams and Snowling, 2001, cited in Deponio, 2005).
- Twenty-six per cent of people with AD(H)D may also be on the autism spectrum (Barkley, 2006, p. 195).
- About 50% of people with ADHD have developmental coordination difficulties or dyspraxia (Gillberg, 2003, cited in Deponio, 2005).
- Specific learning difficulties (SpLD) and AD(H)D 'share similar neurobiological underpinnings, particularly those relating to executive dysfunction' (Denckla, 1996, cited in Bramham and Young, p. 9).
- 'Frontal lobe systems involving cognitive processing difficulties are likely to be affected and can result in additional information processing disorders common to both disorders (SpLD and AD(H)D) (Duncan *et al.*, 1994), cited in Bramham and Young, p. 9.

Characteristics of AD(H)D at University

The following subheadings set out the main characteristics of AD(H)D. No two ADDers are the same and some of the indicators may seem contradictory.

Inattention/Distractibility

Hallowell and Ratey (2006, p. 5) propose that an ADDer's problem is not so much one of attention deficit, but attention inconsistency. In fact, ADDers can over-focus. However, most of the time AD(H)D will manifest itself as a deficit. They are likely to lose all track of time and forget they are meant to be somewhere at a particular time, or that they have not eaten for hours. ADDers may well fail to listen to people or lose track in the middle of a conversation. They are distracted both by internal and external stimuli. It is not that ADDers do not attend; they attend to everything (Derrington, 2005). Furthermore, because focusing on a selected task will be hard, they will tend to make so-called 'careless' mistakes: missing words out and misspelling words they know how to spell perfectly well. If reading, they may lose their place and skip a line.

ADDers may have problems with dividing attention and being able to focus on a conversation with a lot of background noise. Doing two things at once to an acceptable standard may also be hard. They can be easily distracted by irrelevant details. Shifting attention may also be difficult. ADDers may get stuck on one task and not be able to change track. Going from listening to a lecture to taking relevant notes can also be difficult for this reason. Ironically, they can also shift from one thing to another all too easily, as well as dart about all over the place like a butterfly.

ADDers may also have difficulty starting an essay. Procrastination is a major threat. They will put off doing a task till the last possible moment. This is partly because they may set themselves too high a standard and lack confidence as a result. They may only be able to finish a task when there is 'pressure under the gun' – a clear motivating factor or deadline. In these cases there tends to be a rush of adrenaline to help them.

Sustaining attention and completing routine tasks such as scheduling is another problem for ADDers. They tend to lose track in long lectures, particularly on subjects that do not interest them. This may make them wish to walk out, fall asleep or daydream.

I was always falling asleep in long boring economics lectures, especially if I had not slept well the night before. It was so embarrassing. Sometimes I used to skip lectures and go play pin-ball.

Gemma

Organization and memory problems

With attention problems come problems of planning, time management and prioritizing – partly because of short-term memory difficulties. ADDers can find it hard to learn from experience or to foresee or plan things ahead.

They forget and lose things and tend to seem rushed and unprepared. They are also liable to be late and miss appointments, which can be very frustrating for all concerned.

> I am sitting at my desk – my project has to be completed next week. I can't do justice to these ideas, and try and find the advice my tutor gave me. This makes me realise that I was supposed to be meeting my tutor this afternoon, and have forgotten. I don't have a proper project-plan and I'm plunging in all over the place. I can't prioritise or see what's important and what isn't. I'm overwhelmed by all I have to do. I can't remember who I've got to meet and when and where. I've read loads of books – probably too many – I don't know when to stop reading and start acting, what to put in and what to leave out. My work seems very repetitive and goes off at tangents. I've scribbled some notes and references somewhere but can't find half of them and I find it difficult to read the ones I can find.
>
> Patrick

Hyperactivity

Many students seem unable to sit still in lectures. In fact, many will not be able to sit through a whole lecture and will have to go out because of their restlessness. Some may drum or tap their fingers, or rock backwards or forwards. They will fidget excessively or play with things, for example, making paper darts (BRAIN.HE, 2008)). The situation will be exacerbated by thoughts whirling around in their heads. All this can be infuriating for people around them. They also tend to be very enthusiastic about things for a while, but soon lose interest.

Impulsiveness

ADDer students are liable to blurt out things in the middle of lectures or seminars, interrupting the proceedings, which can be very wearisome. What they want to say cannot wait. They do not consider the consequences of their actions or whether their remarks are appropriate. This need for immediate gratification can also lead to addiction problems such as substance abuse, overeating and impulse buying.

They can seek out high-stimulation and high-risk situations, as they have a low boredom threshold. They can change plans a great deal, jumping from one job, or one interest, to another. They always want to take short cuts, starting in the middle of something rather than the beginning, as this can be very boring.

ADDers can also be oppositional and frustrated with rules and procedures. They do not like being told what to do, especially if they do not understand the reason. They can jump in before they make a full evaluation of a situation. They can worry about little things and not see the full picture.

Young and Bramham (2007, p. 15) believe that poor impulse control can have serious – even life-threatening – consequences. Coupled with a 'short fuse' and low tolerance and patience, this may lead to aggressive and antisocial behaviour, including traffic accidents, crime and harm to self and others.

Secondary impairments

According to Kessler (2004; cited in Brown, 2005, pp. 201–2), 88% of adults with AD(H)D have at least one additional psychiatric disorder. These include depression; anxiety disorders including Obsessive Compulsive Disorder; substance abuse disorder; oppositional disorders; and general psychiatric disorders.

Positive characteristics

However, the picture is by no means all negative. In many cases, it is very positive. ADDers often have many strengths, such as creativity and originality. Their high levels of energy can be very productive. Their ability to see the 'big picture' can make them good problem-solvers. Their risk-taking tendency can enable them to make discoveries; and their penchant for hyper-focusing may lead them to see things that others do not.

AD(H)D people can be very determined and never give up. Young and Bramham (2007, p. 11) see them as often overcoming a lot of negativity, because of the adaptable nature of the 'syndrome'. Hallowell and Ratey (2006, p. 5) also see them as very resilient and generous. Many also have entrepreneurial tendencies (Kirby, 2007).

Social issues

Most ADDers have experienced a lifetime of adverse interactions and as a result may have not developed good social skills. They find it difficult to listen and may seem rude to both university staff and their peers. They tend to interrupt and lack the ability to take turns. They are unlikely to pick up on the unwritten rules and have a tendency to 'go on and on', unable to leave a subject alone. They are likely to be anxious, depressed and/or have low self-esteem (Quinn, 2001, pp. 16–18; Young and Bramham, 2007, pp. 7–9). Many will find that taking alcohol and recreational drugs reduces stress, often leading to further substance misuse (Kilcarr in Quinn, 2001, p. 40).

Screening

Screening can be a difficult task, as AD(H)D overlaps with many other types of neurodiversity. When it comes without hyperactivity, it is even more difficult to recognize. Many students arrive at university undiagnosed, as hidden disabilities are often missed at school. Many have also been told that the AD(H)D will go away when they become adult.

It is very important that ADDers are identified, as those who are not will tend to be labelled as 'impossible', 'rude', 'stupid', 'lazy, 'crazy' and similar epithets. This is far worse than having a diagnosis of AD(H)D and contributes to their low self-esteem. A diagnosis is often, but not always, the first step to understanding themselves better and the beginning of an improved lifestyle (Young and Bramham, 2007, p. 13).

When screening for AD(H)D, a history must be taken which includes early childhood. AD(H)D is a developmental impairment present from birth; if its indicators only arise later in life, they will be the result of a different condition, for example, depression. Sometimes, people telephone the United Kingdom's DANDA helpline saying they must have AD(H)D because they cannot concentrate – but that the problem has only occurred recently. In such cases, their problem will not be AD(H)D, but instead will be traced to something else, such as anxiety disorder or depression.

It can be quite difficult to take a history, as one has to rely on the student's memory (and maybe also that of their parents). A good start is going through the DSM-IV Manual. An assessor needs to ascertain the frequent presence of six out of nine 'inattentive' indicators and the same number of 'hyperactive' indicators. If both of these occur, then the combined type of AD(H)D is present.

There are two sets of Adult AD(H)D Scales: the Conners Rating Scales (CAARS; Conners, 2000) and the Brown Attention Deficit Disorder Scales (BADDS; Brown, 1996). The former relies on self-report and an observer's report and has a short version, making it very suitable for screening by disability staff. Brown's scales are thorough in respect of the executive functions, but less so in respect of impulsivity (Young and Bramham, 2007, pp. 39–40). In addition, there are numerous other screening tests available in many books (see reference and resource list at the end of the chapter).

If the screening tests or checklists prove positive, the next step might be to go to a psychologist who knows about AD(H)D for a cognitive assessment. They will administer tests such as the WAIS (see Chapter 3).

Students who wish to take medication will need to see a psychiatrist. It is difficult to obtain a diagnosis on the National Health Service (NHS) in the United Kingdom, so students may have to use a private consultant. The student should start by going to the university GP or mental health team, for referral to the local psychiatric services. Many local psychiatric services in the United Kingdom tend to be ignorant about AD(H)D in adults. They tend to believe that everybody grows out of the impairment, and have no training in it in respect of adults. They may tell the student that he/she has depression or anxiety alone. Of course, many people with AD(H)D do have these conditions to some extent, but it is a secondary problem. Calls to the DANDA helpline (2005–2007) bear this out.

University disability/dyslexia departments will need to support these students. In the best cases, funding can be found so that the ADDer can go to a private psychiatrist who specializes in AD(H)D in adults – or at least knows about it.

Issues in Higher Education

Course and university selection

AD(H)D does not render a student incapable of studying for a degree. This section will be presented as a series of questions a student with AD(H)D (or one who suspects he/she may be an ADDer) might need to ask before going to university.

Many students, of course, do not know that they have AD(H)D – or, if they do know, may not wish to think about it. Nearly all, however, will need a supportive university because of their low self-esteem issues. If they are to achieve high grades, low self-esteem needs to be tackled. Services for AD(H)D tend to be more advanced outside the United Kingdom, especially in the United States judging by the number of books published on the subject (see References).

Questions for a student to ask

1. Does the university have a good disability/dyslexia support department? (It is particularly important to look for a good dyslexia department, as that is where

AD(H)D should be dealt with. In any case, it is rare for an ADDer not to be dyslexic and/or dyspraxic as well; see Chapter 3.)

2.   Does the university disability/dyslexia department have any specialists in AD(H)D? Do they have any experience in teaching/supporting ADDers? Would they help with getting a diagnosis of AD(H)D if relevant? (Specialists may not be common in the United Kingdom, but in the United States it is becoming increasingly common (Quinn, 2001).)

3.   Is the university counselling service aware of AD(H)D? Does it offer Cognitive Behavioural Therapy (CBT)? (There is more on this later in the chapter.) Are there any social skills groups?

> I couldn't get a handle on my studies until my counsellor sat down with me and explained thoroughly ... what areas are affected by ADD.
> A junior history major (in McDonald Richard, 1995, p. 299)

4.   Does the university have mentors/buddies or AD(H)D coaches (see section on coaches) who could offer support with everyday living tasks such as time management and finding the way round? Would the university arrange for these services be to be paid for (in the United Kingdom) by the Disabled Students' Allowance (DSA)?

5.   Would students be able to have a very good look round, individually, before applying? (An opportunity to talk to students and teaching staff before applying to the university may be essential, as general open days may not be enough.)

6.   Are there support groups for people with learning differences at the university?

7.   Is there any help with choosing the right course for an ADDer? (Many will need to choose a course that really motivates them and where their creativity and entrepreneurial skills can be harnessed. It may also be advisable to choose a course where the workload is relatively low and with flexibility as regards needing extra time to complete it.)

> I chose to do a course where there were only a small number of main books to read. Fortunately, it was a course that interested me a lot as well. If this course had not been available to me, I would have ended up on a course where the pages of booklists would have totally overwhelmed me!
> Elizabeth

8.   What sort of general accommodations are made for people with AD(H)D? For example, do they take account of the fact that ADDers find it very difficult to work with distractions? If there is building work going on, how would ADDers be helped to cope? Would they be able to take exams in a quiet room?

9. What is the living accommodation like? Would a student be able to have a quiet room? Do students have to cater for themselves and clean their own rooms? Would it be better to live with parents if there is little help with independent living?
10. What is the library like? Are there carrels where quiet work can be done?

Transition

The change from home to university will probably be particularly overwhelming for ADDers. Apart from the rise in the number of temptations they are exposed to, such as alcohol and drugs, they will have to manage tasks of routine everyday living for themselves, and also have to regulate themselves, probably for the first time. At the best of times, ADDers can find it difficult to 'get it together'. Parents and schools will need to help prepare and encourage students in the year leading up to university (Hallowell and Ratey, 2006, pp. 199–205).

Brown (2005, p. 135) says that the separation from day-to-day contact with parents is hugely challenging for AD(H)D students. Suddenly the 'scaffolding' the student has had from parents and schools is removed. They are entering an unknown zone with nobody to encourage them in all that they do. They no longer have parents to tell them to get up, go to bed or take their medication, and nobody to help them organize their work. In short, they have nobody to help them with self-management. They also have the predilection to make impulsive purchases and there is nobody to hold them back. The extra exposure to drugs and alcohol can present demands on people who have a tendency towards substance abuse. Often they cannot get their medication sorted. They need a friendly, knowledgeable doctor to help sort this out. There may not be one available. They are very likely not to get enough sleep, which will exacerbate all their problems.

Here one ADDer describes his initial experiences at college:

When I actually got to campus it felt good; nobody really cared when I went to bed or when I got up or whether I ever went to class. Most nights I went out for beers with some guys from my dorm and smoked some weed on our way back. Back in my room I would stay on the internet as late as I wanted. … After a while I just gave up on going to classes. I was hopelessly behind. That's how I failed all my classes. I got kicked out at the end of the year.

(Brown, 2005, p. 136)

There are very few studies about the adjustment of AD(H)D students to university. One study (Shaw-Zirt *et al.*, 2005) showed that ADDer students found it much more difficult than their non-ADDer peers, particularly emotionally and academically. They did less well academically despite having equal IQs to the control group. They reported lower levels of self-esteem, but evidence of poorer social skills were less conclusive.

Learning and teaching

1) General Accommodations
The following points offer fundamental advice on making HE courses accessible to ADDers:

- Consider making videos available. Many will find a video easier to absorb than a book and can be repeated when necessary.
- Multi-sensory teaching is essential.
- The provision of session templates is also essential.
- Proof-reading services will also probably be important for some (Hallowell and Ratey, 2006, p. 37). Advise students against trying to spend too much time on what they are bad at.
- Students will need more feedback than average because of problems with memory and self-esteem.
- It is very important that they are given, as far as possible, a distraction-free environment to work in.
- Extra time for exams and coursework is needed.
- Notes should be provided by lecturers before lectures; if not, scribes should be available or notes should be on the Internet or virtual learning environment.
- ADDers should be able to sit in the front where they can concentrate more easily. (Not all ADDers like this; some like to be near a door so that they can go out for a while if they are getting restless.)
- 'Over-teaching' and repetition are also very important; the student might have been daydreaming the first time round!
- The use of headphones and white noise can be helpful to ADDers to cut out background noise.
- Good directions around the library and the campus are necessary.
- Teaching and other material should be available in a wide variety of formats. Fonts should be relatively large. Texts should be broken up into bullet points, headings, tables and diagrams.
- Courses should be designed as flexibly as possible, as ADDers will vary.
- Work will have to be explained more thoroughly to ADDers, ideally on an individual basis. They will also probably be worse at prioritizing than other students; book lists, for example, will need to be explained to them in more detail, as ADDers may find them overwhelming. They will not know where to start – and so quite possibly will not start at all!

Many of the accommodations that need to be made for ADDers will also be appropriate for dyslexic or dyspraxic students: for example multi-sensory teaching, extra study skills, colour-coding, mind-mapping, time-management, memory improvement work and proof-reading, as well as technological support. However, AD(H)D students will tend to be even more disorganized than the average dyslexic student. The use of reminder-alarms may be required much more often as a result. However, ADDers can still struggle with this.

> I use my alarm system on my mobile. The alarm goes off but I'm in the middle of something else so I switch it off. I think I'll do it half an hour later, but by that time I've forgotten all about it, so the system is useless to me.
>
> Shayan

Constant praise and empathy are very important (Cooper and Bilton, 2002, p. 71), because most ADDers have very low self-esteem and have suffered constant criticisms. Maintaining empathy can be very difficult – for example, when the student has forgotten all his notes for a seminar for the umpteenth time. In such cases, it is better to make a neutral remark rather than a disparaging or hostile one. It is also very important to remember to praise ADDers whenever appropriate when marking their work.

In the same way, if the student is being disruptive and keeps interrupting in a seminar, it is better to stay as neutral as possible. Getting angry or sarcastic will only inflame the situation. Often a student will seem rude when in fact they do not mean to be at all.

> I was in a seminar and found the discussion rather boring and not particularly relevant to me. I began to obsess about something somebody said in the last seminar which had annoyed me. I suddenly blurted it out although it was not at all relevant. It seemed like the best thing to do at the time but, my god, it wasn't! Firstly, I found I had completely misunderstood what this person had said; and secondly, I discovered that I more or less agreed with her anyway. I felt such a fool. The facilitator fortunately understood, and told me politely, but firmly to bring such things up at the end of the seminar. I calmed down. If the facilitator had reprimanded me or been angry with me, I would not have done so and may well have continued to interrupt. Fortunately, he understood that I had AD(H)D and dealt with the situation brilliantly.
>
> Elizabeth

2) Learning support staff

First and foremost, it is really important that dyslexia and disability staff should read up and try to understand about AD(H)D. Among other things, they will sometimes need to advocate on behalf of students with academic tutors or lecturers. It is also essential that the rest of the staff are educated, because some will dismiss AD(H)D as just laziness or lack of motivation.

> I found the disability co-ordinator and staff really good, but the lecturers were really ignorant.
>
> Miranda

Many students will not have been diagnosed with AD(H)D before coming to university; others will not have declared it on the application form. Many do not wish to be seen as different from their peers and hope the impairment will somehow 'disappear' as they approach adulthood. For this reason, staff need to be able to support students to get a diagnosis (which is not easy on the NHS in the United Kingdom) and they need to be alert for the signs, so that students can access the support they need.

Often ADDers will start falling severely behind in their deadlines – or fail to complete any work at all. They may produce muddled, untidy work that is well below standard. They may spend their time partying, socializing or taking recreational drugs. They may not turn up for lectures – and when they do attend, they are likely to be disruptive or even fall asleep! It is very important that academic staff look out for signs like this and have good liaison with learning support staff.

> I was so relieved when one of my tutors suggested that I might have AD(H)D and it needed to be investigated. In fact, I had been diagnosed as a child with AD(H)D but was embarrassed to put this on my UCAS form. Anyway, I thought I'd overcome the problems, as I had little trouble with my BTecs. The university arranged for me to be tested and as a result I've got my DSA and all the help I need.
>
> Tim

Educational and support staff will also need to look out for students who are not coping with general day-to-day living, such as hygiene, laundry and organizing their workspace and rooms. Many will need help with debt and money problems, as well as help to live more independently.

There are many ways that students can help themselves, or be advised to help themselves. Learning support staff can advise them of the benefits of good nutrition, regular meals and taking omega 3 fatty acids. Regular exercise and relaxation are also very important for ADDers, as for all types of neurodiversity.

Support staff can also advise students about the availability of interventions for ADDers. Firstly, there is medication which can help ADDers focus better on their studies; this is the only type of neurodiversity for which medication is available. There are two other major interventions or programmes which can be of great use to ADDers: CBT, especially the programme that has been adapted for ADDers; and AD(H)D coaching (see below).

3) Course delivery: teaching styles
Students with AD(H)D tend to favour an active, concrete learning experience (Cooper and Bilton, 2002, p. 68). There are various key points to remember regarding teaching:

- ADDers like to think in the present and are less concerned with theoretical teaching.
- Many like to learn from experience, observation, role play and presentations.
- Student-centred and interactive learning such as Problem Based Learning (Murray and Savin-Baden, 1999) can be beneficial to ADDers, who often do not like authority. It can foster better understanding and retention of facts, and can motivate them.
- It is also important to remember that ADDers can be very stimulating to teach; they can be original and enthusiastic, and can offer stimulating, 'outside the box' thinking.

Not all AD(H)D students will like the above ways of teaching; sometimes their difficulty working with others will get in the way. If a group project is involved, the course tutor should facilitate the group to accept diversity in their peers and seek ways for all to contribute. Group composition can be changed as a last resort.

4) Exams and course assessment
Some key points for assessment are:

- Flexibility is really important: some ADDers prefer exams to continuous assessment, and vice versa.
- Exams may nevertheless be preferable to many ADDers. In coursework, they are more likely to fail to prioritize and include too much irrelevant detailed material;

> I always did much better in exams than in coursework. because of my inability to prioritise, much to the surprise of my teachers.
>
> Katherine

in exams, this is not possible because there is not time to get a great deal written down.

- Others will find continuous assessment better, as exams put too much pressure on memory.

Institutional Policy

General principles

A strategic policy on disability and equality should be in place, with the provision for constant revision and enforcement. There should be a policy regarding neurodiversity in general, with a section on AD(H)D specifically.

Staff development

All staff need training in AD(H)D, especially as many will regard it as another name for bad behaviour – probably to a greater extent than other types of neurodiversity. Many may question whether the 'disorder' exists, as many students are disorganized and impulsive at times. It is also an impairment that more and more students will have been diagnosed with, as rates of diagnosis have increased dramatically over the last 10 years or so (Timimi, 2003). Staff and support workers at every level will need training, including administrative staff, librarians, careers staff, mentors and counsellors. The general student population could also benefit from awareness-raising.

Work placements and careers

Careers staff need to be educated about AD(H)D and how it can affect people in the workplace. Many ADDers end up being self-employed, as they like to work in their own way, and without a boss. This is one of the reasons that they are over-represented in the creative arts and entrepreneurship. Research from the University of Southern California is reported to show that there is a genetic link between entrepreneurship and AD(H)D (Kirby, 2007).

There is less support in the workplace than at university and less money to help. (Work experience is often the place where ADDers have most trouble at university – yet in the United Kingdom, *Access to Work* cannot be used on work placements.)

> I am a student social worker and was given a work placement where they didn't understand my AD(H)D at all or make any accommodations for my enthusiasm and energy. As a result, I failed my placement.
>
> William

It is typical for ADDers to have a series of jobs. They are more likely to face problems in the workplace than their peers (Key4Learning, 2008). Many will find it hard to get on with their boss and follow rules and instructions. They may get bored and frustrated easily, and may walk out of their jobs without thinking of the consequences. They will also find it difficult to follow the unwritten rules of the job and so make many faux pas.

> I can't tell you how many bosses I've told off because they ordered me to do my job like I'm supposed to.
>
> Mark (quoted in Murphy and LeVert, 1995, p. 6)

Medication

Many ADDers find medication extremely helpful. It can help greatly to calm them down, and can benefit their performance in various ways. For example, it can help people concentrate, communicate better and maintain focus, enabling some people to gain their qualifications when nothing else would work.

> I could not have got through university without Ritalin.
>
> Simon

The main medications used in the United Kingdom are stimulants such as methylphenidate (MPH) (Ritalin) or dexamphetamine (Dexedrine). There is a greater variety used elsewhere, especially in the United States. MPH, by far the most commonly prescribed, can be prepared either in immediate release form (Ritalin) or slow release form (such as Concerta). Ritalin takes about 20 minutes to work and wears off after about 4 hours. Concerta can last for up to 12 hours.

There are also various nonstimulant drugs that can help, such as atomoxetine (Strattera) and some types of anti-depressants.

MPH works by counteracting the poor uptake of dopamine and norepinephrine in the brain's frontal lobes. It has been argued that dopamine modulates motivation, and that increasing dopamine 'can act almost as a kind of "Viagra" to encourage the brain's response to the task ... MPH may counter the chronic problem with motivating oneself to do the necessary, but not intrinsically interesting tasks' (Brown, 2005, p. 252).

There are also individual differences in benefits derived from these drugs, and certainly not everybody will benefit. Up to 70–80% of children seem to have a positive response to stimulants (Barkley, 2006, p. 36). However, although the bulk of research has been done on children, Faraone (cited in Brown, 2005, p. 251) found that MPH was just as effective for adults as for children and adolescents.

In spite of the possible positive effects, there are various reasons why some people may not wish to use medication. For some, it will work quite well, but the side effects may prove too much. Commonly reported side effects include nausea, headaches, insomnia, weight loss and anxiety. More serious problems include psychosis and tics. Others avoid medication because they feel it might be addictive. It goes against their desire to be independent. People may also feel they will not be as creative and spontaneous as before, or that medication will cause personality change.

I'm not as spontaneous, funny or as interesting as before. My friends tell me I've become too quiet.

(Applin, 2002, quoted in Quinn, 2001, p. 37)

A lot of fine-tuning of medication is often needed. Some people find Dexedrine works better than Ritalin for them, and dosages for either drug will vary from person to person. Therefore, all medication needs to be carefully monitored by a consultant who knows about AD(H)D. Such people can be very difficult to find in the United Kingdom, even on a private basis.

I found dexamphetamine much better than Ritalin. I took three pills a day – most days. However, after a time the effect wore off and stopped making much difference. Furthermore, my consultant stated that because of my high blood pressure, I should only take the pills when I needed to, i.e. in particularly stressful situations.

Elizabeth

Remembering to take the medication and renewing prescriptions can be a problem. Reminders can be programmed into mobile phones, watches or electronic organizers, or pills can be taken at mealtimes or after a certain cue. Using the slow release variety is another way of dealing with the problem, as it only has to be taken once a day. Mentors/coaches can also help.

Finally, notwithstanding its possible benefits, medication should not be viewed as a magical pill, and other strategies should be used in conjunction with pharmacological intervention.

CBT

The programme 'AD(H)D in Adults: A Psychological Guide to Practice' has been developed by two experienced practitioners in the field, Susan Young and Jessica Bramham (2007). It can be used by other psychologists, mentors, counsellors or disability staff to help adults with AD(H)D to tackle their difficulties, by taking advantage of their resilience and determination. As a last resort, it can also be used as a self-help guide. Dr Sam Goldstein of the University of Utah sees this programme as a 'ground-breaking first step in the standardization of the psychosocial treatment of adults with AD(H)D' (Young and Bramham, 2007, p. xiv). The programme has influenced therapists in the United States and elsewhere (Safren *et al.*, 2005).

Young and Bramham (2007) advocate a combination of CBT and interpersonal techniques, to provide a 'scaffolding' for building skills that were not previously present. Their programme includes social skills training; time management and prioritization; anger and anxiety management; combating negative thinking; problem solving; and relaxation therapy. The programme comes with a companion web site with downloadable materials for clients and therapists.

For example, to tackle impulsivity, they introduce methods of self-monitoring to help adult ADDers learn to identify situations in which they are vulnerable to reacting impulsively, and then to find 'appropriate self-restraint strategies' to use in these circumstances. The programme includes 'stop and think' techniques to maximize self-control, and role-plays to help consider the consequences of impulsive behaviour. Reward systems are used widely to increase motivation.

> My mentor is using this programme with me, and it's beginning to change my life.
>
> William

Coaching

'Life coaching' is increasingly being used to improve skills in the workplace and in relationships (Sutton, 2007). AD(H)D coaching was first introduced in the USA and is now becoming more common in the United Kingdom, including at universities. Much coaching is done by phone and/or email, so geography need not be a problem (Quily, 2008). Phone calls and emails take place at regularly agreed times – at least once a week. It might only be necessary to meet face-to-face at the beginning of the relationship.

A coach acts as a partner (not a parent or counsellor) to provide the structure and support that the college ADDer really needs. This is especially useful if he/she has arrived at university straight from home. Coaches can help students develop daily routines and habits to help them cope with university life – and, in particular, their academic work. Coaches try to encourage ADDers to think and make decisions for themselves.

Coaches and ADDers can work together to identify goals and how to achieve them. Once main goals have been agreed, they can work out the objectives and small achievable steps to reach them. The smaller steps make things seem achievable, as ADDers can all too easily become overwhelmed. Coaches will also help keep ADDers on track by constant monitoring. For example, ADDers may be accountable to coaches for what they have done and not done. Coaches will encourage rather than 'nag'.

Coaches may start by trying to introduce systems into students' daily living pattern, to get them to follow regular routines, systems and rituals. For example, they may try to ensure that a student wakes up and eats at regular times, and takes time to wind down before going to bed. They may develop regular routines for de-cluttering, or systems for handling everyday activities such as financial affairs. Meeting daily routines and developing habits such as these can give students a sense of accomplishment, and thus increase their self-esteem and self-belief.

> I have a love-hate relationship with routines and systems. I know I need them, but find them incredibly boring. But I also know that if I persevere with the systems, I definitely achieve more, rather than living in a state of total confusion. Regular monitoring and encouragement from the coach helps me carry these tasks and routines out which can be such an effort. And it is an effort for an ADDer, who wants immediate gratification and would much rather sit down and eat some chocolate while watching some inane TV programme.
>
> Katherine

Another part of coaching is encouraging clients to take time to think of outcomes. This can help tackle the impulsiveness that is so common among ADDers. Coaches ask questions to make students think ahead about the likely consequences of their proposed actions. A student may feel angry with somebody important to them, and want to scream at them. The coach can help by reminding the student of the consequences, and how it could make everything worse. The coach may also encourage them to think about the last time they screamed at somebody.

Most ADDers have spent their lives being criticized, blamed and misunderstood, and hence generally underachieving. Coaches can champion and listen to students with empathy when things get tough. This support can help a student feel more powerful and less like a victim. Coaches can also help with social skills and use role-play to help with difficult situations. The coach will usually try to help students find their own solutions. Lastly, coaches will help students identify the right coping strategies for them – many of which have been outlined above.

All the interventions above can be used together or alone to help a student achieve their true potential academically and combat a student's underlying sense of underachievement.

Conclusion

AD(H)D often overlaps with other conditions and types of neurodiversity. It has numerous effects on university students, not only academic but also emotional and social. With greater staff awareness, it can be screened for in students. There are a great many undiagnosed ADDers at university who are not reaching their full potential – particularly among those diagnosed as dyslexic – and university staff need to be aware of this.

There are many ways to help AD(H)D students: ways in which university authorities and staff can accommodate, teach and support them and enable them to achieve. Psychological interventions including coaching and CBT, and medical interventions, can be very helpful; however, as with all types of neurodiversity, the most effective way forward is for the HE environment to be as accessible and inclusive to all as possible.

Acknowledgement

Thanks are due to Diana Bartlett for her advice on this chapter, and support with the mechanics of writing it.

References

Adams, J.W. and Snowling, M.J. (2001) Executive function and reading impairments in children reported by their teachers as 'hyperactive'. *British Journal of Developmental Psychology*, **19** (2), 293–306.

American Psychiatric Association (1994) *DSM-IV Diagnostic and Statistical Manual of Mental Disorders 4th revised ed.*, A.P.A., Washington.

Applin, T. (2002) How ADD affects you as a high school student, in *ADD and the College Student: A Guide for High School and College Students with Attention Deficit Disorder* (ed. P.O. Quinn), Magination Press, Washington, DC.

Barkley, R.A. (1997) Behavioral inhibition, sustained attention, and the executive functions: constructing a unifying theory of ADHD, *Psychological Bulletin*, **12** (1), 65–94.

Barkley, R.A. (2006) *Attention-Deficit Hyperactive Disorder. A Handbook for Diagnosis and Treatment*, 3rd edn, Guildford Press, New York.

Barkley, R.A. and Murphy, K.R. (1998) *Attention Deficit Hyperactivity Disorder. A Clinical Workbook*, 2nd edn, Guildford Press, New York.

BRAIN.HE (2008) *Best Resources for Achievement and Intervention re Neurodiversity in Higher Education*, www.brainhe.com (accessed 20 March 2008).

Brown, T.E. (1996) *Brown Attention Deficit Disorder Scales*, Harcourt Brace, San Antonio, TX.

Brown, T.E. (2005) *Attention Deficit Disorder. The Unfocused Mind in Children and Adults*, Yale University Press, San Antonio, TX.

Conners, C.K. (2000) *Conners' Rating Scales – Revised Technical Manual*, MHS, New York.

Cooper, P. and Bilton, K.M. (2002) *Attention Deficit/Hyperactivity Disorder. A Practical Guide for Teachers*, 2nd edn, David Fulton, London.

Deponio, P. (2005) *Inclusion and Supporting Individual Difference: ADHD and Other Specific Learning Differences*. International Special Education Conference, Glasgow www.isec2005.org.uk (accessed 20 March 2008).

Denckla, M.B. (1996) A Theory and Model of Executive Function. In G.R. Lyon and N.A. Krasnegor (ed.) *Attention, Memory and Executive Function* (pp 263–78), Paul H. Brookes, Baltimore.

Derrington, C. (2005) Learning support for students with AD(H)D, in *Neurodiversity in FE and HE: Positive Initiatives for Specific Learning Differences* (ed. D. Pollak), Conference proceedings, Leicester, De Montfort University. www.brainhe.com (accessed 28 May 2008).

Disability Discrimination Act (DDA) (2005) *Her Majesty's Stationery Office*, London.

Duncan, C.C., Rumsey, J.M., Wilkniss, S.M., Denckla, M.B., Hamburger, S.D. and Odou-Potkin, M. (1994) Developmental Dyslexia and Attention Dysfunction in adults: brain potential indices of information processing. *Psychophysiology* **31** (4), 386–401.

Faraone, S.V., Spencer, T.J., Aleardi, M., Pagano, J. and Biederman, J. (2004) Meta-Analysis of the Efficacy of Methylphenidate for treating Adult Attention Deficit Hyperactivity Disorder. *Journal of Clinical Psychopharmacology* **24** (1), 24–9.

Gillberg, C.A. (2003) Deficits in attention, motor control and perception: a brief review. *Archives of Disease in Childhood* **88** (10), 904–10.

Hallowell, E.M. and Ratey, J. (2006) *Delivered from Distraction. Getting the Most out of Life with Attention Deficit Disorder*, Ballantine Books, New York.

Key4Learning (2008) *Skills, Resources and Information to Promote Understanding of Hidden Disabilities* www.key4learning.com (accessed 20 March 2008).

Kessler, R.C. (2004) *Prevalence of Adult ADHD in the United States. Results from the National Comorbidity Study Replication (NCS-R)*. Paper presented to the 157th American Psychiatric Association Annual General meeting, New York.

Kilcarr, P.J. (2001) The risks of Alcohol and Drugs. In P. Quinn (ed.) *ADD and the College Student. A guide for High School and College Students with Attention Deficit Hyperactivity Disorder*. Magination Press Washington D.C.

Kirby, D. (2007) *The Entrepreneurial Tendencies of Young People with ADHD and Traditional Students: Are Those with ADHD Nascent Entrepreneurs?* 8th International ADDISS Conference on Attention Deficit Hyperactivity Disorder: How Do You Solve a Problem Like ADHD? London, ADDISS.

McDonald Richard, M. (1995) Students with Attention Deficit Disorders in Postsecondary Education. Issues of identification and accommodation. In K. Nadeau (ed.) *A Comprehensive Guide to Attention Deficit Disorder* (pp 284–307), Brunner/Mazel, New York.

Murphy, K.R. and LeVert, S. (1995) *Out of the Fog. Treatment Options and Coping Strategies for Adult Attention Deficit Disorder*, Hyperion, New York.

Murray, I. and Savin-Baden, M. (2000) Staff development In problem-based learnIng. *TeachIng In Higher Education*, **5** (1), 107–27.

Quily, P. (2008) www.addcoach4u.com (accessed 20 March 2008).

Quinn, P.O. (ed.) (2001) *ADD and the College Student* (Revised), Magination Press, Washington, DC.

Safren, S.A., Otto, M.W., Sprich, S., Winett, C.L., Wilens, T.E. and Biederman, J. (2005) Cognitive Behavioural for ADHD in medication-treated adults with continued symptoms. *Behaviour Research and Therapy*, **43**, 831–42.

Shaw-Zirt, B., Popali-Lehane, L., Chaplin, W. and Bergman, A. (2005) Adjustment, social skills and self-esteem in college students with symptoms of ADHD. *Journal of Attention Disorders*, **8** (3), 109–20.

Sutton, A. (2007) *52 Ways to Handle It – A Life Coaching Year*, Neal's Yard Remedies www.nealsyardremedies.co.uk (assessed 19 March 2008).

Timimi, S. (2003) The politics of ADHD. *Health Matters*, **52**, 14–15.

Young, S. and Bramham, J. (2007) *ADHD in Adults. A Psychological Guide to Practice*, Wiley & Sons, Chichester.

Sources of Further Information

Web sites

www.adders.org An organization based in the UK. Includes many very useful articles on all aspects of AD(H)D, e.g. on how to go about getting a diagnosis on the NHS in the UK.

www.addiss.co.uk Attention Deficit Disorder Information Services. One of the UK's leading organizations for AD(H)D.

www.chadd.org Children and Adults with Attention Deficit Disorder. The US leading organization on AD(H)D. Has articles on all aspects of AD(H)D including coaching.

www.additudemag.com Contains the latest information and features on AD(H)D.

www.key4learning A UK-based site for matters relating to neurodiversity, especially in the workplace.

www.drthomasbrown.com The site of Dr Tom Brown, with current opinion and information on AD(H)D.

www.lindafox.typepage The website for UK-based coach Linda Fox.

www.oneaddplace.com Contains a comprehensive ADD screening test for adults written by Dr Daniel Amen.

www.add.org The Attention Deficit Disorder Association: a US-based group for adults with AD(H)D.

www.addplanner.com A software planner specially devised for adult ADDers. For example, it tells you exactly what time to leave the house for an appointment and also gives you warnings beforehand as to how much time you have. Some ADDers could find this a bit 'bossy' and may prefer to use programs like Microsoft Outlook.

Support groups

Developmental Adult Neurodiversity Association (DANDA). Runs groups for adults with dyspraxia, ADHD, dyslexia and Asperger's Syndrome, mainly in London but can sometimes put people in touch with groups elsewhere www.danda.org.uk, Tel +44 (0)20 7435 7891.

ADHD Group Harrow (UK) Middlesex (near London), Tel +44 (0)20 8426 1719.

Adult Attention Deficit Disorder UK. A new organization which has groups for adults in London and Bristol. Tel 01934 863556 (Bristol group). www.aadd.org.uk

Books

Kelly, K. and Ramundo, P. (1996) *You Mean I'm Not Lazy, Stupid or Crazy?* Simon & Schuster, New York.

Mooney, J. and Cole, D. (2000) *Learning Outside the Lines*, Simon & Schuster, New York.

Nadeau, K.G. (2006) *Survival Guide for College Students with ADHD or LD*, Magination Press, Washington, DC.

Chapter 9

Mental Well-Being

Kitty McCrea

Introduction

In recent years increasing importance has been given to the issue of student mental health. Traditionally, universities paid little heed to this area, beyond the provision of a counselling service (Tinklin, Riddell and Wilson, 2005). The first part of this introduction traces the developments and changes which have led to the increasingly high-profile and dynamic development of student mental well-being in British higher education institutions (HEIs).

The UK Heads of University Counselling Services (HUCS) (Rana, Smith and Walking, 1999) reported an increase in the number and severity of students with serious mental health problems being seen in their services, based on anecdotal evidence from the counselling services themselves. At the same time, only a tiny proportion of students applying for higher education (HE) indicated on their application forms that they had a mental health disability. Since 1999 changes in legislation, society, government policy and HE itself have raised the profile of student mental health issues. The number of students in UK HE identifying themselves as having a disability based on their mental health increased 326% between 1994 and 2001 (a similar figure to the increase in dyslexic students), but this still amounted to only 1290: just 4% of the total number of students declaring a disability. Between 2001 and 2005/2006, there was a further 45% increase (HESA, 2007). However, these figures will represent the tip of an iceberg as they only include students willing to disclose a mental health difficulty on entry to HE and many more cases are likely to go undisclosed or to emerge at a later date (Tinklin, Riddell and Wilson, 2005). Unfortunately, despite the changes mentioned above, many students are still concerned that declaring a mental health problem will adversely affect their academic career and life chances.

The HUCS Report was followed by guidelines published by the Council of Vice-Chancellors and Principals (CVCP, 2000), which for the first time advised HEIs of the need to be proactive in the area of student mental health. However, the guidance was set within a legal framework and a 'duty of care' which emphasized the legal responsibilities of institutions rather than the rights of students (Stanley and Manthorpe, 2002). The Royal College of Psychiatrists (2003) also reported on the increase in mental health problems in the student population and recommended that institutions increase the funding to their counselling services. The CVCP's report led to the first appointments of mental health advisors in UK universities. These early appointments tended to be Registered Mental Health Nurses mirroring existing National Health Service (NHS) provision, although their roles included Mental Health Promotion, policy development and crisis intervention and management as well as one-to-one support for students with mental health needs. These posts were generally placed within disability teams and less frequently as part of the counselling team. While it was HUCS which identified the problem of students with serious mental health problems, the fact that these mental health posts were generally seen as part of the disability team caused some tensions as HEIs began to come to terms with a much higher profile for students with mental health needs. Mental health advisors have a very different role from that of counsellors: more proactive in terms of advising and guiding students and liaising with a wide range of services both within institutions and externally. They began to fill a gap that traditional counselling services either could not or would not fill.

By 2008, the vast majority of UK HEIs had a mental health advisor (or similar role), but increasingly, the emphasis of the role has begun to change from a medical model of providing support for students with serious mental health problems to a social model, where the mental health needs of all students (not just those with serious problems) are seen as an important part of the institution's mission and where it is necessary 'to examine how the environment is creating or exacerbating difficulties, as well as looking at ways to support people to deal effectively with the environment within which they are operating' (Tinklin, Riddell and Wilson, 2005, p. 498). It has, however, been argued that a more adequate social theory of disability would recognize that everyone may be impaired (Shakespeare and Watson, 2002). This is a convincing argument in the field of mental well-being, where in the general population one in four people will experience some kind of mental health problem in the course of a year (Mental Health Foundation, 2006), with mixed anxiety and depression the most common mental disorder in Britain. The government has recently responded to this need by providing £170 million of funding for the Improved Access to Psychological Therapy Project as recommended in the Layard Report (2004). In some universities, the tensions between a traditional counselling service and a separate Mental Health Support Service located within a disability team is being resolved by the provision of a more integrated approach, where a single department provides a range of support services including counselling, mentoring, support workers and mental health practitioners. This approach is likely to best meet the needs of all students, including those who have learning differences such as dyslexia and dyspraxia.

What Is Mental Well-Being?

One definition suggests that it is 'a state of well-being in which the individual realizes his or her own abilities, can cope with the normal stresses of life, can work productively and fruitfully, and is able to make a contribution to his or her community' (World Health Organization, 2007). More specifically, mental well-being is:

- feeling in control;
- being able to make rational decisions;
- being in touch with one's feelings;
- being able to form positive relationships;
- feeling good about oneself; and
- knowing how to look after oneself.

(Oxford Student Mental Health Network, 2007).

Mental well-being has been described as a continuum, with good mental health at one end and poor mental health at the other end (Leach and Birnie, 2006). Most of us will find ourselves at different points on this continuum at times in our lives. It is therefore not particularly helpful to think of individuals with mental health problems as a separate group. While it can sometimes be helpful to have an understanding of the main diagnostic categories such as anxiety and depression, the most important task from the point of view of an academic member of staff is to understand the barriers that can prevent students from reaching their full potential in HE.

There is some evidence to suggest that students have poorer mental health than the non-student population (Fox, Caraher and Baker, 2001). Studies include Webb *et al.* (1996), who found that 12.1% of male students and 14.8% of female students had measureable levels of depression. Surveys at the University of Leicester (2002) showed that 10.5% of first years and 1% of second years had significant levels of distress. However, the Royal College of Psychiatrists Report (2003) found no evidence that students are more likely to suffer from a diagnosable mental disorder. They do identify, however, that stressful events associated with student life such as the transition from home to university, the demands of independent study, financial pressures and study and assessment demands may contribute to the higher rate of emotional symptoms evidenced in a number of reports and studies. A scoping review (Connell *et al.*, 2006) found that much of the available research regarding the severity of mental health problems within the university population is of variable quality and general applicability. A number of studies have looked at the impact of factors such as the transition from home to university, the demands of independent study, and financial pressures on student mental health and well-being, including the impact on student mental health at different points in the academic year. With data collected from a cohort of students on four occasions (during the August prior to their starting at university, week 4 in semester 1, the end of semester 1 and the end of semester 2), Cooke *et al.* (2006) demonstrated that greater strain is placed on well-being once students start university compared with pre-entry levels. This strain rises and falls across the year but does not return to pre-university levels. The findings suggest that attendance at university can be an anxious time for many students, especially at the beginning of the year. The study also identified a vulnerable group of students for whom elevated anxiety may be a precursor of subsequent depression.

Within the same project, an analysis of the relationship between attitudes towards debt and mental health among university undergraduates indicated, not surprisingly perhaps, that students with significant financial concerns felt more 'tense, anxious or nervous', more 'criticized by other people' and found it more 'difficult getting to sleep or staying asleep' than students with low financial concerns (Cooke *et al.*, 2004). Other studies have tended to support this (Jessop, Herberts and Soloman, 2005), although there is also some evidence to suggest that while financial and other difficulties can increase students' levels of anxiety and depression (and affect academic performance), university life may also have a beneficial effect for some students with pre-existing conditions (Andrews and Wilding, 2004).

For some students, their experience of living with neurodiversity such as dyslexia and dyspraxia will affect their self-esteem and this will impact negatively on their mental well-being. Low self-esteem is a vulnerability factor for a range of difficulties including depression, anxiety, relationship difficulties, lack of assertiveness, underachievement, eating disorders and substance abuse (Fennell, 1999). Students with ADHD or Asperger's Syndrome will often experience difficulties with social isolation and problems with forming relationships, which can make the transition to university particularly challenging.

Undoubtedly, the transition from school to HE is a stressful experience for many students, with large numbers dropping out or performing well below their potential. Research in the United States has suggested a strong correlation between what has become known as emotional intelligence and students' ability to make the transition successfully between school and university and to succeed academically (Vella and Schlatter, 2006). Emotional intelligence is a relatively new area of psychological research and is still developing as a concept. One model has defined emotional intelligence as being concerned with understanding oneself and others (intrapersonal and interpersonal skills) and being able to adapt to and cope with environmental demands and stresses (Bar-On, 1977). What does seem clear is that academic success goes hand in hand with emotional well-being, so there is a case to be made for universities to develop a range of strategies to enhance personal development for first year students in particular to tackle dysfunctional coping strategies and behavioural patterns, of which binge drinking and substance abuse are just two examples. It has been argued that universities have a duty to promote the well-being of students through systematically assisting students with their social and emotional growth and the acquisition of personal and interpersonal skills (Vella and Schlatter, 2006). As with learning and study skills, the skills of emotional intelligence should be seen as an integral part of the university curriculum for all, rather than remedial help for those who are not coping.

Common Mental Health Problems

This section provides a very brief guide to the main types of mental health problems. These are difficulties that can affect many of us at some time in our lives; they do not always require medical or other treatment and often get better by themselves without any particular interventions.

Depression

We all experience days when we feel a bit down; however, if the low mood persists this may be defined as depression (which may be mild, moderate or severe) and can affect about one in six adults at some time in their lives. While most episodes of depression do clear up by themselves, the symptoms can be quite distressing and include constant sadness, feelings of hopelessness, self-criticism and lack of energy and interest in life. Students who are experiencing depression may find it hard to get up for lectures; they are likely to find it hard to concentrate and to complete work on time and may consider giving up or leaving their course. They may avoid seeking help from tutors and lecturers, feel that they are to blame for their problems and therefore be reluctant to seek help. Non-attendance at lectures and classes might be one of the signs you notice that someone may be struggling with depression.

Anxiety

Anxiety often goes hand in hand with depression, but can also be a common problem on its own. It is important to remember that anxiety is a normal part of the human condition and something we all experience from time to time. It only becomes a problem for students when it causes difficulties in their lives, for example, because they have developed avoidance strategies (such as not attending lectures because of the fear of having a panic attack). Within the general umbrella of anxiety there are a number of different recognized problems such as panic attacks, phobias and obsessive–compulsive tendencies. For many students, anxiety levels will naturally be raised by standard academic requirements such as assignments, presentations and examinations. Social anxiety is also very common among students and can make university life very stressful and sometimes lonely for vulnerable individuals. It has been argued that to understand HE student retention, attention needs to be paid to ways in which students can be assisted to integrate into the social world of the university (Wilcox, Winn and Fyvie-Gauld, 2005).

Stress

Stress is a normal part of human functioning and serves useful purposes in enabling individuals to respond effectively in an emergency or when extra effort is required (such as an interview or examination), but too much stress in vulnerable individuals can lead to more serious problems such as anxiety and depression. Many aspects of student life can cause stress including: the transition from home and family to university; the pressures involved in managing a new lifestyle, environment and housing situation; the pressures of coursework and assessment; difficulties making friends; financial hardship and relationship problems. For a review of the available research on stress and student life, see Robotham and Julian (2006). With increasing legal obligations on employers to take responsibility for employees' health and welfare and an increasing awareness within society of the negative effects of stress, this is an area that universities cannot afford to ignore. Again, as with other areas of well-being, the responsibility is shifting from that of simply expecting the individual to seek better ways of managing their stress to the view that it is the institution's responsibility to ensure through good practices that the environment is one that promotes well-being and discourages environmental and other factors which can impact adversely on an individual's ability to cope (Robotham and Julian, 2006).

Other types of mental health problem

More serious and less common mental health difficulties include illnesses such as schizophrenia and bipolar disorder, but students with these conditions are likely to arrive at university with their conditions under control. It is important to remember, however, that students with these conditions are vulnerable to stress, which can cause a relapse or deterioration in their ability to function effectively.

Various types of self-harming behaviour are also common among student populations; in this category would fall excessive use of alcohol or drugs, some eating disorders, self-cutting and suicide attempts. These usually represent maladaptive coping strategies for individuals who are not coping well in other ways with mental health issues. Although there is no evidence to suggest that self-harming and suicidal behaviour are any more prevalent in student populations than in the rest of the community (RCP, 2003), there has understandably been increasing concern over student suicides in recent years, and several reports have recommended good practice for higher institutions in preventing student suicides (UUK, 2002; RCP, 2003; Stanley *et al.*, 2007). Most HEIs will have policies and procedures for staff to follow if they become concerned about student well-being and in crisis situations involving student mental health (CVCP, 2000; Ferguson, 2002).

Issues in Higher Education

The rest of this chapter looks at the learning and teaching environment and what tutors, lecturers and other university staff can do actively to promote well-being among students. In line with the social model of disability, the aim should be to provide an environment which supports the mental health and well-being of all students. Good practices for students with existing mental health difficulties will in themselves be good learning and teaching practices for all students (and especially for those with learning differences) and will go a long way to improving the mental well-being of all students in HE. This section of the chapter also includes case studies illustrating the difficulties that students face and the ways in which these can be addressed by the institution and by individual staff. There is no intention that academic staff and tutors should become counsellors or experts in mental health. It is more important to be aware of the boundaries of your responsibilities and know where to seek advice, or send students for referral. However, what you can do is to understand what the world of lectures, seminars, assessments and examinations looks like from the point of view of a vulnerable and anxious student. In so doing, you will be better placed to ensure that the learning and teaching environment is one that promotes the mental well-being of all students.

Promoting Mental Well-Being

The recent UK Disability Discrimination Act (HMSO, 2005) brought a corporate duty for HEIs actively to promote disability equality through:

- the promotion of equality of opportunity;
- promoting positive attitudes towards disabled people; and
- encouraging participation by disabled people in public life.

HEIs have a responsibility to develop policy, not only for supporting those with mental health difficulties but also for promoting the mental well-being of all students (Crouch and Scarffe, 2006). The aims of mental health promotion at an institutional level should include:

- Providing a supportive environment that promotes a sense of inclusion and provides opportunities for social inclusion and interaction;
- The introduction of structural changes to reduce unnecessary stressors and increase support for both staff and students;

- The provision of clear and widely accessible information about the availability of resources and support;
- Strengthening pastoral care and support services;
- The promotion of healthy lifestyles;
- A pleasant working environment; and
- The review of course and programme design to reduce unnecessary stress.

In terms of mental health promotion for students with mental difficulties, the recommendations of UUK (Crouch and Scarffe, 2006) are that strategies should include:

- Promoting awareness of the requirements of relevant legislation;
- Clear guidance to staff as to how to respond to a declaration of disability/mental health;
- Challenging any discrimination and stigma directed at those experiencing mental health difficulties;
- Making reasonable adjustments to provision to prevent academic disadvantage for students with mental health difficulties consistent with the maintenance of academic standards – preferably through anticipation (see next section below) rather than post-hoc adjustment;
- Developing procedures that allow health-related breaks in study with assessment of readiness to return;
- Offering intermediate qualifications at suitable points of a degree;
- Promoting equality of opportunity for students with mental health difficulties in terms of recruitment and admission;
- Promoting and maintaining effective contact and co-operation between the institution and external helping agencies, including the NHS;
- Providing support for staff dealing with mental health difficulties; and
- Making available informed financial and careers counselling when appropriate.

Guidance on how to set up a health-promoting university project has been published by the World Health Organization (Tsouros *et al.*, 1998). Examples of projects in the United Kingdom can be found at the University of Central Lancashire and Lancaster University.

Learning and Teaching

'Learning and teaching that respects the mental health and well-being of students is good practice for everyone' (Burgess, 2007). This section suggests good practice which will help to reduce anxiety and stress among all students, but with particular benefits for students with mental health vulnerabilities. Little has been published in this area, but there are a number of Higher Education Funding Council for England (HEFCE) funded projects focusing on student mental health (DART, 2005; Leach and Birnie, 2006), including detailed student case studies which cover the transition to HE, learning and teaching experiences and the impact of those on learning and academic progress. Although focused on good practice in specific subject disciplines (Geography and Engineering and the Built Environment), the good practice identified is relevant to all subject areas. The section that follows draws upon these projects and the reader is recommended to consult them for a more detailed exploration of the issues.

Lectures

Many students find the lecture theatre environment daunting: the formality of the setting, the relative remoteness of the lecturer, the need to enter the room in a very public way (especially if a late arrival) and the difficulties involved in slipping out unobtrusively if necessary all contribute to a potentially intimidating environment for vulnerable students. Students with mental health difficulties may have genuine problems with attending early lectures (depression and associated insomnia in particular give rise to this), so it is helpful to remember this when dealing with late arrivals. It may be useful to consider whether the first few minutes of the class time could be used creatively to allow for latecomers.

There may be little that can be done to change the environment (although sometimes it may be possible to request a more suitable room if it is too large for the size of group for example, or not suitable for the type of teaching taking place), but you can make sure that your approach is welcoming and informal rather than intimidating (Leach and Birnie, 2006).

Evidence suggests that attention spans in a lecture environment vary from 5 to 30 minutes (Bligh, 1998) and students with mental health difficulties may find concentrating for any length of time particularly challenging. They may rely on handouts or recordings of lectures to enable them to go over material outside of the lecture. For example, one student 'finds that grasping the points made is now a process that happens after the lecture rather than during the lecture, as was previously the case. During lectures he needs to listen more but given his shorter concentration span, finds it increasingly difficult to remember the salient points to be able to write them down and expand upon them afterwards' (DART, 2005).

Ideas for breaking up lecture delivery to provide changes of activity which allow students opportunities to reflect on and process information include:

- Giving students the opportunity to discuss their objectives for the lecture;
- Providing opportunities for students to relate the lecture material to their own experiences;
- Using incomplete handouts for students to complete;
- Using buzz groups (timed tasks and discussion for small groups, followed by feedback to the whole group);
- Setting small problem-solving activities; and
- Breaking the lecture into sections and running a short quiz to emphasize the main points made (Leach and Birnie, 2006).

Working in groups

Collaborative group work is an important learning and assessment tool in many subject disciplines and can be a major issue for those with a variety of mental health issues. Too often such students can become isolated as groups form, and it is important to use a variety of 'ice-breakers' to help students get to know each other. Teaching staff need to ensure that no one is isolated or disadvantaged, and therefore allowing groups to self-select their members is not always the best policy. A more formal approach may be needed to ensure that everyone is given the opportunity to take part effectively.

Assessed group work can also present difficulties for students who feel that they cope best when they can work on their own at their own pace. One student, for example, 'would rather not do assessed groupwork ... the pressure he feels is even greater when he feels others are relying on him. He fears that any failing on his part will have a knock on impact on others' (DART, 2005). Another student, however, feels differently about group work: 'If anything, it helps him in that others can make up for his failing organizational skills and a shared workload actually relieves the pressure which has such an adverse impact upon him.' In group discussions '(he) is able to contribute when he feels well, but if he is particularly affected by stress and anxiety he will tend to go quiet' (DART, 2005). It would be helpful to allow time for all students to share their fears and worries about group work.

Presentations

Most students with mental health issues will have no difficulty with the research and reading that goes into preparing for presentations and seminar discussion, but the performance anxiety that is present for most people in public speaking can present huge difficulties for them. The high level of interpersonal skills required to manage these situations can be daunting for those who find social situations difficult, or whose confidence and self-esteem are fragile. For one student:

> *Verbal presentation leads to stress and he does not feel comfortable and becomes more introverted. His ... strategy for dealing with this is to trade an increased contribution to the preparation of the presentation for dispensation on standing up and presenting verbally. This is only possible where flexibility in the assessment criteria allows for it. (DART, 2005)*

However, all students will benefit from building up skills through practice in nonassessed or 'safe' situations. It may be possible to build these skills into the curriculum, or students may be encouraged to access study skills support which provides help in these areas. Essentially what students need is an opportunity, through coaching and effective feedback, to build confidence gradually. For those students, however, who really cannot manage the public speaking element of a presentation, it is possible to provide alternatives which still meet the learning and assessment outcomes. Examples include:

* poster presentation or webpage;
* PowerPoint presentation (without the verbal commentary);
* taped or videoed presentation put together in relative privacy; and
* delivery of presentation to tutor only (Leach and Birnie, 2006).

Feedback and assessment

The receiving of constructive feedback is an integral part of academic life, but can be particularly challenging for students with mental health difficulties. Those who are vulnerable include students with low self-esteem and those with perfectionist tendencies, who will tend to feel that it is their worth as an individual that is being judged rather than their work. This fear of being judged may lead to attendance problems, withdrawal, reluctance to talk to tutors and a failure to complete work. Receiving feedback may also be very challenging for neurodiverse students, especially those struggling with low self-esteem as a result of their experiences at school. Older students may find it particularly difficult to accept that mistakes are inevitable when learning something new and may have perfectionist tendencies and a reluctance to admit that they are struggling. However, giving good feedback is a skill that tutors and lecturers can learn and when done well it can increase motivation and self-esteem. When giving feedback it is important to make it clear that the comments are about the work and not the individual. So, for example, instead of saying 'You haven't …' try 'The assignment would benefit from …' Suggestions for changes should always be balanced by positive comments which are both supportive and suggest a way forward (Leach and Birnie, 2006, p. 56).

At the same time as giving well-structured feedback, it would be helpful to take the time to listen to the student so that they have an opportunity to talk through any difficulties they may be experiencing. Being listened to, and understood, will help to reduce anxieties and restore self-esteem. A common problem for all students is the length of time it can take before receiving feedback on work. For students who are vulnerable to mental health problems, having to wait a long time (e.g. over a vacation) for their marks and feedback can feel intolerable and lead to considerably elevated levels of anxiety and even dropout. Some universities operate a semester-based system where the first formal assessment takes place at the end of the first term, but no feedback is available to students on their performance until formal teaching begins again at the beginning of semester two. In these circumstances, anxious students who fear they may have done badly may not return after the Christmas and New Year break.

Examinations and other forms of assessment are naturally anxiety-provoking for all students, but strategies to minimize unnecessary anxiety experienced by students with mental health difficulties will be of benefit to all. Students may have unrealistically high expectations of themselves, so it is important to help them develop a more realistic idea of what is being looked for. Other sources of anxiety include: the examination room itself (a reasonable adjustment for a student with mental health difficulties could be to take the exam in another room); having to recall a great deal of factual information (open-book exams or seen questions may be appropriate alternatives here). There may be changes which will benefit all students; others may be appropriate as reasonable adjustments for students with particular difficulties. Sometimes the process students have to go through to be granted reasonable adjustments in examinations can be extremely stressful. For example, one student pointed out how different members of staff reacted to his being granted extra time and open-book examinations as a reasonable adjustment in assessment, following the assessment of his disability by the University Disability Services team:

At first the changes were resisted, referred to the Professional Body that accredits his course and only later accepted. During this period of uncertainty, Dave did not know whether to prepare for a traditional

2 to 3 hour exam or to start preparing permitted material to take into the exam with him. In consequence, the uncertainty caused him even greater stress and the ultimate adjustments made largely failed to assist him in a meaningful way.   (DART, 2005)

Exams are a major hurdle for many students, and especially for those with mental health difficulties and learning differences, so it is worthwhile considering alternative assessment methods wherever possible.

Summary

In summary, to promote mental well-being, protect those who may be vulnerable to mental distress and provide optimum conditions for learning generally, it will be helpful to:

- Avoid undue stress in the design of the curriculum:
  - Learning opportunities should be balanced through the day and across the week.
  - Assignments should be spaced rather than bunched at the end of semesters.
  - Feedback should be timely, especially in the first term.
- Provide plenty of information in different formats that can be accessed at different times and continually signposted, for example expectations (especially in relation to assessment) and detailed and timely information about different kinds of learning opportunities (such as practical work, fieldwork and external visits). Many students will not have read or understood the information.
- Provide opportunities to rehearse assessed work before it is formally assessed. This is particularly important for presentations and role plays.
- Build small group work into the first term, with experienced seminar leaders who can enable students to develop confidence in speaking and learning together.
- Provide the programme with a human face, especially an effective tutorial system so that students have an early link with someone who knows them, who can help build confidence and provide appropriate support. Tutors should make sure they are well informed about the range of student support services and that the department maintains links with these services and has a commitment to student well-being (Burgess, 2007).

Student Support

The support needs of students with mental health issues will vary enormously and each individual will cope with their situation differently.

Some students will declare their needs before university entry, maybe on their application form, and in this case can be invited to discuss their needs. Often, however, students will not have declared any mental health needs at application or prior to entry, as they may have concerns over the stigma that is still attached in society to mental health. It is important that all course pre-entry literature makes positive statements around the institution's commitment to student mental health and well-being, to encourage declaration. Some students who do declare mental health issues may not need any particular adjustments. For others a detailed assessment of needs should be carried out by staff who are trained to do this. The areas which may need to be discussed with the student include:

- learning support needs;
- examination/assessment arrangements;
- accommodation options;
- financial support (such as eligibility for Disabled Students' Allowance in the United Kingdom); and
- contact with student support services such as counselling, health service and mental health support.

Where students do not declare their needs prior to entry and these subsequently become known (either through a crisis developing or because the student is finding it difficult to cope), or where these develop during a student's university career, academic staff may find themselves offering support directly to students. It can often be hard for teaching staff to decide how much support they can or should be offering a student themselves and when to refer to other services. Action tutors can take includes:

- Being clear about what you can and cannot offer; listen to the students' problems and offer tea/coffee and a chat, but beware of straying into trying to be an amateur therapist;
- Taking action to reduce the barriers to achievement that they may face (see learning and teaching section above);
- Helping the student find other sources of support; be aware of the services available in your institution;
- Being prepared to refer them to health, counselling, mental health or disability support services within the institution for help; and
- Being aware of your institution's policies and procedures with regard to confidentiality and the sharing of information and procedures to follow in the event of a crisis situation (Leach and Birnie, 2006).

Case Studies

The following case studies illustrate how students with very different mental health needs can be supported during their studies. These are fictional examples based on real-life situations.

Case study 1: James

Background

James is 38 years old. He has been unemployed for many years as his illness has made it difficult for him to find work. James did attend university in his early 20s but dropped out and has not studied full time since then. He has a long history of bipolar depression and has been receiving treatment as an outpatient for many years. At the time of applying to study as a nurse, he was receiving support and treatment from his psychiatrist and a community psychiatric nurse. James will be moving from another part of the United Kingdom to attend university. He currently lives in supported rented accommodation, which is a small, self-contained flat. He receives benefits which support him financially. In his community he is well established and has a small group of close friends who give him a lot of support.

Application to university

A chance to visit the university and explore its suitability is essential for James. People who have experienced mental health difficulties for long periods have often lost confidence and find negotiating new and complex places and situations stressful. James may be ready to study but the environment may be much more daunting than he realizes. Other points to consider include:

- An interview, which is essential for someone applying in this situation before being offered a place on a course. There may be issues of suitability for professional practice (in this case nursing).
- Confidentiality: who needs to know this sensitive information? Once the student has declared his disability, the university as a whole is deemed to know under UK law and will be required to make reasonable adjustments. Against this needs to be set the sensitivity of the information and the student's rights under the Data Protection Act (HMSO, 1998).

- The balance between equality of opportunity, risk of dropout, risk to the student's well-being and potential risk of a relapse, the risk to the general public and the reputation of the profession and/or institution needs to be considered against the applicant's abilities and potential to practise within their chosen field.
- A meeting to discuss support needs and whether the institution can meet those needs will be essential for James. In the United Kingdom, assessment for eligibility for the Disabled Students' Allowance (DSA) and any environmental or learning adaptations will be required. The following areas will need to be involved in this process:
  - Accommodation: this is a mature student who is accustomed to having his own home but also supported accommodation. Should he be offered a place in a hall of residence? If so it will be necessary to consider the nature of the hall, the other students and whether the university can offer him an appropriate living environment.
  - Finance: James could experience financial hardship as he will no longer be able to claim some of his benefits, but as he is applying to do nursing he will lose out on some of the funds available to other students. He will also incur extra costs for things such as medication and transport for hospital visits.
  - Social: this student may need more support than other students to integrate into student life. He would benefit from a mentor or buddy, who may be available through the Students' Union or could be paid for through the DSA.
  - Study skills: James has not studied for many years. He may have lost his study skills and certainly will have lost confidence. His ability may also be affected by his medication and the symptoms of his illness. He is unlikely to remain totally symptom-free for long periods even with medication.

On entry to university

- Current support and medical services will need to be involved. It is essential that this student is encouraged to register with a GP. There is a danger that James could slip through the net if the transfer between health and social services in his area and the new area is not done quickly and smoothly.
- The student should be encouraged to make himself and his needs known to academic staff to ensure that extra time and care are given to him during the induction process. He will need more support and reassurance than most students.
- It is crucial that James is made aware of the range of support services and how to access them. It will be especially important for him to have a personal tutor whom he can meet with regularly.
- The Faculty Disability Officer (or equivalent) will need to liaise with appropriate support staff (such as the Mental Health Advisor or Disability Officer) to discuss

any further academic support that may be required, such as copies of lecture notes or extra time for deadlines. Consideration will have to be given to practice placements. James's support needs must be balanced against the need to ensure that he has an appropriately robust and rounded training and education.

Progression

- James will benefit from special exam arrangements for a multitude of reasons.
- The student will also benefit from having a key worker within the university to ensure that he is remaining well, coping with his studies and accessing all the necessary support services. James is at increased risk of dropping out of the course without this support, which could be provided through the DSA or a mentoring scheme.
- Ideally James will also have a key worker from the statutory health or social services sector. There should be careful liaison between all services throughout his academic career.

Achievement

- This student will benefit from specialist input from the careers service, to advise him on issues such as employment discrimination as well as the normal processes of finding suitable employment. Research shows that mental health is one of the last workplace taboos, with fewer than 4 in 10 employers saying that they would consider employing someone with a history of mental health problems (Shaw Trust, 2006).

Case study 2: Rima

Background

Rima is a 21-year-old Humanities student who was helped by the University Counselling Service. A friend recommended counselling, and when a tutor recommended it too, she finally made an appointment. Rima was feeling pretty low when she arrived for her first session. She had been assessed as dyslexic in her first year and her confidence and self-esteem had been badly affected by this. In particular, she talked about feeling very isolated, having withdrawn from her friends of two years, skipping classes, and spending a lot of time on her own, often under the duvet, crying and unmotivated to do anything.

Progress

At her first counselling session she completed an Outcome Measure (Evans *et al.*, 2000), which reflected quite a high level of depression and anxiety. Counselling drew her into a dialogue where she was able to look at her negative evaluation of herself against her own extremely high standards. She was very self-critical and consumed by negative thinking.

As counselling progressed, Rima was able to couple this awareness of herself with a growing appreciation of what she *did* do well, felt good about and enjoyed, and what she was prepared to do differently to increase her sense of well-being. With the encouragement of her counsellor she began to access the appropriate learning support and to re-evaluate her negative appraisal of her dyslexia.

An interim Outcome Measure completed at the third session highlighted progress towards a greater sense of mental well-being. Rima evaluated her marks more positively, became more relaxed and fun-loving with friends, and grew more involved again. The depression lifted.

The final Outcome Measure completed at the sixth and final session showed her how she was able to maintain a happier lifestyle and reach her full potential in her studies.

Case study 3: Laura

Background

Laura is a first year Computer Science student who came for coaching, as she had seen the posters, seen the service advertised on the Counselling Service website and did not know what else to do. Generally, she felt she was coping well but was getting very 'panicky' about delivering a presentation to her peers in the next few weeks. She said she had done a couple of presentations at school and felt they had gone really badly. She was very worried about 'showing herself up' in front of her university peers.

The coach agreed with Laura on what would be the main focus for the work and that they would work together for three sessions. Generally, Laura described herself as fairly confident in most settings but said that she tended to wait for others to start a conversation with her first, rather than making the first move. However, she was clear that her main coaching goal was to improve her presentation skills.

Session 1 focused on the technical aspects of what makes a good presentation. By Session 2, Laura was beginning to feel more confident about the presentation and clearer in her own mind about how she could structure it, how she would make notes and what visual aids she could use. Session 2 focused on identifying Laura's negative thoughts about delivering presentations and helping her to learn techniques to challenge such thoughts, as well as helping her to understand her anxiety response and ways of managing her symptoms.

By Session 3 Laura was feeling more prepared and confident about delivering her presentation and practised delivering a 10-minute presentation in the session which was videotaped by her coach. Although still nervous, Laura was pleased with how she had got on; better than she had thought, with some specific learning points to carry forward. Laura was now prepared to deliver her presentation to her peers in three weeks' time, using presentation skills and anxiety management techniques she learnt in coaching.

(These case studies are based on materials developed at De Montfort University, Leicester for use as part of staff training.)

References

Adrews, B. and Wilding, J.M. (2004) The relation of depression and anxiety to life-stress and achievement in students. *British Journal of Psychology*, **95** (4), 509–21.

Bar-On, R. (1997) *The Emotional Quotient Inventory (EQ-i): A Test of Emotional Intelligence*, Multi-Health Systems, Toronto.

Bligh, A.D. (1998) *What's the Use of Lectures?* Jossey Bass, San Francisco.

Burgess, H. (2007) Promoting mental well-being in the curriculum, in *Developing an Inclusive Curriculum*, Higher Education Academy (unpublished), York.

Committee of Vice-Chancellors and Principals, now Universities UK (CVCP) (2000) *Guidelines on Student Mental Health Policies and Procedures for Higher Education*, CVCP, London.

Connell, J., Chaill, J., Barkham, M., Gilbody, S. and Madill, A. (2006) *A Systematic Scoping Review of the Research on Counselling in Higher and Further Education*, BACP, Rugby.

Cooke, R., Barkham, M., Audin, K. and Bradley, M. (2004) Student debt and its relation to student mental health. *Journal of Further and Higher Education*, **8** (1), 54–66.

Cooke, R., Bewick, B.M., Barkham, M., Bradley, M. and Audin, K. (2006) Measuring, monitoring and managing the psychological well-being of first year university students. *British Journal of Guidance and Counselling*, **34** (4), 505–17.

Crouch, R. and Scarffe, P. (2006) *Guidelines for Mental Health Promotion in Higher Education.* Universities UK/Guild HE Committee for the Promotion of Mental Well-Being in Higher Education, www.uwic.ac.uk/disability/useful_resources.asp (accessed 28 February 2008).

DART (2005) *Disabilities Academic Resource Tool,* http://dart.lboro.ac.uk/tool/ (accessed 28 February 2008).

Evans, C., Mellor-Clark, J., Margison, F, *et al.* (2000) Clinical outcomes in routine evaluation: the CORE-OM. *Journal of Mental Health,* **9**, 247–55.

Fennell, M.J.V. (1999) Low self-esteem, in *Treating Complex Cases: The Cognitive Behavioural Approach* (eds N. Tarrier, A. Wells and G. Haddock), John Wiley & Sons, Ltd, Chichester.

Ferguson, S. (2002) *Student Mental Health Planning, Guidance and Training Manual.* HEFCE funded project at Lancaster University, www.studentmentalhealth.org.uk (accessed 28 February 2008).

Fox, P., Caraher, M. and Baker, H. (2001) Promoting student mental health. *The Mental Health Foundation Update,* **2**, (11).

Higher Education Statistics Agency (HESA) (2007) Disability 2005/6, www.hesa.ac.uk (accessed 28 February 2008).

HMSO (1998) *Data Protection Act,* www.opsi.gov.uk/acts (accessed on 28 February 2008).

HMSO (2005) *Disability Discrimination Act,* www.opsi.gov.uk/acts (accessed 28 February 2008).

Jessop, D.C., Herberts, C. and Soloman, L. (2005) The impact of financial circumstances on student health. *British Journal of Health Psychology,* **10** (3), 411–20.

Layard, R. (2004) *Mental Health: Britain's Biggest Social Problem?* Department of Health, London.

Leach, J. and Birnie, J. (2006) *Developing an Inclusive Curriculum for A) Students with Mental Health Issues B) Students with Asperger Syndrome.* Geography Discipline Network, University of Gloucestershire, www2.glos.ac.uk/gdn/icp (accessed 28 February 2008).

Mental Health Foundation (2006) *Statistics on Mental Health,* www.mentalhealth.org.uk/information/mental-health-overview/statistics (accessed 28 February 2008).

Oxford Student Mental Health Network (2007) *Support for Student with Mental Health Problems,* www.brookes.ac.uk/student/services/osmhn (accessed 28 February 2008).

Rana, R., Smith, E. and Walking, J. (1999) *Degrees of Disturbance: The New Agenda.* A Report from the Heads of University Counselling Services, BACP, Rugby.

Robotham, D. and Julian, C. (2006) Stress and the higher education student: a critical review of the literature. *Journal of Further and Higher Education,* **30** (2), 107–17.

Royal College of Psychiatrists (RCP) (2003) *The Mental Health of Students in Higher Education.* Council Report, www.rcpsych.ac.uk/publications (accessed 28 February 2008).

Shakespeare, T. and Watson, N. (2002) The social model of disability: an outdated ideology? *Research in Social Science and Disability*, **2**, 9–28.

Shaw Trust (2006) *Mental Health – The Last Workplace Taboo*, www.shaw-trust. org.uk/mentalhealth (accessed 23 February 2008).

Stanley, N., Mallon, S., Bell, J., Hilton, S. and Manthorpe, J. (2007) *Responses and Prevention in Student Suicide*, University of Central Lancashire, Preston.

Stanley, N. and Manthorpe, J. (eds) (2002) *Students' Mental Health Needs: Problems and Responses*, Jessica Kingsley, London.

Tinklin, T., Riddell, S. and Wilson, A. (2005) Support for students with mental health difficulties in higher education: the students' perspective. *British Journal of Guidance and Counselling*, **33** (4), 495–512.

Tsouros, A.D., Dowding, G., Thompson, J. and Dooris, M. (eds) (1998) *Health Promoting Universities: Concept, Experience and a Framework for Action*, World Health Organization, Regional Office for Europe, Copenhagen.

Universities UK (2002) *Reducing the Risk of Student Suicide: Issues and Responses for Higher Education Institutions.* UUK, London, www.universitiesuk.ac.uk (accessed 28 February 2008).

University of Leicester (2002) *Student Psychological Health Project: Undergraduate Student Survey Results.* EDSC, www.le.ac.uk/edsc/sphp/ (accessed 22 May 2008).

Vella, P. and Schlatter, N. (2006) Student retention and success – the emotional intelligence factor. *AUCC Journal*, December, 7–9.

Webb, E., Ashton, C.H., Kelly, P. and Kamali, F. (1996) Alcohol and drug use in UK university students. *The Lancet*, **348**, 922–25.

Wilcox, P., Winn, S. and Fyvie-Gauld, M. (2005) 'It was nothing to do with the university, it was just the people': the role of social support in the first-year experience of higher education. *Studies in Higher Education*, **30** (6), 707–22.

World Health Organization (2007) *Mental Health: A State of Well-Being*, www. who.int/features/factfiles/mental_health (accessed 28 February 2008).

Sources of Further Information

www.studentdepression.org/site/ (aimed at students)
www.rcpsych.ac.uk/ (aimed at the general public as well as professionals)
www.studentsinmind.org.uk (aimed at students experiencing mental distress)
www.student.counselling.co.uk/ (aimed at students and staff seeking information on available support and easy links to sources of information)
www.mind.org.uk/ (aimed at the general public)
www.rethink.org (aimed at people with severe mental health difficulties, with specific information for students)

Chapter 10

Assistive Technology

E.A. Draffan

If you are dyslexic and you use a computer to write it is assistive technology but if you are not dyslexic and you use a computer to write with it is not? (Wanderman, 2003)

Introduction

The term 'assistive technology' conjures up different ideas related to the use of devices, computers and services depending on where you work. In the medical world it may be thought of as 'any product or service designed to enable independence for disabled and older people' (FAST, 2001). In higher education we should perhaps be looking at a definition that incorporates the idea that it can be 'any item, piece of equipment, or product system whether acquired commercially off the shelf, modified or customized, that is used to increase, maintain, or improve functional capabilities of individuals with disabilities' (Individuals with Disabilities Education Act (IDEA), 1997).

However, assistive technology is not the only term used for devices and electronic hardware and software that can enable students to access the curriculum more easily. In the United Kingdom, the Royal National Institute for the Blind tends to use the term 'access technologies' and the National Institute of Adult Continuing Education (2004) has used the term 'enabling technology' in its reports. Both terms have been used in the titles of online resources and centres to support students.

Terms such as 'adaptive technologies' may imply that the task of the individual is to adjust to the environment, rather than vice versa. Such language may also indicate that an item has been adapted by a specialist for an individual with a particular need. Yet in today's world, where scientists talk about 'pervasive' or 'ubiquitous' computing and where minute chips are embedded in all manner of devices with ever-increasing connections via invisible networks, it would be more appropriate to reverse this scenario, so that the technology adapts intuitively to the user's preferences without expert help.

The idea of technology being 'assistive' or helpful may not always be the case. This chapter will illustrate this and other issues by quotations from several students. When asked about using her assistive technologies, Stephanie said: 'Before I had my training, I did feel like I was doing two courses and that was, frankly, too much. I had to stay with my old bad habits because I just didn't feel I had the time to take out to learn something new to help me. It was a vicious circle, really.'

One problem with assistive technology is that like many other commonly used technologies, it has tended to become over-complex and 'bloated'. This is a term used by those in the computer world to describe the bulky software programs that have so many features that they may confuse, so that people tend to use only around five or six menu items. Additional features may be used by a few and one can understand how products grow as users ask for more facilities. A simple program to read text from the screen has spell checking added, homophone checking, dictionary, scanning, optical character recognition, font wizards, colour changing, highlighting text and pausing. You can see in an instant how easy it is to make a simple idea into a complex program that requires skills from the user to navigate the various menus and buttons. The default settings often show everything, but with a bit of knowledge, buttons and menus can be hidden and complexity reduced. So in this case the assistive technology is initially difficult, not unlike many of the general programs available on most computers. However, in Stephanie's case, once she had completed her training, her final comment was: 'I think it's great – for me personally. It's enabled me to be more focused. I used to think I was organised. But when I had my first year, with the reading and everything, it just seemed like I was studying 24/7 and didn't have a work/life balance.'

Those who advise, assess and train students in the use of assistive technologies have the enormous burden of considering all aspects of their skills, abilities, preferences within their working environment, before offering a shopping list of handheld devices, software and hardware. Figure 10.1 incorporates ideas from 'Match of Person and Technology' (Scherer, 2004) and 'Human Activity Assistive Technology' (HAAT) (Cook and Hussey, 2002).

This is easier said than done especially when there are so many devices and software programs on offer. It is not possible to know them all, and

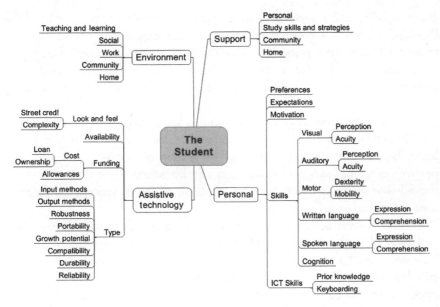

Figure 10.1 Mapping the areas that need to be considered when making assistive technology choices

there is very little time for trials and a full understanding of the context in which they will be used, let alone getting to know the student's preferences and skills in one meeting. It is rare to have the chance to offer more appointments when assessing for the use of these technologies. There is therefore a need to understand the true complexity of some assistive technologies and the fact that the user may be required to have a considerable amount of expertise if they are to take full advantage of the support they may offer.

There is also an issue with the fact that the assistive technology may be considered a very specific type of technology; it may have a 'label' that can be matched to a type of difficulty. But when we are looking at learning differences across a wide spectrum for instance, the computer that is invaluable to many is not considered an assistive technology by the Inland Revenue in the United Kingdom, but the spell checker or word prediction program may be exempt from value added tax (VAT) as they can be seen to help with spelling and vocabulary difficulties. This may be seen as a bonus (for those who are willing to sign a waiver form), but there are some technologies that are incredibly helpful that fall into the general technology domain, where there is no tax relief. They may even be classified as course-specific and therefore rarely come under consideration as part of the Disabled Students' Allowance assessment. An example is EndNote for referencing academic papers. This tool not only puts the names of authors in alphabetical order, which can be difficult for some, but also provides the appropriate layout for the citation and automatically places it at the end of the paper as references are inserted, thus helping organizational skills. In recent years, the boundary between what is specifically designed for those with disabilities and what is helpful for all has less clarity than it had in the past. There is also a need to accept the merging of mobile, online and desktop technologies where documents can be edited while on the move, shared with others online by using such applications as Google Docs, and finally e-mailed to tutors for marking.

In a neurodiverse world, the way all learners can be supported by some of the very latest technologies can be both empowering and enabling. We must not allow the divisions between what is considered assistive and what may be fashionable to blur our vision as to how successful these applications can be in supporting study strategies. Ease of use is as important as accessibility; for example, if you are reading a web page on one of the latest touch screen phones (such as the Apple iPhone) and you find that the text size on the screen when reading a web page is too small – with a flick of the fingers it will enlarge. This ability to effortlessly adapt to the user's preference is a feature that should be seen in all technologies.

We now have a growing trend of moving between various types of technologies to enable learning: taking notes with pen and paper, digital pen or tablet computer, texting on a mobile phone or sending messages using Skype or Microsoft Live Messenger (MSN), researching using journals or online resources. I believe that students need to become agile technology users. In this case I have taken this idea from software engineers and paraphrased a statement by Ambler (2007):

Agile is an iterative and incremental (evolutionary) approach to technology use, which is performed in a collaborative manner by people with 'just enough' ceremony that produces successful outcomes in a cost-effective and timely manner meeting the changing needs of its stakeholders.

Mobile Technologies

(See Resources list at end of chapter for web addresses giving information on all items.)

In the higher education learning environment, when we examine the ways in which students are organizing their world, we must consider assistive technologies in the widest sense of the term, not just those carrying the VAT waiver or devices that lack 'street cred' so they are never used. Popular mobile technologies that are rarely lost include mobile phones such as those owned by Sarah: 'Having a Smart Phone basically allows me to carry a mobile phone, personal organiser, laptop and MP3 player all in my pocket. I can access information, or do work anytime I please. I've even sat in nightclubs writing essays! Having the ability to sync the phone means all my information is up to date with the records on my computer. If I have something I need to be doing or attending to, my phone will alert me.'

The mobile phone, when synchronized with the computer and online timetables, can support those with organizational difficulties such as Attention Deficit (Hyperactivity) Disorder (AD(H)D) and dyspraxia by having alarms for approaching deadlines, notes for tutor meetings, seminars, and contact lists for e-mail and text messaging.

The mobile phone also has the ability to recognize your voice, so that you can dictate messages if typing is an issue due to coordination or spelling difficulties and even have them read back. This applies to many generally available mobile phones. There are assistive technologies that can be added to phones, such as the Nuance Zooms software and Code Factory Mobile Magnifier, offering general screen content enhancement when the graphics or text are too small, and Nuance Talks and Code Factory Mobile Speak providing screen reading. Dolphin has also developed Smart Hal (Figure 10.2) for those who wish to have every element of the phone's menus and text read back to them. This can be incredibly useful when concentrating on something else, not just for those who are unable to read the screen.

So screen reading, first seen on the computer using synthesized voices to read anything from menus to text in documents, has now migrated to a mobile platform and is also available on many personal digital assistants (PDAs), such as the iPAQ which runs Microsoft Mobile software. As Geneve says: 'I'm using my PDA for everything to keep me organised, and I can download my timetables onto the PDA, so that I don't actually have to access the web.'

It will be interesting to see how long the PDA survives as a support item when the Smart Phone is offering similar features, in particular those with large screens, good data support and MP3 audio file sharing. The latter allows students to listen to their lectures and podcasts (broadcast audio files on the Internet that were initially designed for the iPod, hence 'podcast').

Figure 10.2 Smart Hal

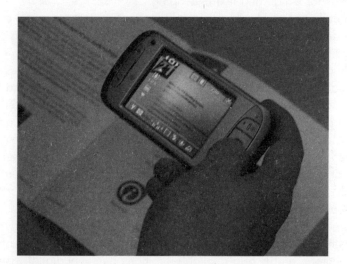

Figure 10.3 CapturaTalk

It is not just the mobile phone that has become an aid to learning but also the digital camera, especially when twinned with scanning and optical character recognition (OCR) such as that offered by CapturaTalk (Figure 10.3) from Iansyst and Kurzweil from Sight and Sound. These devices allow the user to take a picture of text, choose the area they wish to have recognized and have it read aloud. In an ideal world, this would work with every type of text, but there are times when the clarity prevents a true representation and the layout upsets the sequence of words. It will be a skilled user that needs to decide when and where to use this technology.

This could also be said for the digital recorder, which is offered to many dyslexic students. The Olympus DS-30 (also DS-40 and DS-50) (Figure 10.4) digital recorder provides audio feedback for all its menus, not just when recording and playing. These palm-sized recorders have tactile buttons, are easy to link to the computer and can be used for speech recognition as well as for downloading podcasts. It is important to appreciate that the memos and notes taken by the user who has trained in the speech recognition software such as Dragon NaturallySpeaking will be transcribed relatively easily, but the lecturer's voice from the recorded seminar will not necessarily be recognized with great accuracy at present.

These small recorders can be very helpful, as Andrew pointed out: 'When it came to revision I'd listen to the lecture again and I'd go and make my own recording of myself. If I'm on the bus, I'd just listen to that with my anatomy cards in front of me.' But not all students work well with audio materials and some need more visual or kinaesthetic ways of working. A quote sent to me by e-mail and used by a student (who admitted losing her recorder and PDA) stated: 'Tell me, and I will forget. Show me, and I may remember. Involve me, and I will understand' (Confucius, around 450 BC).

Figure 10.4 Olympus DS-40

Audio Notetaker (Figure 10.5) from lansyst can offer the visual element to a recording and is useful for those who wish to store quotes and find it hard to work their way through their recordings without a visual cue. The program can also help those who are researchers, having undertaken interviews and needing to store sections of audio recordings with keywords, times and lengths. It is a program that is hard to explain; the text window on the left holds the transcription or notes and on the right the audio file is seen as a series of dashes and spaces representing words and phrases.

However, the recorder can also become a burden, as typing up notes from the recordings made may more than double the time of the actual lecture. There are technologies in the pipeline that will hopefully resolve these issues, such as Via Scribe, being used by those working with Liberated Learning Consortium whose technology centres around two core applications: 'automatically transcribing spoken language and creating web accessible multimedia notes' with automatic speech recognition plus text and visuals to enhance learning (Wald and Bain, 2005, p. 436).

Handheld spell checkers have been used for many years to support students' vocabulary and spelling issues in libraries, while working on handwritten work and when out and about (Figure 10.6).

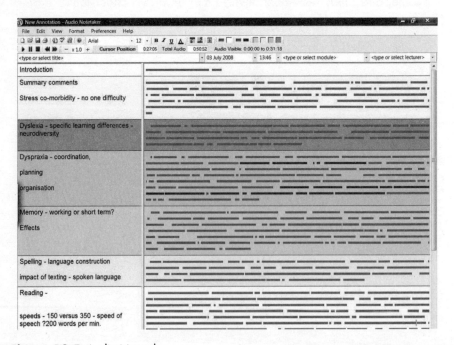

Figure 10.5 Audio Notetaker

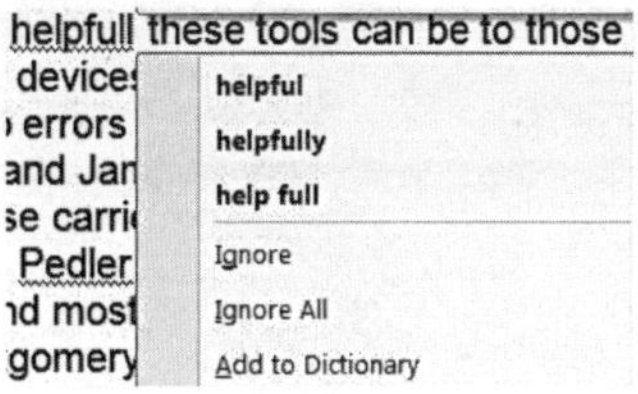

Figure 10.6 Using Microsoft Word Spell Checker

A study on how helpful these tools can be to those who have spelling difficulties showed that the devices that had large vocabularies were not always the most successful in picking up errors or making it easier for the user to choose the correct word (Draffan and James, 2004). The authors go on to say that 'studies such as those carried out by MacArthur *et al.* (1996), Nisbet *et al.* (1999), Montgomery *et al.* (2001) and Pedler (2001) found that spell checkers' ability to correct misspellings varied greatly and most could not correct a significant proportion of the errors. ... Montgomery *et al.* also concluded that the correct spelling must appear in the top three of the suggestion list for the spell checker to be effective' (ibid., p. 2). So with around 30% of spellings remaining incorrect, it means that the human proof-reader is still going to be busy! The study undertaken also looked at computer-based software for spell checking and found that those using the Microsoft Word spell checker, Texthelp Read and Write, ClaroRead and other packages experienced a similar success rate.

There are also digital 'pens' such as the Wizcom Reading pen with Oxford Dictionary to aid comprehension. These pens scan the word as the device is drawn across the page and it appears on the small display. It may be spelt out or broken into syllables with synthesized speech as well as having a definition. The problem for undergraduates is that many of the words they require are more complex than those offered by the dictionaries. This also applies to many handheld and computer-based spell checkers. The top end pens will not only read out words and provide the meanings but some will store data for use later. They will synchronize with the computer so that a quotation may be carried from a reference book to a document.

Digiscribble and other electronic notetaking devices, that work with a receiver connected to a digital pen and ordinary paper, can also help those who have relatively good handwriting. These technologies are useful for making mind-maps or drawing diagrams and equations, which can then be transferred to the computer. It is also possible to use handwriting recognition in much the same way that you can use Tablet PCs with

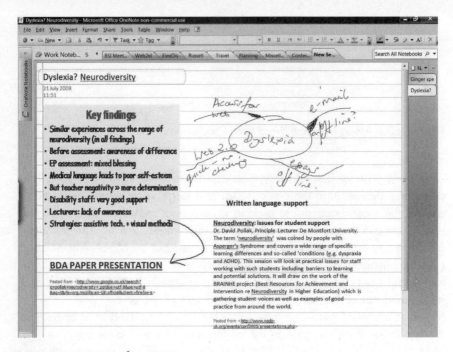

Figure 10.7 Microsoft OneNote

Microsoft OneNote (Figure 10.7) or the Journal for taking notes in a lecture.

Computer technologies

It is vitally important to remember to ensure that the user is comfortable using aspects of hardware, not just the software. The type of monitor available varies enormously from the latest shiny screen laptop to the large flat screen for a desktop computer. Many students with autism notice flicker on some of the older cathode ray tube monitors and are distracted by the pixels (Figure 10.8) or tiny dots of colour seen on pictures on screens; this is demonstrated on the TechDis web site called Sim-dis, where the advice is to offer vector-type graphics which are not confined to a rectangular shape. Those with any visual sensitivity may find the shiny reflective screens offered on some laptops affect readability, but they do work better in sunlight when compared to the nonglare screens.

Keyboard size may be an issue for those with coordination difficulties, for example, dyspraxia, and it is important to check typing skills. It may

Figure 10.8 Laptop with mobile phone

Figure 10.9 Laptop stand

help to have a separate standard keyboard and mouse, which, with a laptop stand, will also help to avoid any repetitive strain issues. A sensitive glide pad is often set at the front of the keyboard on laptops (see Figure 10.9) and this may also cause problems for those with any form of tremor. As Jim points out: 'With my shakes I end up double-clicking everything.

Also, I can only use an optical mouse. I can't use a touchpad, so when I got my computer, I asked specifically for a separate mouse rather than a touchpad.'

Ergonomic height-adjustable chairs can also have an enormous impact on the length of time a student can concentrate on their work, along with a large desk area for files, printer, scanner plus snacks and drinks. Obviously, the working environment itself must suit learner preferences, so distracting noises may affect those with autism, Asperger's Syndrome or AD(H)D, but music of the type preferred by the student may be beneficial. The latter should, however, be avoided when working with speech recognition systems such as Dragon NaturallySpeaking, which is sensitive to external noises (the user dictates into a microphone and text is transcribed).

It is important to remember that students regularly switch between paper-based reading and digital text. In fact, as monitors are luminous with backlighting and paper is reflective, paper copies might make reading easier for some students with Meares-Irlen syndrome. When asked about reading from paper compared with the screen, Andy said: 'I find it easier to read off paper than I do off a computer screen, because I think at times I get eye strain and tiredness from looking at a bright screen too long. Having been to the assistive technology lectures, I'm seriously considering changing my text backgrounds to a pale blue rather than bright white, to see if that makes life any easier. I tried it the other day and it was a bit easier to read.'

It may also be useful to keep a copy of articles for later reference, as well as encouraging annotations and even graphical note taking. This learning strategy was adopted by many of the students who took part in the Edge Hill study (Blankfield, Davey and Sackville 2003), where it was found that multiple representations of learning content can be beneficial.

Journals, articles and books are usually printed in black ink on white paper. Coloured overlays, glasses and lamps with coloured films can help those with visual processing difficulties where letters appear to jump, swirl or fall in rivers down a page (Evans, 2001). These issues may not necessarily be linked to poor visual acuity, but can result in the student skipping sections of text or poor comprehension (Figure 10.10).

Coloured overlays may prevent the glare of black text on white paper having such an impact on readability. Some students find the Visual Tracking Magnifier (Figure 10.11) can help to steady the tracking along a line across the page.

Both colour changes and tracking with a virtual ruler can be achieved on the computer. The program that offers the 'ScreenRuler' has been

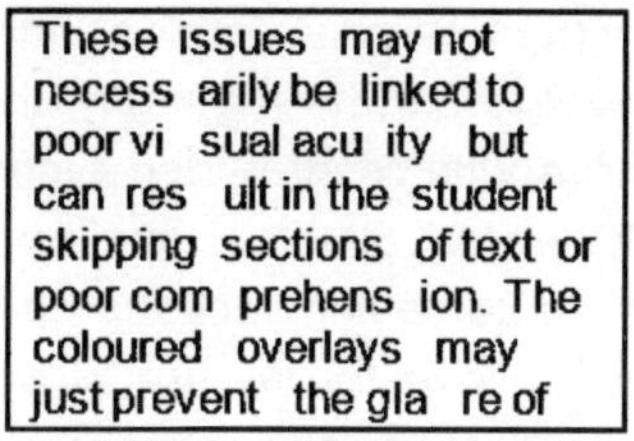

These issues may not
necess arily be linked to
poor vi sual acu ity but
can res ult in the student
skipping sections of text or
poor com prehens ion. The
coloured overlays may
just prevent the gla re of

Figure 10.10 Rivers of text

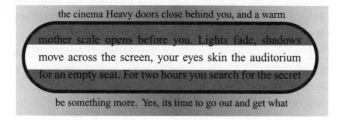

Figure 10.11 VTM Line Reader

Figure 10.12 ClaroView
Source: Copyright Claro Software Ltd. Reproduced with permission.

developed by ClaroSoftware; it allows for areas of the screen to be
masked off and/or magnified.

There are several assistive features found on computers as standard,
such as the options for changing colour backgrounds and the appearance
of the screen as part of the operating system in Mac, Windows and Linux
computers. It is possible to change text size, font type and colour, but there
are also specialist assistive technology programs that may make it even
easier. ClaroView (Figure 10.12) enables the user to cover the screen with

what could be called a 'virtual overlay', offering many different hues and depths of colour in a similar fashion to the many shades available in acetate. This may help those with Meares-Irlen syndrome.

A simulation of the various text effects is available on the TechDis Sim-Dis web site. There is also a computer package called DyslexSim (Beacham and Szumko, 2005), which allows for the user's own text to be represented as a way of showing the impact of various types of visual stress or perceptual difficulties.

The fact that text can be enlarged for many students is another powerful adaptation for clarity, along with increasing the distance between the lines of text in a long document and at times the space between letters. All these attributes are available in Microsoft Word, but the user has to navigate through several menus. A software package called 'ReadAble' (Figure 10.13) from Iansyst makes it easier, as there is just a single screen to reach the features with an easy way to return items to the default view if mistakes occur.

There are many other assistive technologies offered by the operating systems on computers. In Windows XP they can be found under the Accessibility Wizard or Control Panel; in Vista there is the Ease of Access Centre. Apple Macs have similar settings along with Voice Over that will read text in many applications. However, students have criticized the Mac voices and it may be worth investing in extra text-to-speech synthesizers that use the Acapela voices, offered by ClaroRead for Mac (Figure 10.14). To some, these voices sound less robotic and make for easier reading. The

Figure 10.13 ReadAble

Figure 10.14 ClaroRead for Mac
Source: Copyright Claro Software Ltd. Reproduced with permission.

same is true of the basic Windows voices; it may help to invest in programs that offer RealSpeak alternatives such as TextHelp Read and Write or ClaroRead 2007.

It should be noted that where desktop settings are locked down and user preferences cannot be reached, for instance in some public computer labs where operating system settings are not available, then specialist software is the only option.

The most commonly used software for those with reading, spelling and written language difficulties tends to be 'text-to-speech'. It allows the user to have text spoken as they type, to check the content of their sentences and to provide proof-reading support once the document has been written. As has been mentioned, the problem is that some students find the voice offered by the computer rather annoying and the way the punctuation is not always accurately heard (with pauses in odd places) can be distracting. But others seem to become used to these vagaries. Sarah said: 'I change it (the voice) daily, depending on "Daniel" or "Emily". Normally, I find the men speak in a lower tone. I sometimes find it clearer to understand. You can change the speed, and punctuation is interesting sometimes. It runs along, and it will go over the comma and stop three words later, and then ... I have just got used to it, but sometimes it will run really fast and then it will slow down again. But you can vary it.'

Those who are dyslexic may have particular difficulties with auditory perception and find any voices that are not to their liking particularly distracting, especially if they are not clear. Hogan and Dooley (2004, pp. 73–75) found that the ability of students to cope with different speaking rates varied from student to student, and state that 'audio quality seems to negatively affect students with LD far more than those with other types of disabilities.' Some students find it helpful to increase the pauses between words and this is possible with many of the software packages.

As has been indicated, several software packages with text-to-speech features also offer the ability to check spelling and homophones. One point to highlight is that if you are checking a very long document for homophones it will take time, and it is always wise to check documents at a paragraph level when using this feature for a speedy result. It may also help to use the dictionary offered by these programs, as it will provide the meaning of the word in a sample phrase.

Texthelp Read and Write Gold (Figure 10.15), ClaroRead Plus and Kurzweil 3000 offer additional help to those who find it hard to copy type lengthy quotes or sections of text for notes. These programs all have scanning with OCR options. This may also help those who have reading difficulties and wish to transfer documents from paper to digital format and have them read back from the computer screen. Once the document is on the screen, it can be adapted to suit the user with larger text, changes in colour and other types of adjustment. However, it should be pointed out that not all documents scan in particularly well: for instance, those with columns and tables can lose their layout, equations can become 'alphabet soup' and pictures can be misplaced. Generally the layout can be maintained more successfully when saved in Adobe Portable Document Format (PDF).

But it is the PDF that is saved as a picture that often causes the most problems. A document with diagrams may be rendered unreadable.

Figure 10.15 Texthelp Read and Write Gold

However, this is when Abby FineReader scanning software, used by TextHelp, allows the student to make the most of 'Screenshot Reader' (Figure 10.16) which provides the facility to read this text as a screen grab. In other words, the user can use the mouse to gather the text into a virtual box and the program will read the text if possible. The system is similar to those offered on the mobile digital camera and optical character recognition systems discussed earlier.

It is perhaps the planning of written documents that often causes the most concern for those who experience dyslexia and various written language difficulties. Those assessing study needs within higher education often recommend mind-mapping software such as that demonstrated by the first diagram in this chapter (Figure 10.1). But as one student commented: It's like 'if you have dyslexic people, give them a "mind map," though it doesn't (always) work.' The concept- or mind-mapping software available both online (such as Mind Meister) or free (such as Freemind), or at a more complex level such as Inspiration, Mind Genius, Claro Mindfull, Spark Learner or Mind Manager, may offer a way to generate ideas in a diagram. The default diagrams produced vary depending on the program used, but as Figure 10.17 shows, most can be adapted to appear in a similar fashion.

So when making a choice about which software suits the student's preferences, it is important to note whether they prefer to use the mouse and drag links and symbols or whether they want to use mainly keyboard input with links being generated automatically in a more hierarchical fashion. The degree to which the program can be used to prioritize thoughts and export them to other programs is also important, as well as work with multimedia files and other text-to-speech programs.

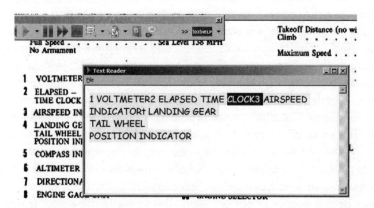

Figure 10.16 Screenshot Reader

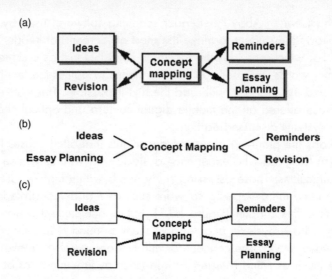

Figure 10.17 Mind-maps made with Inspiration, Mind Genius and Spark Learner

Most mind-mapping programs offer the chance to see one's thoughts in a linear fashion, and this can be exported to any word processing program. The ideas can be shuffled into different positions and used as an essay outline. There are those students who find it easier to shuffle their ideas in a PowerPoint slide layout, as suggested by Reena: 'I'd get journal articles and then start finding the theme. I'd go on PowerPoint and type the themes out. ... I'd put more content in there to write it up, and then to make sure that it's coherent, I would do a pretend presentation.'

For those who find creating text difficult, and typing even harder, it may help to use a speech recognition system such as Dragon NaturallySpeaking: this will work with Windows and Mac computers and can be used online in text forms, e-mail and even some mind-mapping programs such as Inspiration. A good headset is required (with a well-positioned microphone), relatively clear speech but more importantly the ability to dictate in phrases or sentences. It is the composing of academic written language that often poses problems, rather than the simple dictation of text. The other difficulty is that speech recognition software does not 'make' spelling mistakes, but merely attempts to change the word to suit the context; unless this is appreciated, whole sentences can be misconstrued. Very often, those who have written language difficulties fail to notice the changes or are unable to correct them. The software allows for a replay of all that has been dictated as well as proof-reading with text-to-speech.

Working on the Internet

Many of the aforementioned assistive technologies were originally designed to work with word processing software and Microsoft or Mac-based applications, rather than Internet browser applications that might be viewed through Opera, Mozilla Firefox or Safari and Internet Explorer. Students of today are spending more of their study and leisure time interacting with web-based technologies. A recent study of student expectations (Ipsos Mori for JISC, 2007) showed that 'young university hopefuls expect unrestricted access to the Internet' where:

- Sixty-five per cent 'regularly' use social networking sites, such as Facebook, MySpace or Flickr (females more than males – 71% and 59%, respectively) and only 5% 'never' use them
- A quarter (27%) 'regularly' use wikis, blogs or online networks
- Of those who had at least begun the process of preparing for university application, 50% had looked at or asked for information about the types of IT provision
- Of those who had looked at or asked about IT provision, 42% said that there was more IT provision than they expected (Ipsos Mori for JISC, 2007).

Several students interviewed during the LexDis project (LexDis Project, 2007–2009) at the University of Southampton (United Kingdom) commented that they do not use their assistive technologies when writing e-mails, working in Facebook or chatting in MSN, because these text-based applications allow for a more relaxed mode of writing. However, as more academics use wikis and blogs, spell checking becomes more essential (Figure 10.18).

If students do not wish to use their specialist assistive technologies, it is possible to use a browser add-on such as ieSpell for Microsoft Explorer with UK spelling, or Spellbound for Mozilla Firefox, and Opera which has a built-in spell checker. The latter also has text-to-speech and there is a speech add-on for Firefox called Fire Vox, or Accessibar which also provides colour, font and zoom options. ReadingBar 2 offers additional features for Internet Explorer, with text highlighting and the ability to save the output to MP3 files, but it has to be purchased for around $79.

Lecturers use the Internet or the intranet within their universities as a system for sharing their teaching materials, with discussion lists and interactive media. Lecture notes are posted within virtual learning environments such as Blackboard. These resources can be invaluable if they include options for the way notes can be viewed. As Sarah points out: 'The

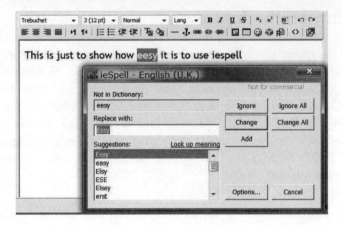

Figure 10.18 ieSpell used with an online text editor

fact that we have Blackboard, and you can put all the lectures on there ...
makes it so much easier to go back – with Impatica sessions.' These
sessions are ones that may contain a video of the lecture with narration,
animation and text linked to the PowerPoint slides. Blackboard software
does not include its own screen reader, so users who wish to use one have
to copy and paste text into another program, or download files to be read
in their native applications such as Word or PowerPoint. However, it does
allow the user a limited range of colour schemes for changing the look and
feel of the menus.

Without using any extra tools, the most accessible part of a PowerPoint
presentation, for those using screen readers or text-to-speech programs, is
very often the speaker notes which a lecturer may have written below the
slides. It is worth also remembering that if the Microsoft templates offered
in PowerPoint are used, the outline view can also be read with text-to-
speech and easily exported to Microsoft Word for annotation. A program
such as 'The Accessible Web Publishing Wizard for Microsoft Office' offers
the student the greatest choice of text and graphics but does not have
audio or video support. This is offered by LecShare Pro, which generates
notes in Word, HTML, Quicktime movies and video podcasts.

Many students have grown up with technologies and are happy to
experiment. To quote Andy once again: 'Having been fairly proficient from
a young age ... I'm not afraid to poke all the buttons and click all the
settings and see what things do. I know the extent to what you can do with
the software, and I know I'm not going to break it and I know I can always

reinstall it.' However, this does not necessarily prepare them for coping with the amount of data available for research purposes. This requires a high level of organizational skills, not always a strength for those with learning differences. As a participant in one of Morkes and Nielsen's (1997) usability trials said: 'You can't just throw information up there, and clutter up cyberspace. Anybody who makes a web site should make the effort to organise the information'.

Wikis, blogs and many Web 2.0 type web page layouts, which offer user interaction, sometimes lack accepted Web 1.0 type navigational organization. They may be just a stream of information with very few categories, headings, subheadings or white space. The text-to-speech engines hardly pause between sections. Tag clouds, which may be based on the types of words most searched for on a web page, are seen as a mass of words that the speech engine rattles through in a meaningless way (Figure 10.19).

Nevertheless, there are students developing skills who are willing to share with others how they have organized their work. An example has been provided by Robert, participating in the LexDis project (see Resource list at end of chapter). He has produced a method for making tab groups on his browser to access specialist journals quickly and easily (Figure 10.20).

Figure 10.19 Tag Cloud

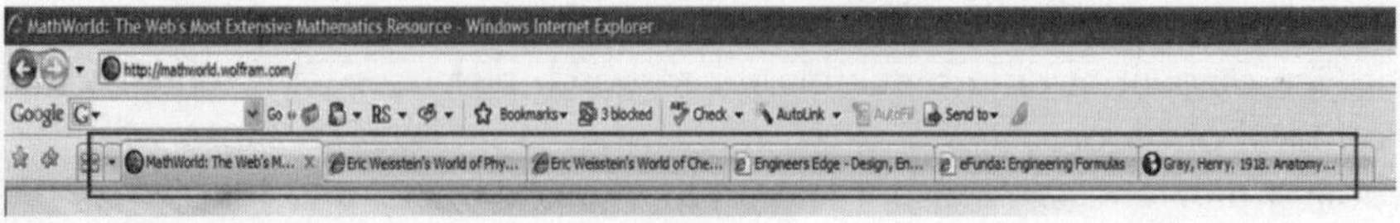

Figure 10.20 Tab groups

Conclusion

Today's learner is required to be agile in choosing technologies, and it is a wise assessor who 'thinks out of the box' when it comes to what qualifies as an assistive technology. The technologies learners use also need to be developed in an agile fashion – working with many different course-related applications – as well as being easy to use in a very flexible manner. If it takes too long to set up, it will remain on the shelf.

There is also the issue that those supporting students need to be aware of the vast array of teaching and learning tools that students are using on a daily basis. Not all work well with the technologies supplied to support their organizational and written language difficulties. These learning tools are changing and merging, as are the assistive technologies, so that students switch from portable to desktop with ease. Being able to synchronize content is more important than it was a few years ago, and we have not even mentioned the fact that many text-to-speech programs now work from a pen drive (memory stick) and so are, in themselves, a portable technology.

Despite a growing awareness that students can receive support for study skills and are able to benefit from the use of assistive technologies, there remains a general lack of awareness that inaccessible curriculum materials increase the barriers to learning, let alone the problems of copyright laws for those with print impairments. The complex PDF document or hastily photocopied journal article in font size 8 to save paper can greatly increase the study time for a student, who may need to rescan the document to access the content with text-to-speech software. The book that cannot be scanned for those with specific learning differences because of present legal issues in the United Kingdom (unless you also have visual or mobility impairment) is yet another barrier to overcome.

There still remains the urgent need to augment an inclusive teaching and learning environment with rich media content. This content needs to be intuitive and accessible to a wide range of learning preferences while allowing for the use of assistive and enabling technologies in the widest sense.

Acknowledgements

With grateful thanks to all those students taking part in the Joint Information Systems Committee funded LexDis project at the University of Southampton.

References

Ambler, S.W. (2007) *Agile Software Development: Definition*, www.agilemodeling. com/essays/agileSoftwareDevelopment.htm (accessed 19 March 2008).

Beacham, N. and Szumko, J. (2005) *DyslexSim*, English Language Study Unit, University of Loughborough.

Blankfield, S., Davey, J. and Sackville, A. (2003) *Supporting Students with Dyslexia in the Effective Use of C&IT in Their Academic Studies.* Ormskirk, Edgehill College, www.edgehill.ac.uk/tld/research/ (accessed 20 March 2008).

Confucius (around 450 BC) Quote taken from Experiential Learning Cycles web pages, http://wilderdom.com/experiential/elc/ExperientialLearningCycle.htm (accessed 18 March 2008).

Cook, A.M. and Hussey, S.M. (2002) *Assistive Technology: Principles and Practices*, 2nd edn, Mosby, St Louis, MO.

Draffan, E.A. and James, A. (2004) *The Accuracy of Electronic Spell Checkers for Dyslexic Learners.* PATOSS bulletin in 2004, www.dyslexic.com/spell-checker-accuracy (accessed 15 March 2008).

Evans, B.J.W. (2001) *Dyslexia and Vision*, Whurr, London.

Foundation for Assistive Technology (FAST) (2001) *Definition of the Term Assistive Technology*, www.fastuk.org/about/definitionofat.php (accessed 18 March 2008).

Hogan, B.J. and Dooley, P. (2004) The computerized audio library, part 2: its uses for gathering statistics on students with dyslexia. *JSET E Journal*, **19** (1), 73–75, http://jset.unlv.edu/19.1/asseds/ashton.pdf (accessed 10 January 2008).

Individuals with Disabilities Education Act (IDEA) (1997) 20, USC, Chapter 33, Section 1401 (25) US, www.ed.gov/offices/OSERS/Policy/IDEA/regs.html (accessed 11 March 2008).

Ipsos MORI for JISC (2007) *Student Expectations Study: Key Findings from Online Research and Discussion Evenings Held in June 2007 for the Joint Information Systems Committee*, www.jisc.ac.uk/media/documents/publications/ studentexpectations.pdf (accessed 19 March 2008).

LexDis Project (2007–2009) JISC funded project, University of Southampton, www. lexdis.ecs.soton.ac.uk (accessed 19 March 2008).

MacArthur, C.A., Graham, S., Haynes, J.B. and DeLaPaz, S. (1996) Spell checkers and students with learning disabilities: performance comparisons and impact on spelling. *Journal of Special Education*, **30**, 35–57.

Montgomery, D.J., Karlan, G.R. and Coutinho, M. (2001) The effectiveness of Word Processor Spell Checker Programs to produce target words for misspellings generated by students with learning disabilities. *Journal of Special Education Technology*, **16** (2), 2, http://jset.unlv.edu/16.2/Montgomery/two.html (accessed 22 May 2008).

Morkes, J. and Nielsen, J. (1997) *How to Write for the Web*, www.useit.com/papers/webwriting/writing.html (accessed 20 March 2008).

National Institute of Adult Continuing Education (NIACE) (2004) *Enabling Technology Conference*, www.niace.org.uk/Conferences/archive/EnablingTech.htm (accessed 20 March 2008).

Nisbet, P., Spooner, R., Arthur, E. and Whittaker, P. (1999) *Supportive Writing Technology*, Edinburgh, Call Centre, p. 223.

Pedler, J. (2001) Computer Spellcheckers and Dyslexics – a performance study. *The British Journal of Educational Technology*, **32** (1), 23–38.

Scherer, M.J. (2004) *Connecting to Learn, Educational and Assistive Technology for People with Disabilities*, American Psychological Association, Washington, DC.

TechDis Sim-dis website www.techdis.ac.uk/resources/sites/2/simdis/index.htm (accessed 19 March 2008).

Wald, M. and Bain, K. (2005) *Using Automatic Speech Recognition to Assist Communication and Learning*, in HCI International 2005: 11th International Conference on Human-Computer Interaction, 22–27 July, Las Vegas, http://eprints.ecs.soton.ac.uk/10730/ (accessed 19 March 2008).

Wanderman, R. (2003) *Tools and Dyslexia: Issues and Ideas*, www.ldresources.org/?p=171 (accessed 18 March 2008). This article first appeared in the Fall 2003 issue of Perspectives, the newsletter of the International Dyslexia Association.

Further Reading

Higgins, K. and Boone, R. (eds) (1997) *Technology for Students with Learning Disabilities*, Austin, Pro-ed CD-ROM of the text available with the book.

Seale, J. (2006) *E-learning and Disability in Higher Education: Accessibility Theory and Practice*, Routledge, Oxford.

Resources

Accessible Web Publishing Wizard for Microsoft Office	www.virtual508.com/
Apple iPhone, Safari Browser	www.apple.com
Blackboard Virtual Learning Environment	www.blackboard.com
CapturaTalk, VTM Line Reader and Readable	www.dyslexic.com

ClaroRead and Write, ClaroView, Screen Ruler and Claro Mindfull — www.clarosoftware.com

Code Factory S.L. Mobile Magnifier and Mobile Speak — http://www.codefactory.es/

Digiscribble — www.scanningpens.co.uk

Dolphin Smart and Pocket Hal — www.yourdolphin.com/productdetail.asp?id=26

Dragon NaturallySpeaking — www.nuance.com

EndNote Bibliographic Software — www.adeptscience.com

Freemind — http://freemind.sourceforge.net/wiki/index.php/Main_Page

Google Docs — www.google.com/

Impatica — www.impatica.com

Inspiration — www.inspiration.com

Kurzweil Reader — www.sightandsound.co.uk/

LecShare Pro — www.lecshare.com/

Mind Manager — www.mindjet.com/uk/

Mind Meister — www.mindmeister.com

Mindgenius — www.mindgenius.com

Mozilla Firefox add-ons such as Accessibar and Fire Vox — www.mozilla.com/en-US/firefox/ and http://accessibar.mozdev.org/

MSN – Windows Live Messenger and Internet Explorer, PowerPoint, Microsoft Office — www.microsoft.com

Nuance Zooms and Talks mobile phone software — www.nuance.co.uk/zooms/

Olympus DS-30, DS-40 and DS-50 — www.olympus.co.uk

Opera Browser — www.opera.com/

Reading Pen and Oxford Dictionary — www.wizcom.com

ReadingBar 2 — www.readplease.com/english/readingbar.php

Skype — www.skype.com

Spark Learner — http://spark-space.com/

TextHelp Read and Write Gold — www.texthelp.com

Chapter 11

Teaching, Learning and Assessment: 'It's Not Like You Think'

Heather Symonds

In this chapter I aim to offer educationists the opportunity to meet the challenges of neurodiversity and alter pedagogic practice. The discussion begins by assessing the impact of neurodiversity on current policy and practice in higher education (HE). The chapter goes on to propose positive changes.

Some individuals manifest differences in processing information concerning the world, and these differences constitute a neurological pluralism within the sphere of cultural diversity. The blog site Autism Diva (see web site list at end of chapter) has a strapline which reads: 'It's not like you think'. Understanding the diversity of thinking within the audience of learners sets the agenda for inclusive education. Differences of thought and perspective can lead to constructive challenges for lecturers and students, resulting in positive re-interpretations of the learning outcomes of programmes, interesting debates and lateral thinking in relation to subject areas or, conversely and less pleasantly, can end in destructive stress for all.

Being different may lead to troubled learning (Sagan, 2007); this is not surprising given that the educational world offers largely linear, text-led, exam-based, time-focused, standardized learning. The authors of this book wish for trouble for learners to be minimized. If tutors examine the issues arising from thinking differently and critically reflect on the possibility that they may be practising troubled pedagogy, new learning opportunities may arise.

The notion of diverse learners is not new, but this pedagogic acknowledgement has not led to radical changes within the syllabus.

I would describe many initiatives as apologist in their attempts to redress the balance for students (Konur, 2002). Choices of assessment are often limited, nodding at alternatives. Commitment to a choice of assessment is reflected firstly in the number of credits attached to the activity. In the United Kingdom, a BA degree award consists of 120 credits per year, amounting to a total of 360 credits over three years. If the assignment or activity being assessed in a non-text-led form amounts to a mere 10 credits, there appears to be little pedagogic commitment to significant change. In addition to the notion of 'credit-worthiness', diverse assessment needs to be supported by a curriculum designed to focus on preparation for it. Oral performance, for example, needs to be taught in the same manner as writing. Tutors also need to be trained to deliver new assessments. All those with the power of speech can talk, but it does not make us all orators. Physically, many of us can 'work a floor' and engage an audience with our eye contact, but in order to deliver an enhanced performance, expert tuition is required in this area. Rodenburg (2005) is an expert praised by actors for her work in improving vocal performance.

Art by itself can be assessed without being wrapped in extended writing. Visual communication is powerful and instantaneous – material may not be actually subliminal but the reading can be as effective. If this were not true, then multinationals are mistaken in paying millions for the inclusion of their logos in Hollywood films. It is interesting to read accounts of how viewers perceive an image, but a visual image stands alone with polysemic interpretations and does not require text to enhance meaning. Creative media need not require words, but still the majority of academic assessment appears bound in text.

Students who are dyslexic are still required to be assessed directly within the field of their disability by being asked to *write* about their knowledge, interpretation of the subject and understanding. In order to write at the level expected, they often have to read inaccessible texts. Creative artists, for instance, are asked to read semiotics and comprehend the *jouissance* of a text, presented with polysyllabic and unfamiliar words, which stretch the memory and auditory processing facilities. Diagnosticians are fully aware that reading for meaning at speed reduces accuracy and comprehension and will be an onerous task for many students with specific learning differences (SpLDs). Still the emphasis within teaching and learning remains focused on strategies for intervention to raise the standard of reading – not for conceptualizing diverse ways of accessing the curriculum.

Writing, a recognized challenge for many types of specific learning difference, requires students to overcome mental blocks based on past academic pressure, while struggling to organize thoughts and words, hoping that in proof-reading, one error is not corrected at the expense of another being made. Assistive technology, though impressive, still fails to address sequencing difficulties sufficiently and is not always reliable in offering dictionary replacement words. Staff asked to consider students' dyslexia in grading scripts may try to disregard spelling and grammar mistakes, but are often unsure of their remit as regards feeding back on structure, style and content. The tutor's toolbox does not include specific awareness of the nuances of the specific learning difference, limiting understanding and feedback.

Knowledge has to be the platform for change in pedagogy. Staff training would have to be introduced before the start of the validation process for a new course. Validation processes require market research into the need for a new degree and the probable student target audience. This model, required for initiating academic programmes, needs to be adopted for disability and specifically, neurodiversity. Consider admissions: if they are by art portfolio, what might constitute evidence that the student had experienced difficulties while still demonstrating promising work? How do admissions adapt the entry criteria for those with specific learning differences?

Self-esteem is lowered and competitive educational goals are formed when an individual is 'other' than a standard learner. Their 'otherness' is often presented to them, not as a positive attribute – their diversity perhaps contributing to lateral thinking in the creative individual – but underscoring difficulties. Their 'otherness' is perceived only in a negative light, as the perception is that additional teaching may be required. What meets with approval in the institutional meritocracy is the student's ability to fit in and be less 'other'. Lateral thinking is part of diversity, which is needed by society; such students invent different avenues and methods for reaching goals, acknowledged by the National Aeronuatics and Space Administration (NASA) in their high proportion of employees who are dyslexic (Brazeau-Ward, 2005) or by Disney in his enthusiasm for animators with lateral thinking ability (West, 2000).

Committed educators are aware that educational research into dyslexia centres on literacy intervention for dyslexic students, measuring the gap between successful remediation and academic attainment. The future goal, like the best intentions of 'No child left behind' policies in the United States, is often to eliminate the gap between dyslexics and neurotypicals. The gap for older students appears too hard to fill as 'catching up' has been left too late, leaving little room for change. The deficit model of learning difference has to date lent itself to awareness and best intentions but has not offered solutions, particularly in dealing with the legacy of emotional and social factors from a society presenting academic goals that for some are hard to attain.

Accommodated assessment was introduced to rationalize the uneven differences between candidates pursuing an academic goal. Early accommodations were often unwieldy: applying for extra time, eking it out, fighting for a space to undertake exams without distraction. Even today, extra time is usually granted only after forms have been filled out (form-filling is harder for many students with SpLDs) at the correct point in time (a poor relationship to time and calendars being one of the indicators) and handed in to the right person (remembering names and places often being another indicator). These actions require the students to raise the issue of their disability and underscore difference – always with the fear that 'extra' may not be given.

Universities exercising a duty of care should ensure it is automatic; it is not a favour or an extenuation. Imagine a visually impaired student being told they may be granted assistance to move around the building but it was not automatic. Or a student with serious mobility issues being told that access to the lift might be considered. In some institutions, it is still likely to be the case that accommodations sit within an atmosphere of unspoken prejudice against those who have invisible differences and that the accommodation does little to truly enable the student or progress the arguments of equality.

In the United Kingdom, the last decade has seen a substantial increase in student numbers within the disability sector. Dyslexia is the single largest category, but there is a distinctive growth in the UK category 'other' – particularly mental health (HESA, 2007). Professional organizations have grown with the rise in the number of students. As a founding member of the Association of Dyslexia Specialists in Higher Education (ADSHE), I can report that it was formed in direct response to HE needs; members have produced valuable resources advising on reasonable adjustments to teaching, learning and assessment (Hargreaves, 2007).

The United Kingdom also has a Professional Association of Teachers of Students with Specific Learning Difficulties (PATOSS). The number of PATOSS-registered assessors has grown to meet the demand for reports for the Disabled Students' Allowance (DSA). The Dyspraxia Foundation and the Developmental Adult Neurodiversity Association (DANDA) also support the community in the United Kingdom. In addition there has been a steady rise in literature aimed at supporting students in HE, which will support the sector in managing its new duties towards a diverse student body (Jamieson and Morgan, 2007; www.brainhe.com).

In the United Kingdom, projects with proven ideas and suggestions for the classroom have been initiated from Learning and Skills Council (LSC)-sponsored work, for example, 'Into Art with Dyslexia' (Symonds, 2004), and the Ladders Project (2004). Inclusive teaching and learning approaches for sixth form and further education (FE) were promoted by the AchieveAbility project, sponsored by the Higher Education Academy (Achievability); at the time of writing, this is being developed via a three-year (2007–2010) National Teaching Fellowship Scheme project called InCurriculum also sponsored by the Higher Education Academy (see website list pp. 266–7).

Such initiatives have been supported by professionals working directly within the area of support and guidance for students, but it is the absence of significant change in the United Kingdom that has led to the introduction of the Disability Equality Duty (DED) (HMSO, 2005) as a development from the 1995 Disability Discrimination Act. This legislation aims to move from a strategy of asking not to discriminate to an imperative of a duty of care. The DED requires that a clear policy is publicly available, stipulating all current codes of practice and operation. For HE this requires universities to consult users, present their policies in public arenas and offer solutions working towards a five-year plan. Implementing change then becomes monitored via an annual progress report. This differs from previous legislative requirements in that it demands a proactive perspective.

Responding to the DED

A dual approach is required to introduce change: firstly, senior management having specific responsibility for promoting and monitoring difference and secondly, constant involvement with students presenting as neurologically diverse. Goals need to include staff awareness training and the funding of pedagogic projects initiated by student-expressed needs and led by experts in the field.

Plans must be made following consultation with students and staff, or there will be errors which could culminate in litigation if needs are ignored or marginalized. Simple implementations include every member of staff having access to a copy of the university policy, or a summary booklet signposting key contacts. Other important features include proactive committees (with clear references to them on the university web site); indeed the Disability Equality Scheme itself should be flagged up on university web sites in a prominent position. This should be the home page, not a linked page; for example: 'We welcome students with diverse needs

– if you think differently you have come to the right place'. Such proactive initiatives represent the spirit of a duty of care.

Awareness training is seldom mandatory, but when it is, it becomes a valuable platform for understanding the issues at hand. Induction training often includes disability awareness; still the volume of information received can marginalize this. In order to create fresh teaching, learning and assessment, a structured permeable approach is welcome. This can be attained by using existing staff appraisal systems, staff development records and peer observation forms. Appraisals should include staff participation in disability awareness and training on an annual basis. Exemption should only be available for those with professional qualifications in the field. Staff development sessions are more often attended by the 'converted'; the responsibility would lie with managers to encourage staff who have not attended. It is no longer an option simply to consider disability, and such an approach acknowledges the importance of diversity.

The DED is acknowledged by the United Kingdom's University and College Union as 'a positive duty, which builds disability equality at the beginning of the process of teaching' (UCU, 2006). Critical reflection needs to start after disability awareness training by considering the role played by an academic member of staff. Examine the feedback from student questionnaires in relation to the course. Also, examine the course with regard to the Equality Duty: how well is disability, specifically neurodiversity, taken into account? If such reflection were not carried out as part of a regular course review and monitoring process, it should form part of a stage-one action plan.

Assuming a comprehensive diversity investigation is in place, embedded feedback should inform the course planning for the forthcoming year and any validation work being prepared. If minor changes need to be made, the course team may seek a minor modification which can, for example, alter assessment to an inclusive model by automatically offering students a choice of vehicles of assessment. The assessment can then be reviewed for improvement as part of the next review. Amendments and accommodations can be introduced immediately, as they are not inclusive of all but are designed to support students with a disability. Institutions may decide to use the accommodations route as a pilot or model for some changes, before developing an inclusive model for all students. The rationale for this is that wholesale changes, central to an academic programme, will be subject to Academic Affairs or Academic Quality inspections (or equivalent). This process is lengthy and expensive and, depending on the run of the programme, could be five years away. Making a start can be achieved by unit/module modification and staff training which is working towards change.

It should be remembered that the current trend (in the UK) is towards single equality legislation and single equality schemes. However, the principle remains that relevant groups must be involved, not just consulted. This suggests a role beyond focus groups; there should be direct involvement at all levels and in all groups, for example, student inclusion in a University Diversity Committee and even perhaps selected visiting status at University Management Team meetings (or equivalent).

The DED sits well with the Student Enhanced Learning through Effective Formative Feedback (HEA, 2006) principles of effective practice (National Professional Standards Framework HEA), as it encourages teacher and peer dialogue about learning and promotes clear performance descriptors. Ethically, HE welcomes extensions to positive pedagogic changes; UK law requires universities to introduce change strategically or face the consequence that the Equality and Human Rights Commission (EHRC) is at liberty to issue compliance notices, which could result in court proceedings.

Course Design and Curriculum Development

It is not the role of the EHRC to dictate the nature of the curriculum, but if a curriculum is to engage a diverse student body, it should hope to interest and inform. An androcentric and ethnocentric curriculum alienates a diverse student body, as does failing to raise the profile of those with differences within the curriculum. Citing Leonardo da Vinci's dyslexia or the specific learning difference of contemporary photographers is both interesting and motivational for students with dyslexia. Biographical information on leading figures within disciplines or projects with disability as a focus will involve the whole student body and raise everyone's awareness.

Planning the curriculum includes citing references in advance for material to be ordered and available. Ensuring varied learning resources supports diverse student needs and facilitates access to the curriculum. Providing audio books, downloadable material and video logs may require research into the subject matter and/or recording selective material from text-based resources, but this work will increase the accessibility profile of the course. Advice from specialist librarians, together with members of diversity groups, can be invaluable to tutors in heightening learning opportunities for students. All validation panels should check references with the DED in mind.

In constructing responses to the DED, universities should incorporate National Assessment Centre programme requirements forms as part of the validation process (National Network of Assessment Centres – see Table 11.1). This should allow the course team to indicate its understanding of the diverse needs of students with disabilities. This framework can then be employed in feeding back as part of Annual Course Monitoring Reviews. Monitoring processes would then organically create appropriate course changes in the minor modification to programmes that are available to course teams who wish formally to alter practice during the life cycle of a degree.

Assessment

Completing the NNAC form (Table 11.1) should prompt course directors to indicate 'reasonable adjustments' that may be made, or better still, stimulate the possible development of universal design for learning (CAST. org). Professional development might require adapting the form to suit course needs, for example, specialist work placements. The long-term aim would be to collate a bank of 'needs', which would inform new curricula and possibly be distributed across national networks (in the United Kingdom, through the Higher Education Academy and subject centres).

In the United Kingdom, copyright is not automatically surrendered for all those with disabilities; however, consent from publishers is rarely withheld if

Table 11.1 Checklist for adjustments to assessments. Please indicate which methods of assessment are used, or will be used in the future and provide further details where appropriate

Method of Assessment	✓	Further Details
Essays/Assignments		
Presentations		
Orals		
Group Work		
Reports		
Placement Reports		
Written Exams		
Practical Exams		
Dissertation/Extended Project		

(Extract from an NNAC Needs Assessment Questionnaire)

the access is restricted and is selective, that is, a section of a recommended chapter. Individuals with visual impairment are granted exemptions, but it is not automatic (Royal National Institute for the Blind (RNIB), 2008) as it is in the United States (Reading for the Blind and Dyslexic (RFB&D)). In the United Kingdom, the National Bureau for Students with Disabilities (SKILL) also offers valuable advice and information on many of the above issues. (See web site list for links to all these organizations.)

Assessment is a vehicle to demonstrate the efficacy of teaching and learning. Assessment appears as the end product for students, but should be the starting point for teachers. The questions to ask are: 'Where am I going? How am I going to help the students get there?' In starting the journey of designing a new programme, it is advisable to begin by considering how the knowledge presented and its uses are to be assessed. The formula offered by the TLC web (creativeassessment.org) is an excellent starting point.

TLC Project Assessment Case Study Template

Assessment Strategy

Subject and module

Useful for which students?

Keywords

Assessment activity

How does this assessment improve student learning?

Underpinning assessment theory links

What went well

What could be improved

What support for staff is needed to implement this method of assessment?

What support for students is needed to implement this method of assessment?

What are the time implications?

Other resource implications?

What are the risks?

How can these be minimized?

Implications for dyslexic students?

Institution where this was trialled

Lecturer

CATS Level (Credit Accumulation and Transfer Scheme)

Compulsory/optional

Relationship to other modules

Delivery pattern

Student profile

Learning outcomes assessed

References

Classic models of text-led assessment involve building blocks from 500 words to 1,500 or 2,000-word essays, and ultimately the 8,000 to 10,000-word extended essay. Alternatives generally carry fewer credits. Even within creative practice, it is common to maintain this posture. Research inquiries have revealed that scripts as assessment are perceived as familiar, having observable standards and as being relatively time-friendly for tutors (Symonds, 2006a). In reality, the standard of script marking is often highly questionable. Grading, despite grading descriptors, is variable. Examiners strive to be fair, but subjectivity in interpreting questions, responses and the actual criteria creates diversity. This allows other assessment models to compete in establishing excellence, as tutors strive for parity but do not always award equally.

Being familiar with the vehicle of assessment might sound reassuring; as a student who was dyslexic told me:

> Better the devil you know. I am really bad at essays, but at least I have trained to plan this sort of assessment. I could be really bad at another sort of assessment.

Introducing new assessment tools is not readily welcomed because they are unfamiliar, but this is not a reason to withhold the offer of choice. Students who have teacher-directed learning are often insecure in their first experience of group discourse or being asked to initiate discussion; the benefits of change remain worth the effort of introducing different assessment. In any case, assessment should be an integral part of the creative process of pedagogy. Being aware of the learning differences among students creates a legal imperative to accommodate, but opportunities exist to consider what actually works for the learner, rather than force the learner to adapt to a given mode, like a square peg in a round hole.

Before completing the details of new programmes, when the themes and learning outcomes are in their early stages, it is advisable to seek assistance in formulating assessment, whether attempting inclusive models or focusing on accommodated assessment. Staff development on new practices, adaptations and best national practice can afford interesting and supportive avenues for testing the efficacy of teaching and learning. National developments can be useful and may even present themselves as 'off-the-shelf' models. My own work on the viva voce is offered with handbooks and exemplars, guiding staff and students through new processes, answering questions and offering resources and assistance (Symonds, 2006b). There is also a podcast (see web site list). The research and administrative checklists are outlined, affording quality assurance and saving tutors' time.

Contents of the Viva Guide (Symonds, 2006)

- What is a viva?   3
- Who will be present at the viva?   4
- Why are dyslexic students allowed to undertake a viva?   5
- Suitability of a viva and consent   7
- Process of a viva   8
- Consent form exemplar   9
- Liaison with Study Support staff-structure   10
- Performance assessment   12
- Narration versus analysis   15
- Building blocks to a viva   16
- References   18

extract from Viva Voce Guide UAL©

Dedicated and approved projects are being designed in the United Kingdom (InCurriculum 2007 and others – see web site list) to offer inclusive models of assessment. Towards Learning Creatively (creativeassessment.org) as outlined above has a web site which offers case studies, and the HE subject centres explore contemporary best practice, which may not be dedicated to disability but often present suggestions and accounts of new knowledge in this area. Other agencies and organizations such as FEDORA (the European Forum for Student Guidance) or AHEAD (the USA's Association on Higher Education and Disability) are exploring new possibilities. Writing PAD (Figure 11.1; see web site list) offers interpretations of assessment and is an art-based web site which has striven to encourage innovative ways of presenting information to creative arts, media-based communities of students with a higher neurologically diverse profile than other subjects. Assessments are being explored that used to be seen as risk taking, but have become established and accredited. Dedicated and supported projects have opened new doors and the successful realization of assessments lends strength to the argument for change (Herrington and Simpson, 2002).

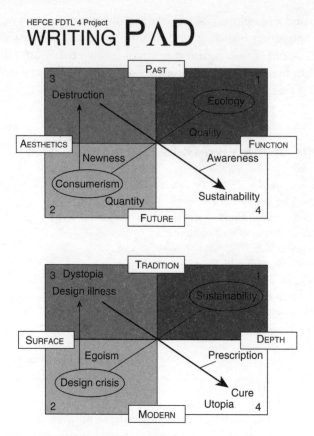

HEFCE FDTL 4 Project
WRITING PΛD

Figure 11.1 Sequence of the design process
Source: www.writing-pad.ac.uk

Figure 11.1 is used to rationalize the sequence of the design process. The pattern has different colour schemes to represent the essential quadrants of importance and interrelationship between ideas. The areas can be seen individually if the paper is physically segmented (folded over in four) but then revealed as a conceptual framework when unfolded.

New assessments take time to implement. Higher education institutions and organizations need to enable staff critically to reflect, by offering extra time for new developments and offering future inclusive models of education. Inclusive education requires investment or tutors will stumble at the first hurdle.

Proactive responses and planning are what is required, both by legislation and as basic good practice; however, universal design for learning (CAST.org) can still leave some learners struggling, unless distance-learning packages are designed to accompany classroom-based attendance. Individual needs will still require exclusive considerations, even within a comprehensive offer with choices of assessment.

Course handbooks should include diagrams (such as an assessment map) and should be available to all students in an accessible font and with minimum dense text. Clarity and legibility are paramount. Students commonly misconstrue the objective of their course when assessment dates seem to suggest that all deadlines converge at the end of term, rather than realizing that while the hand-in date suggests this phenomenon, the reality is that assignment work needs to be submitted, on average, every two weeks in a single term. Staging assignments may therefore be a better model. It is vital to decide on an assessment map that does not require any translation but is utterly transparent, staged and designed to minimize anxiety.

Work-Based Learning (WBL) and Work Placement

Industrial and vocational links require course teams to think beyond suitability for the discipline and beyond general legality in allocating or approving vocational placements or practice. The DED (in the UK) asks that policy in this area be comprehensive and consider the possibilities arising from working for a given company. The work placement officer needs to carry out a risk assessment. Staff risk assessment training may be required to ensure that they are exercising a duty of care. This circumvents some areas of controversy related to disclosure of disability or learning difference. A universal design approach may be sufficient as a starting point in evidencing care.

Formulating a policy on disclosure is critical in maximizing obligations to students and employers. Confidentiality cannot be broken; however, should the university know of a disability that could substantively affect a student's abilities to perform, let alone risk damage to property or others, then they are legally at risk (SKILL, 2000 – see web site list pp. 266–7). Students should be encouraged to disclose, as in any case it may affect their performance, for example, note-taking from the telephone, working in an open office with distractions, or being required to undertake alphabetic mapping in filing and appearing slower than others at undertaking these tasks.

Workloads for tutors with major WBL or placement duties should take into account the variation and diversity within any given group, as time is required to match students' needs assessments with employers who will maximize vocational experience and promote self-esteem. Liaison with disability officers or coordinators may be required, together with employability or careers specialists in the field of difference. Attention should also be paid to the student voice presented at the course review, where feedback from work placements will inform new strategies. Students should also be made aware of their future employee rights (in the United Kingdom, under the government's Access to Work practice).

Teaching Strategies

Much can be learned from the work of those professionals within the spheres of neurodiversity; it is worthwhile exploring both web sites and texts, as texts (while providing a base for strategies) can become outdated. In addition, organizations and web sites offer strategies that have been tried and tested in HE; the AHEAD and the ADSHE both provide examples of best practice, and BRAIN.HE contains key teaching principles for a wide range of neurodiversity (see web site list).

There are some excellent textbooks which offer study skills suggestions. Cottrell (1999, 2003, 2007), Hargreaves (2007), Price (2006) and Price and Maier (2007) offer HE suggestions based on their direct experience as tutors and trainers. The references at the end of this chapter are designed to inform the reader of accessible texts helping with stress and dyslexia, self-esteem, assistive technology and maths. A wealth of material exists in relation to secondary school classroom interventions; recently LSC projects have encouraged FE perspectives (Ladders Project, 2004) and HE has supported AchieveAbility (see web site list pp. 265–7) as part of widening participation.

All pedagogy requires research and one model will not fit all; adaptations, negotiations and advocacy will have a role to play in establishing a strategy that enables the majority to be supported but does not exclude difference. Piloting strategies will require asking the students and reviewing performance: what works for the student? Establishing a shadowing fellow student to observe and appreciate difficulties experienced is also effective involvement.

Appointing buddies or mentors is a possible pedagogic route to fill the gap for some students, although ideally, all teaching should promote autonomy and confidence for the learner who will otherwise not 'hit the ground running' in employment (Dearing, 1997). Buddies can help read articles into sound recorders or read directly for a student; this is dependent on the tutor preparing accurate page numbers in referenced texts in advance of a lecture or seminar.

Wherever possible, demonstrations and (even more effective) participative kinaesthetic learning will enable students to learn. This active model has been refined by Raven and Barnett (2007); originally designed to cope with large numbers of students on foundation courses, the Creative Learning in Practice Centre for Excellence in Teaching and Learning project (CLIP CETL, 2005) has been extended and is being monitored for effective teaching. Kinaesthetic learning is appreciated on most vocationally based programmes, as the students feel they have come 'to do' and 'watch others doing' rather than write about the doing. Several experienced tutors have offered examples of health studies students appreciating demonstrations and active work (ADSHE web site – see web site list).

> Asking the students with neurodiversity to identify two areas that worked well for them in every session, and tracking this feedback, is a positive starting point.

Visual learning methods have been developed by creative arts media tutors and may require staff training in delivering video logs and podcasts and employing interactive media (Raein, 2006). The Writing PAD project is inspirational, as is the work of the International Society for Education through Art (INSEA, 2008 – see web site list pp. 265–7) in promoting creative responses to pedagogy, which may engage those with neurodiversity as the focus is on senses and stimuli.

Students with Attention Deficit Disorder are easily distracted and may want to change locations or spaces, or occupy them differently. Planning for interaction and haptic movement improves learning, accessing long-term memory; physical activity like brain gym improves performance; visits and field trips – however short – have an impact. Physical symbols can have a lasting effect. I once attended an MA lecture where the tutor presented physical artefacts to illustrate romance and our interpretations of objects; I can remember the input after 20 years.

Olfactory memory can be incorporated into teaching strategy; eating foods or offering smells can trigger memory. Associative smell is primeval; spraying papers for revision with perfume and smelling that perfume on the day will increase memory for revision – a good exam tip.

Multi-sensory teaching is enjoyable and works wonderfully in nurseries. The printed and written lexicon is then signalled as king and the joys of different learning channels become marginalized, to the detriment not only of many neurologically diverse students but (I believe) all students. Revisiting kinaesthetic, auditory and visual channels in teaching situations is useful and fun.

In course delivery, it is advisable to review the possibility of providing off-white paper for all students to avoid high white glare; this will require ordering in advance from reprographic units. Offering readable material is a preferred choice for all students and attention should be paid to guidelines on 'readability', for example, from the RNIB (www.rinb.org) and dyslexia specialists. This strategy can be mirrored in the use of software, such as Blackboard or other virtual learning environments (VLEs); choosing a pastel-coloured background and a clear font in quite a large size (and good spacing) will go far in pleasing all students. General ease of reading and legibility minimizes stress. Ultimately, it should be made easy for the student to alter the appearance of any electronic resource to suit his or her preference, but being committed to help and illustrating action is also much appreciated. If material is online, provide an introduction to adapting it on systems like Blackboard. Almost half of UK dyslexics in HE are newly diagnosed and may not have sufficient IT skills to adapt the material to be user-friendly. Online material should be compliant with accessibility protocols such as the W3C (www.w3.org). Liaise with IT specialists where possible to maximize materials.

Summarize the key points, names and references at the start of a session and never at the end, when students who have higher levels of inaccuracy may not grasp what is written on the board. Copying in the presence of distraction is one of the highest-order skills. In delivering lectures, it is also important to consider that students may be audio-recording. Tutors are familiar with placing emphasis on their authority by writing on the board, but adding an audible tap at the same time can make playing back easier for the student. Use of pauses and tonality, rather like voice-over training, also assists the listener. Staff may wish to consider improvements in their own oral presentations as part of their professional development.

Student Selection and Diversity

In the United Kingdom, admissions to universities have altered as a response to the widening participation initiatives of the Schwarz Report (Schwarz, 2004). Marketing departments should have had appropriate training, and this should have ensured a profile for any university which clearly invites all students, regardless of difference, to apply for places. Fair admissions have been on the agenda for several years and should be reflected in admissions and staff/tutor handbooks. Course directors need to consult disability representatives if they have difficulty in interpreting fair entry criteria. Criteria for entry are adjusted to reflect disadvantage, such as offering a student admission with a 'C' grade and not a 'B' in a text-led assignment. The student clearly needs to be able to complete the course, but candidates should be considered who may access curriculum differently, for example, those with issues arising from learning differences, concentration, memory, sequencing, literacy and organization. Strategies for fair admissions may include sensitive reading of the applicant's statement or tutor reference, offering interviews to allow the student to express himself or herself outside of literacy, or asking for additional information.

International Students

Admitting international students requires that the same rules be applied. Unfortunately, as with many home students, learners are not always aware of their difference until after the course has started. This can be problematic, as language interference presents a difficulty in assessing neurodiversity. In formulating a profile for assessment, the consistency of education, the quality of tuition in the English language, the number of years studied and immersion in the language are all variables. This does not even touch the surface of differences of culture, where disability may traditionally be perceived as a weakness or dishonour on the family. Screening provides an insight into the learner and may suggest difference; the University of the Arts in the United Kingdom has transliterated the Bangor Dyslexia Test into five languages, including Japanese. These screens are not perfect but have been devised as a practical attempt to face the challenge. Although there has been research in this area (Smythe, Everatt and Salter, 2004), a universal assessment tool does not exist.

That dyslexia is universal was well established at an International Dyslexia Association conference (IDA, 2000) and students may be referred to experts in their own languages. The European and International Dyslexia Associations provide additional advice (see web site list).

Post-screening, the student wherever possible should be referred to his/ her own country for full assessment to eliminate language difficulties from the profile. This does not prevent a full examination of the differences and how these might affect the student while studying. Spanish speakers benefit from the Woodcock Muñoz test (Woodcock *et al.*, 1996) and the work undertaken by Davidson and Strucker (2002) at Harvard University.

Extraordinary Dyslexic Gifted and Eclectic (EDGE), the Japanese dyslexia association, provides guidance for Japanese students in HE abroad, and participated in the first ever dyslexia conference in Japan (Rifkin, 2004). Accessing advice from EDGE will assist International Officers and Disability Officers in other countries.

SKILL (see web site list) provides information for admissions tutors as a good practice guide for international students with a disability, and importantly has information on the support students can expect. International students have rights under the law to be treated equally; the same rights of disclosure, reasonable teaching and learning and assessment apply, even though this does not usually extend to funding. The United Kingdom's DSA is awarded to home students, while other students have to seek assistance from their own government or include the support as part of their international costs (UKCOSA, 2007 – see web site list). The more inclusive a curriculum is and the better the provision in relation to Blackboard or other VLE, decisions to have nonglare paper and improvements in audio facilities will enable all students, including internationals.

The international face of dyslexia is uneven; certain countries are very supportive of their students, for example, Denmark, where students are awarded grants similar to the United Kingdom and support personnel are happy to liaise and receive invoices and advice from the chosen country of study. The United States offers no such grant and neither does Australia.

Staff Awareness Training as Mandatory

Staff development or staff awareness is the first recommendation for any institution. Training may not be mandatory as such, but it should be made clear that without certain credits for in-service diversity training, the likelihood of promotion or an award of excellence in a staff appraisal would be fairly low. Individual programmes and personal development plans should include participating in neurodiversity training in HE at all levels, including senior management. A rolling programme should be offered to include a full range of diversity: for example, race, gender, sexual orientation, mental health, hearing impairment, visual impairment, autism, HIV and mobility.

Staff choosing to undertake external training or programmes should be awarded Accreditation of Prior Learning. This would be a cost-effective option for Human Resources and Faculty budgets. Expertise in the subject discipline is an obvious person-specification for a member of staff wishing to design a new HE programme, but if not coupled with contemporary pedagogic understanding of the diverse needs of the learners, the programme will promote troubled learning for an increasingly large number of students. Not only is this no longer ethically, politically or legally acceptable, but it is also liable to store up long-term difficulties for the course team.

The United Kingdom's Schwarz Report on admissions (Schwarz, 2004) has ensured changes to admissions procedures, but enthusiasm to increase student numbers by taking a wider section of the population is not synonymous with universal design for learning. Planning for the future is integral to success in ensuring every student has learning opportunities.

Specialist Dyslexia Staff

Specialist staff generally do try to monitor the changes in disability legislation and in practices; indeed those that are registered in the United Kingdom as PATOSS assessors are required to undertake professional development as an integral part of their practice certificate. Unfortunately, some visiting tutors are not made aware of developments within the university as a whole regarding teaching, learning and assessment. Delivering alternative or accommodated assessment, or encouraging different assessments giving students choice, requires additional training. Preparing to write and preparing to deliver orally are naturally distinct. Adapting requires assistance. Investigating vocal coaches and professional orators as trainers may be useful in addition to the correct resources and materials being made available.

New Staff

The Inner London Education Authority (long abolished) had a compulsory question at interview for all candidates for teaching posts, which centred on equal opportunities. With the new EHRC profile, this type of question needs to be re-introduced. Inserting a diversity question at interview, not just within the person specification, highlights the importance of diversity and ensures that candidates are aware of the issues within the student body; the phrasing should illustrate an understanding of the manner in which equality needs to be addressed. HE tutors need to reflect on this question: 'If I were to walk into your classroom, what evidence would I be presented with of equal opportunities (diversity) in action?'

The Impact of Change

Describing 'reasonable adjustments' and change for students can appear dry and even bureaucratic. It is in student narratives that the true impact is observed and valued. In 2006, I supported an undergraduate in Sound Arts Design who wanted to be assessed orally; he was afforded this opportunity by new handbooks designed to validate the 'viva voce' model (Symonds, 2006b). Costas is dyslexic and all of his life had felt that writing, his greatest weakness, never represented his ideas or feelings. Written assignments took him much longer than his peers and his frustration was overwhelming. His life was spent checking word counts, spell checking and proof-reading. He wanted to interpret and evaluate to the best of his ability and had expressed this view since his days as a Foundation student:

> I know I can get B averages in my essays but it is torture. I spend ages planning and never like the look of it. The spelling, the sentences – all of it is stressful. Because I can get a 'B', they think my dyslexia is not all that bad. They don't see the stress, the time I put into that 'B'. Why can't I just answer questions? They want me to know what it's all about? Well let them ask me.

Costas Kontos: BA (Hons) Sound Arts Design 2006

Costas was aware that one tutor, who believed that he would not have difficulty submitting work, was not entirely happy; for the tutor it was 'the shock of the new'. Costas started to record interviews, to record his notes and thoughts and to use Protools software to refine his recordings and edit work. I applied for additional DSA funding from his Local Education Authority and bought technical time and additional tuition time.

Working in real time meant placing emphasis only on the truly vital, and placing supportive material – even discographies – in the portfolio. There were few audio texts available ironically, even in Sound Arts, but I read extracts, he thought about extracts and he then planned his theoretical response in audio form. He involved his flatmates, friends and family in rehearsing his performance. This new learning experience involved preparation, patience and creativity. As his degree was in the relatively unusual area of 'Sound Arts Design' he felt that people 'really got it', that is, they understood his dissertation and his field.

I supported Costas with the vehicle of assessment, gave him confidence and listened critically. His supervisor was the professional expert and the work belonged to Costas. As I constantly reminded him, what I knew about Japanese rock guitarists could cover the back of a postage stamp. He took control of his learning as he navigated his way around the learning outcomes of his programme. He negotiated with his supervisory tutor and made responses aiming at 'real time' delivery with supportive materials.

Costas co-presented a session with me at the WritingPAD 2006 conference (see web site) at which he argued passionately for the viva voce and maintaining the defence element, which he believed was an integral part of the delivery. His perspective on oral discourse is stressed in a vocational text for artists, 'Life's a Pitch' (Bayley and Mavity 2007).

Tessa: Foundation Degree Student 2008

Tessa had a measurable low spelling age, which would have made being assessed in written form impossible. Material from the viva voce handbook was adapted to meet her needs and the course requirements. She had short vivas, the shortest piece being five minutes, which addressed a 500-word submission. The subject matter was deconstructed and then rationalized and created within the time frame to respond to key questions asked of the learners. At the time of writing, Tessa has nearly completed the first year and gains in confidence with every viva. She has good diction and has relied on being loquacious and conserving information in long-term memory for several years, as she had no other way of offering others information or evaluating knowledge acquired. Now the learning experience best reflects the difference:

I am learning to think like a presenter. I listen to the radio and consider how they might plan presentations. Sound-bites and interviews on my ipod have become part of how I learn.

The role of the educator is to enable learning to take place and to maximize student capabilities; it seems fitting to let a student with a neurodiversity have the final voice:

If I learnt anything it was that I had been struggling with my learning for a very good reason. This has completely changed my perception of self and my understanding of what I am potentially capable of.

References

Bayley, S. and Mavity, R. (2007) *Life's a Pitch*, Bantam Press, London.

Brazeau-Ward, L. (2002) *Dyslexia and the University*, Canadian Dyslexia Centre, Ottawa.

Cottrell, S. (1999) *The Study Skills Handbook*, Palgrave Macmillan, Basingstoke.

Cottrell, S. (2003) *Skills for Success*, Palgrave Macmillan, Basingstoke.

Cottrell, S. (2007) *Exam Skills Handbook*, Palgrave Macmillan, Basingstoke.

Creative Learning for Excellence in Teaching and Learning (CLIP CETL) (2005) University of the Arts London (HEFCE sponsored project 2005), Chelsea.

Davidson, R.K. and Strucker, J. (2002) Patterns of word recognition errors among ABE native and non-native speakers of English. *Scientific Studies of Reading*, **6** (3), 299–316.

Dearing, R. (1997) *Higher Education in the Learning Society: The Dearing Report. National Committee of Inquiry into Higher Education*, Her Majesty's Stationery Office, London.

Hargreaves, S. (2007) *Study Skills for Dyslexic Students*, Sage, London.

Herrington, M. and Simpson, D. (2002) *Making Reasonable Adjustments with Disabled Students in Higher Education*, Nottingham University, HEFCE project.

Higher Education Academy (2006) Student Enhanced Learning through Effective Formative Feedback (SENLEF), www.heacademy.ac.uk (accessed 20 May 2008).

Higher Education Statistics Agency (HESA) (2007) *Disability 2005/6*. www.hesa.ac.uk (accessed 5 October 2008).

HMSO (2005) *Disability Discrimination Act 2005*, Her Majesty's Stationery Office, London.

International Dyslexia Association (2000) *Multilingualism*, IDA Washington, DC.

Jamieson, C. and Morgan, E. (2007) *Managing Dyslexia at University – A Resource for Students, Academic and Support Staff*, David Fulton, London.

Konur, O. (2002) Assessment of Disabled Students in Higher Education: Current Public Policy Issues. *Assessment and Evaluation in Higher Education*, **27** (2), 131–52.

Ladders Project (2004) AimHigher Central London Partnership. Learning and Skills Council.

Price, G.A. (2006) Creative solutions to making technology work: three case studies of dyslexic writers in higher education. *Research in Learning Technology*, **14** (1), 21–38.

Price, G. and Maier, P. (2007) *Effective Study Skills: Essential Skills for Academic and Career Success*, Prentice Hall, London.

Raein, M. (2006) *Holding Patterns – Theory and Overviews – Writing PAD (HEFCE TDL4) Conference: Where Do We Go from Here: A Platform for Past and Future Initiatives.* Goldsmiths College, University of London, 21 October 2006.

Raven, D. and Barnett, N. (2007) *Oven-Ready – Exploring the Learning Context in Art and Design.* CLIP CETL Learning and Teaching Symposium, London.

Rifkin, C. (2004) *Dyslexia in Japanese, Chinese and English.* Brain Science Institute and the 5th Oxford-Kobe Biomedical Science Joint International Symposium.

Rodenburg, P. (2005) *The Right to Speak: Working with the Voice*, Methuen, London.

Royal National Institute for the Blind (RNIB) (2008) Disabled People in Further and Higher Education (www.rnib.org.uk).

Sagan, O. (2007) An interplay of learning, creativity and narrative biography in a mental health setting: Bertie's story. *Journal of Social Work Practice*, **21** (3), 311–21.

Schwarz, S. (2004) *Fair Admissions to Higher Education: A 'Widening Participation' Perspective*, Action on Access, Ormskirk.

Smythe, I., Everatt, J. and Salter, R. (eds) (2004) *The International Book of Dyslexia*, Wiley, London.

Symonds, H. (2004) *Project Report: Into Art with Dyslexia*, Learning and Skills, London.

Symonds, H. (2006a) *Teaching and Learning Fellowship Report*, University of the Arts, London.

Symonds, H. (2006b) *Implementing the Viva as Accommodated Assessment for Art and Design Students with Dyslexia. Writing PAD (HEFCE TDL4) Conference, Where Do We Go from Here: A Platform for Past and Future Initiatives.* Goldsmiths College, University of London, 21 October 2006.

University and College Union (UCU) (2006) *Some FAQs on the Disability Equality Duty*. www.ucu.org.uk (accessed 5 October 2008).

West, T.G. (2000) *Dyslexia and Creativity.* Dyslexia in Higher Education in Art and Design: A Creative Opportunity Conference, Surrey Institute of Art and Design (7 April 2008).

Woodcock, R., Munoz-Sandoval, A.F., Ruef, M. and Alvorado, C.G. (1996) *Woodcock-Munoz Test of Cognitive Ability*, Riverside Publishing USA (UK version available at Nelson.Assessment@nelson.com).

Useful Web Sites

http://autismdiva.blogspot.com (accessed 28 May 2005)

www.skill.org.uk SKILL: Information for international disabled students (No.8: Support) (accessed 21 May 2008)

www.equalityhumanrights.com Equality and Human Rights Commission (EHRC) (accessed 27 May 2008) www.ahead.org Association On Higher Education and Disability (AHEAD). Columbus, USA. Promoting Mental Well Being in the Curriculum (accessed 26 May 2008)

www.jobcentreplus.gov.uk/jcp/customers/helpfordisabledpeople/accesstowork Access to Work (UK) (accessed 26 May 2008)

www.bbc.co.uk/ouch BBC Ouch Disability Magazine (accessed 23 May 2008)

www.adshe.org.uk Association of Dyslexia Specialists in Higher Education (ADSHE) (UK) (accessed 22 May 2008)

www.interdys.org International Dyslexia Association (IDA) (accessed 20 May 2008)

www.fedora.eu.org FEDORA The European Forum for Student Guidance (FEDORA) (accessed 16 May 2008)

www.heacademy.ac.uk/resources/videoandaudio HE Academy UK. Developing an Inclusive Curriculum: Seminar at HE Academy York (accessed 15 May 2008)

www.heacademy.ac.uk/ourwork/learning/assessment HE Academy assessment information (accessed 30 April 2008)

www.achieveability.org.uk/index.html AchieveAbility A national network formed to promote awareness of the needs of those with Dyslexia, Dyspraxia and Dyscalculia or Specific Learning Differences (SpLD) in the learning environment (accessed 30 April 2008)

www.dotheduty.org Disability Equality Duty – Code of Practice UK (accessed 30 April 2008)

www.mhhe.heacademy.ac.uk MHHE: enhancing learning and teaching about mental health in higher education [accessed 29 April 2008)

www.leeds.ac.uk/educol/ncihe Dearing R (1997) Full reports submitted of the National Enquiry into Higher Education (accessed 28 April 2008)

www.dyslexia.eu.com/conferences.html European Dyslexia Association (accessed 26 April 2008)

www. admissions-review.org Schwartz Report (2006) Higher Education Review. Fair Admissions to Higher Education: Recommendations for good practice (accessed 25 April 2008)

www.writing-pad.ac.uk WritingPAD Writing Purposefully in Art & Design. (accessed 25 April 2008)

www.cast.org/index.html CAST (2007) Universal Design for Learning (accessed 24 April 2008)

www.heacademy.ac.uk/projects/detail/ntfsproject_norwichartdesign HE Academy National Teaching Fellowship Projects (accessed 26 April 2008)

www.incurriculum.org.uk InCurriculum. Developing the AchieveAbility of an inclusive curriculum in Higher Education drawn from learning and teaching strategies for students with specific learning differences (accessed 24 May 2008)

www.rnib.org.uk/wacblog/flash/accessible-flash-banner-ad-guidelines Royal National Institute for the Blind (RNIB) UK. *See it Right – Readability print checklist* (accessed 24 April 2008)

www.arts.ac.uk/itrdu/podcasts/baphoto.xml Kontos, C. (2005) Personal communication – London College of Communication, University of the Arts London, University of the Arts, London: BA Photography podcasts (accessed 24 April 2008)

www.writing-pad.ac.uk Symonds, H. (2006) *Accommodated Assessment for Dyslexic Students in Art and Design* (accessed 23 April 2008)

www.creativeassessment.org.uk Towards Learning Creatively (TLC) (accessed 23 April 2008)

www.ukcosa.org.uk UKCOSA: The Council for International Education. Provides advice and information to international students studying in the UK and to staff who work with them (accessed 23 April 2008)

www.insea.org International Society for Education through Art (accessed 26 April 2008)

www.brainhe.com Best Resources for Achievement and Intervention is Neurodiversity in Higher education. (accessed 23 April 2008)

Chapter 12

Conclusion: Constructing the Whole Picture and Looking Forward

David Pollak

The contents list for this book could be seen as implying a fragmented view of the learning and teaching issues associated with neurodiversity. Should such students be regarded as having 'special needs' which can be addressed in a compartmentalized way? The answer is 'no'. This book may appear to have perpetuated the individual labelling of students, but there are many commonalities among the students depicted here. Furthermore, a great variety of learning styles are represented in the student body as a whole. That does not mean that HE staff can ignore neurodiversity – quite the reverse. The point is that pedagogy (or andragogy) for all can only be an effective philosophy if it is supported by specific knowledge about student diversity (Powell, 2003).

This chapter identifies a number of themes which emerge from the book; these are drawn together in order to sum up the present situation in HE and to make recommendations for future policy, particularly regarding inclusive learning, teaching and assessment.

Disability, Diversity and Inclusion

The moving and perceptive student voices included in this book support what Powell (2003, p. 3) calls 'the right for all to be able to access appropriate education'. These students are currently categorized (in several countries) as disabled; regardless of their labels, they constitute a challenge to higher education in relation to course design, learning, teaching and assessment (Riddell, Tinklin and Wilson, 2005). Neurodiversity poses its own particular challenge to individual students, as a result of the current system. In many countries, legal and administrative procedures advocate a medical model of disability and learning difference: students are required to be formally diagnosed and identified, and adjustments are made so that they can fit in to existing approaches to learning and teaching. This process is better than leaving them to 'sink or swim', but the assumption is that the procedures of HE are immutable. Students must basically adapt themselves to the system, and it will make some concessions, but only to those who have been 'certified'.

Alongside this policy, there exists legislation such as the UK's recent Disability Discrimination Act (HMSO, 2005), which requires the representation of disabled people and also requires institutions to have Disability Equality Schemes. Riddell and Watson (2003, p. 2) draw attention to the belief that abandoning 'an agenda of redistribution and equality in favour of an emphasis on difference and diversity' perpetuates deep-seated structural inequality. The tension between these viewpoints has yet to be resolved; it will be revisited later in this chapter.

Chapters 3 to 9 of this book have made clear that students identified with learning differences do experience impairments. Riddell, Tinklin and Wilson (2005, p. 16) discuss the distinction between disability and impairment, stating that some campaigners believe 'that impairment does not necessarily result in disability, and in an ideal society, where all barriers were removed, disability would cease to exist'. On the other hand, many of the students portrayed in this book would agree with Crow (1996, p. 58) that 'for many disabled people personal struggle related to impairment will remain even when disabling barriers no longer exist'. This book has also demonstrated that 'impairments fluctuate and are experienced in different ways over an individual's life course' (Riddell, Tinklin and Wilson, 2005, p. 132).

There remains however a clear analogy between physical impairment and neurodiversity in terms of access. If a student using a wheelchair is confronted by a staircase to the library, the building is inaccessible; the student's academic ability (having met the entry requirements) is irrelevant. In the same way, if the course is delivered and assessed in ways which disadvantage a student similar to those described in this book, that course is inaccessible. I will return to inclusive approaches to learning and teaching later in the chapter.

Overlaps between Types of Neurodiversity

There are many ways in which the types of student included in this book resemble each other. The UK's Developmental Adult Neurodiversity Association (DANDA) has produced a Venn diagram (DANDA, 2005) which shows some aspects of these overlaps. It focuses on the difficulties people often experience. Members of DANDA had a dual aim in compiling it: to show how the various types of neurodiversity are part of one picture, and to convey the range of problematic areas of their experience. It uses the expression *'we are people of extremes'*, which may be seen as evidence of a degree of frustration resulting from years of struggle with educational institutions. Although the diagram represents a simplified view and is capable of further refinement, it makes clear that the indicators of each type of neurodiversity cannot be compartmentalized.

It may be that eventually a 'grand unifying theory' of neurodiversity will be formulated, but current attempts at this are predominantly medical in nature (Frith, 2002; Stein, 2004). Grant (Chapter 3) proposes a model based on the neurocognitive processing of information, and believes that there are many cognitive aspects of the overlap between types of neurodiversity. Colley (Chapter 8) refers to four of many different studies which have found considerable overlap between AD(H)D and other specific learning differences. However, it is always important to take note of what students have to say; Grant and Cooper (Chapter 4) both refer to compelling student accounts of visualization. Having been focused on assessing HE students for several years, Grant has data on many hundreds of people; this unique body of work is showing striking incidence not only of visual thinking but also of synaesthesia (Grant, 2007), which is likely to yield further insight in the future.

This book also demonstrates a number of similarities between the types of student covered as regards learning strategies. All students need a high level of metacognition in order to succeed in HE, but the students in this book have particular need of this. There is a dual reason for that: their intrinsic cognitive structure and the way HE is currently organized. The same applies to the degree of determination they require in order to graduate, a factor mentioned in several chapters here. Working in learning support in the United Kingdom, it is often humbling to hear of the challenges students are facing, in addition to the pressures of earning money (and in many cases, family responsibilities).

Similarities between the students are also evident in respect of personal organization. Potential to be imprecise about time (Cooper, Chapter 4) can also be experienced by ADDers, Aspies and those who are dyspraxic and dyscalculic. Trott (Chapter 6) is particularly clear about the 'life skill' aspects. As Drew (Chapter 5) adds, a mentor can be a great help. However, part of the mentor's role (like that of the learning support tutor) should be to facilitate the student to develop her own strategies, be they for life management or study.

Another aspect which all types of neurodiversity have in common is the dilemma about disclosure, particularly in the workplace. Students are of course conscious of their 'probationary' status in a work setting in any case, but this is added to by uncertainty as to the level of ignorance or prejudice regarding neurodiversity which they might find there. McCrea (Chapter 9) refers to mental health as 'one of the last workplace taboos', but in the United Kingdom the tabloid press is still ready to perpetuate the notion that dyslexic (or as they persist in saying, wordblind) people all read backwards and spell upside-down. Trott (Chapter 6) points out that promotion at work can often involve management, which usually brings responsibility for budgets, so dyscalculia may present particular issues if the individual is not assertive and senior management is not aware of reasonable adjustments.

As regards such adjustments at university, this book makes clear that there are many overlaps between what is good practice for all the students covered, in terms of both mainstream provision and individual support.

Research by the BRAIN.HE project in the United Kingdom (Griffin and Pollak, 2008) involved participants identified with eight different types of neurodiversity. A clear finding was that regardless of their identification, the students reported the following:

- Being formally identified ('diagnosed') was a complex experience, including positive aspects (such as relief and explanation) and also discomfort regarding the label.
- While there is evidence of increased awareness of neurodiversity among education professionals, students are still called 'lazy' and told to 'try harder'.
- There is a lack of communication at universities between academic staff and learning support/disability staff.
- Students receive the clear message that they must make arrangements to fit themselves to the system, that is, it is they who have the 'problem'.

This was a very small-scale study (there were 27 participants), but it reflects the findings of Pollak (2005), whose cohort of dyslexic students reported similar issues regarding self-concept, self-esteem and identity. UK law refers to 'reasonable adjustments' and US law to 'accommodations', but in order to obtain these, students have to be pathologized and labelled.

Admissions and Transition

Powell (2003, p. 112) believes that one challenge for HEIs is 'how to guide choice of course without being constrained by any preconceptions of limitations imposed by condition'. Riddell, Tinklin and Wilson (2005, p. 75) surveyed all HEIs in England and Scotland, and found that at interview, some institutions effectively put disabled students off continuing with their application by stressing the potential challenges of the course (although their published policy stated that admission was based on purely academic grounds). There is clearly a balance to be struck between giving a student realistic advice and accepting that university policy could often deliver greater accessibility than current arrangements allow.

Students do not, however, seek a qualification which they perceive to be of less value than those of their peers; some choose not to pursue examination arrangements, for example, because 'I don't want any special conditions, I don't want special exceptions; if I've got it wrong, I've got it wrong' (Pollak, 2005, p. 225). In Powell's (2003, p. 3) reference to 'the right for all to be able to access appropriate education', the key word is 'appropriate'; students should not be 'set up to fail'. Inclusive practice does not mean that any person is entitled to enrol for any course; there must be a match between ability and course requirements, even when disability and neurodiversity are taken into account.

Unfortunately, increased participation in HE has meant that most students are admitted without interview, and thus opportunities for mutual exploration are lost. Trott (Chapter 6) demonstrates that students need to think beyond the entry requirements. There is a responsibility for students to inform themselves about the demands of the whole course (which would still apply even if it were highly inclusive); for example, some dyslexic people applying for Fine Art do not realize that the final year of the course currently involves a substantial dissertation. However, as Symonds points out in Chapter 11, course specifications should be drafted in such a way that alternative assignments are available which meet the learning outcomes in different ways. Cooper (Chapter 4) puts it succinctly: 'Universities would become more inclusive if they provided clear and meaningful entry criteria based on a thorough course analysis that identifies the nature of the learning journey, the learning environment and the capacity of the organisation to respond to diversity.' As this happy situation is not yet widely seen (in the United Kingdom at least), students would do well to make use of Colley's checklist of questions to ask about a university (Chapter 8) or Cooper's in Chapter 4.

Transition into HE can challenge any student's personal organization skills. As Chapters 4 to 9 here show, this is a particular issue for neurodiversity. At the opposite end of the working life-course, pre-retirement workshops usually advise people to consider aspects of their employment which they enjoy and seek ways to replace these in retirement; the kind of student covered in this book should do the same with practical arrangements at university. If someone has always reminded him about events in his diary, what alternative system can he devise? If somebody has always proof-read her work, where will this support come from? The message of this book is not simply that universities must be pro-active about developing inclusive practices; students should also be pro-active about applying for the right course and exploring accessibility arrangements.

This is where university open days play an important role. They offer students a chance not only to meet disability and welfare officers, but also to ask course tutors about key issues such as course delivery styles, accessibility of materials and assessment modes. Such conversations can reveal a great deal about staff awareness of inclusive practice. Some universities also offer pre-entry courses, such as the three-day preparatory residential course for dyslexic students run at the UK University of Middlesex just before the academic year begins (Parker, 2007).

In a speech about widening participation delivered in April 2008, John Denham, UK Minister for Innovation, Universities and Skills, said: '... the time is right to bring together higher education institutions' widening participation and fair access policies, including transparent admissions systems, into a single document' (Denham, 2008). It will be essential for such a document to include the issue of fair access for neurodiversity as well as for types of applicant frequently referred to as 'disadvantaged'. The trend in the United Kingdom towards single documents of that kind is also evidenced by the Higher Education Academy, which now has a 'Single Equality Scheme' (HEA, 2008) described as setting out 'a framework for mainstreaming equality and diversity practice across the work of the Academy'. More on this approach below.

Identification

Riddell, Tinklin and Wilson (2005, p. 153), writing of dyslexic students, comment that: 'In order to obtain the support they require, they actively seek a diagnosis, but at the same time they resent and reject the stigma associated with the category of disability'. This arises partly because of the way society in general still tends to use the language of within-person deficit and personal tragedy, and partly because such students often wish to avoid victim status. But as Grant points out (Chapter 3), the process of identification has the potential to be empowering and enabling, as long as it is much more than just an exercise in labelling. Participants in the BRAIN.HE project (Griffin and Pollak, 2008) reported that identification was a relief, because they had a reason for their experience; they also expressed awareness of their strengths – but at the same time, the majority of them used language which revealed a medical view of neurodiversity. This may result from the fact that these are the only terms they have been offered (Pollak, 2005). It was sobering, early in 2008, to see a 13-year-old boy on UK television saying: 'The trouble is, I suffer from dyslexia'.

Nevertheless, there are what Hurst (Chapter 2) calls 'reasons to be cheerful'. There is a gradual increase in academic staff awareness: BRAIN.HE participants (Griffin and Pollak, 2008) spoke of lecturers advising them to seek assessment for learning difference, having recognized the indicators in them. They also reported excellent support from disability and learning support staff, and that work is underpinned by the availability of checklists for screening such as those provided here by Drew (Chapter 5) and Martin (Chapter 7). The pioneering work by Trott and Beacham (Chapter 6) on a dyscalculia screening tool for FE and HE is also encouraging.

The process of identification, both screening and full psychological assessment, must take account of the student's sense of self. If self-esteem is defined as the result of comparison between self-image and the ideal self (Lawrence, 1996), then the potential of the identification process to damage self-esteem is clear. As Martin (Chapter 7) points out, identification takes place over time, both in bureaucratic terms and in terms of the student's adjustment to a change of identity. Both Colley (Chapter 8) and Griffin and Pollak (2008) refer to the long-term emotional effect of epithets used by school teachers, which often forms an important part of the emotional hinterland a student brings to being identified. Chanock (2007, p. 40) writes of 'practices that both enable and disable students' in present systems regarding dyslexia in HE. She calls for people working in different discourse communities, one of which is focused on a medical model of learning difference, to learn from each other. This is relevant to every stage of the identification process, from the way it is proposed to the student to the way it is conducted and the language used in reports.

Singleton (1999) reported that at the time of his working party's survey, 43% of known dyslexic students at UK universities had been so identified after enrolment. There may be many reasons for this, but one interpretation is consonant with the social model of learning difference: such students struggle at university because the disability of dyslexia is constructed by the practices of higher education institutions (HEIs).

Learning and Teaching

Probably the most striking similarities between Chapters 4 to 9 are evident in respect of recommended learning and teaching approaches. Yet the strategies called for are not outlandish or 'special' – they are listed in many publications about HE teaching. For example, Horgan (1999, p. 89) suggests the following: 'As the lecture proceeds, continue to show students the lecture outline on an overhead transparency so that they can chart their way through and note the significant elements'. Horgan also recommends linking the lecture with previous course elements, providing activities and variety for students, summarizing the main points at the end of each section, providing good handouts – all elements listed by authors in this book.

Cooper (Chapter 4) refers to lecturers 'owning up to making mistakes'. This is an example of what Rogers (1983) calls 'congruence' – being a real person in the relationship with a student. Cowan (1998, p. 144) stresses the importance of this, but adds that Rogerian 'unconditional positive regard' can also contribute to successful teaching: 'This is expressed when the teacher has a positive and accepting attitude to whatever the student is, or is thinking or doing, at that moment. It is a prizing of learners as imperfect human beings', even when they seem to behave erratically. A key aspect to add to this is that in the context of neurodiversity, such an attitude leads to student confidence in the lecturer, which in turn leads to willingness to disclose learning difference issues.

Disclosure is vital if good communication, and hence successful learning and teaching, are to take place. For example, Ferguson (2003, p. 85) refers to the 'commonness of mental ill-health'. Indeed, just as cancer used to be 'unmentionable' but this has changed, so in the United Kingdom at least people are now beginning to be more open about mental 'issues'. It is likely that most families have at least one member who is, or has been, a service user regarding mental well-being. As this book shows, there is a lack of reliable data as to the prevalence of many types of neurodiversity in the population as a whole; in HE, there is always a contrast between numbers who have disclosed a learning difference and numbers who are either unaware of it or who choose not to disclose (and some of the latter may be choosing not to opt in to the medicalization of neurodiversity).

This implies a need for what Martin (Chapter 7) calls empathy with the student, and this in turn requires flexibility (which Aspies are usually said to lack, and Martin has shown to be frequently lacking in academic staff). Powell (2003, p. 112) set a 'task for educators': 'how to think creatively about different ways of learning that can be employed to achieve the same learning outcomes'. The point was made above that accessible approaches for neurodiversity often amount to no more than good learning, teaching and assessment practice. McCrea's summary (Chapter 9) of ways to address student mental well-being issues is an example. Cooper (Chapter 4), Drew (Chapter 5) and Martin (Chapter 7) all refer to barriers to learning; Drew provides a long list of practical suggestions for removing or minimizing such barriers. Some lecturers might take exception to individual items, for example: 'Do not expect the student to read an article at speed in order to discuss it'. They might respond that this is the nature of HE, and that those who cannot manage it should not be present. Rapid reading (and comprehension) is indeed a traditional HE expectation; however, the diversity agenda invites course leaders to re-consider the core learning outcomes. Are rapid reading and comprehension essential – or is it in fact the ability to understand and debate the concepts in the article? An inclusive lecturer places all such material online and provides advance notice of session content, so that students can prepare; those who need to take longer over reading, or access the article via assistive technology, can do so. Such a lecturer also lets students know that she is aware of learning diversity.

However, as Cooper points out in Chapter 4, strategies for individual students and lecturers, though important, are only part of the picture. There should be an institutional policy which facilitates the removal of barriers to learning (see Chapter 11). Validation procedures should include enquiries about the accessibility of the proposed course and levels of staff awareness of student diversity. Members of validation panels should be prepared to question assessment methods. Cooper's comments about linear thought should be taken into account: assignments which demand this are disabling for most dyslexic students. Could patchwork text (Winter, 2003) be used to meet the learning outcomes? Would a non-linear portfolio be acceptable?

This is not to ignore the fact that some courses are vocational or professional. Journalists must be able to produce grammatically correct, accurately spelled English under time pressure. Lawyers must be able to read lengthy briefs and judgements and produce extended arguments. The key factor is that the policy of both professional bodies and HEIs should be to make procedures as accessible as possible – but there is a difference between blind adherence to academic tradition and the realities of the professional or vocational workplace. Having said that, research for a recent presentation to a conference of UK Pharmacy course leaders (Pollak, 2006) revealed that dyslexic pharmacy students are particularly careful, have very successful placement experiences and worry their tutors much less than the over-confident (male) students who sit in the back row of the lecture theatre and think they know it all.

Drew (Chapter 5) and Martin (Chapter 7) provide useful checklists for course leaders and managers who are aware of the need for systems to ensure inclusive practice. Symonds (Chapter 11) offers checklists for programme design, which are particularly useful for assessment factors. This is challenging material; it implies a questioning of the very nature of HE. In the United Kingdom, there is a long history of elitism. Until the last 18 years, HE was attended by a tiny minority of the population. It is still being run by senior academics whose own university experience (as students) was elitist. In many Faculties, their instinctive view of it involves attending numerous lectures, reading large numbers of (printed) books and journals and writing large numbers of three-hour examinations and long essays (using a fountain pen, or if very modern, a typewriter). When preparing for my PhD viva, I was warned that the examiners would probably insist on some re-drafting of my thesis because they had experienced that themselves and would not want me to 'get away with it' (although I did in fact do so); I believe there is still an element of 'it was good enough for us' about course design.

Symonds (Chapter 11) presents an alternative view which chimes with that of Cottrell (2001), who believes that too many lecturers address the students whom they wish were in the room (i.e. people resembling themselves), rather than those who are actually present. HE is attracting a wide diversity of people with a similar diversity of approaches to learning. Their presence should be seen as a stimulus and an enrichment, rather than as a problem.

One way of creating courses which are accessible to all is to adopt Universal Design for Learning (Rose and Meyer, 2002). This approach posits that as the brain's recognition, strategic and affective networks are all involved in learning, then course design should offer multiple means of representation, of expression and of engagement. Hall and Stahl (2006) give a succinct exposition of ways in which this can be achieved, and their suggestions are remarkably consonant with the approaches recommended in this book. For example, they suggest presenting content in multiple formats, using images and video as well as text; using concept maps and making clear links with previous elements and across the course; offering a variety of means of assessment.

Universities will soon be enrolling 18-year-old students for whom the internet has been part of life since before they were born. E-learning already plays a hugely greater role in HE than it did as little as five years ago. Pearson and Koppi (2006, p. 57) state that course developers should not only be aware that many students will be using assistive technology, but also that 'resources need to be carefully designed and offered in alternative formats'. They add the point made by many authors in this book, that in developing accessible courses, academic staff are creating a more inclusive learning environment for all students, not just for a minority who are 'different'. Pearson and Koppi offer a useful checklist of accessibility elements; further material of that nature is available from TechDis (see list of national projects at the end of the chapter).

It must not be forgotten that learning and teaching have significant affective dimensions. Students will not learn if they are not emotionally able to do so. Oxford (2008, p. 34), writing about academics who offer students emotional support, quotes a Fellow of the British Association for Counselling and Psychotherapy: 'Any tutor who doesn't want to do that is in the wrong job. Teaching is a people's game, not a process. Go and do some research with rats.' This is not to say that tutors should attempt to be capital 'C' counsellors; they should be aware of boundaries and refer students to professionals – but being emotionally aware should be part of their repertoire. There is great resistance to this (mostly from males). 'I didn't come into this field to do pastoral work – I am an academic' is a common view. Just as future academic staff will need to move away from the traditional view of HE described above, they will also need to accept that teaching has an important affective dimension.

Finally in this section, we must not forget the issue of academic and professional competence standards. These have extensive implications for curriculum design, course delivery and admissions, and their relationship with potential discrimination against students classed as disabled is often tense. Competence standards involve not only criteria set by professional bodies, but also any standards which universities set in academic terms. These standards are set when courses are designed and marketed, when decisions are made about student admissions, when students are assessed and when qualifications are awarded. The University of Edinburgh (2006) offers the following definition in respect of the UK Disability Discrimination Act (DDA):

> *For a standard to be a competence standard within the meaning of the Code of Practice for Part IV of the DDA, it needs to satisfy all of the following 3 conditions:*
>
> 1. *It must be 'an academic, medical or other standard applied by or on behalf of an education provider for the purpose of determining whether a person has a particular level of competence or ability' (5.71).*
> 2. *It must be relevant to the course, that is, a genuine standard (5.73).*
> 3. *It must not lead to direct discrimination against a disabled person when it is applied.*

A key fact here is that under this legislation, there is 'no duty to make reasonable adjustments to a provision, criterion or practice which the Act defines as a competence standard' (ibid.) There is however, and this is very important in the light of the points made in this book about inclusive practices, a necessity to look for alternative ways in which disabled students can show that they have attained the competence standard. In addition, as Hurst points out (Chapter 3), professional bodies external to a university are also bound by disability legislation.

> *If the standard is applied equally to all, it would not be direct discrimination. But it might be less favourable treatment for a reason related to the person's disability. While less favourable treatment leading to direct discrimination can never be justified, there may be justification for disability related discrimination in the application of a competency standard.   (ibid.)*

If any discrimination is to be justifiable and lawful, it would need to be applied equally to people who do not have the particular impairment in question, and it must be a proportionate way of achieving a legitimate aim (e.g. there must be a pressing need that supports the aim, and there must be no other way of achieving the aim which would be less detrimental to disabled people). For example:

> *A course in dentistry requires the students to execute various manual procedures to a very high level of accuracy. A student develops a persistent manual tremor, and so fails the assessment and the course. This appears to be less favourable treatment for a reason related to a person's disability; however, if it is applied equally to all students*

*examined whether or not they have this impairment, and if it is
'proportionate to the requirements of the course', then the requirement
is a relevant competence standard. (ibid.)*

It is important to devote space to this issue, because it is highly topical
and the cause of much discussion among academic staff, particularly those
running professional courses such as those in the medical field. If institutions
are to avoid discrimination with regard to competence standards, the Code
of Practice to the UK Disability Discrimination Act Part 4 (Disability Rights
Commission, now EHRC) states:

In advance of it becoming an issue of disadvantage:

- *Identify the specific purpose of each competence standard applied and
  examine how the competence standard achieves that purpose.*
- *Consider the possible impact of each competence standard on disabled
  people, and ask of any which might have an adverse effect whether the
  standard is absolutely necessary.*
- *Review the purpose and effect of each competence standard in the light
  of changing circumstances, such as developments in technology.*
- *Examine whether the purpose for which a competence standard is applied
  could be achieved without adverse impact on disabled people.*
- *Document discussions and conclusions on above points. (6.31).*

Staff Development

Biggs (1999) has long been regarded in the United Kingdom as a
'standard work' on HE teaching. He states: 'The key to reflecting on the
way we teach is to base our thinking on what we know about how
students learn' (p. 11). He goes on to write about deep and surface
learners and alignment between curriculum, teaching methods and
assessment procedures. What the present book demonstrates is that
knowledge about how students learn needs to be more detailed than this.
As Cooper (Chapter 4) makes clear, the key component of the type of
brain we currently label dyslexic is usually a preference for non-linear
thought. Cooper and Grant (Chapter 3) also have much to teach the
academy about visual thinking. Why is linear text the predominant form of
assessment, given that there are so many students who would prefer not to
express their ideas in such a manner?

Such a question raises the issue of what is required of staff development
events. First of all, there should be an end to segregation. There tends to

be an 'us and them' attitude; academic staff often regard student services, disability teams and learning support units as 'remedial' centres to whom students can be sent – and support staff tend to complain about academic staff's reluctance to engage with accessibility training and practice (Riddell, Tinklin and Wilson, 2005, p. 68). Mortimore (2008) refers to the presence of a 'glass wall' between them.

In the United Kingdom, the passing of part 4 of the Disability Discrimination Act in 2001 ushered in an era of 'shroud-waving', where members of disability teams were wont to issue dire warnings of the danger that the institution would be sued. While awareness of the law remains important (and legislation has contributed to a gradual cultural shift), that is not a way to enthuse staff about inclusive practice. Symonds (Chapter 11) is nevertheless clear that pressure should be put on staff to attend development sessions, recommending that the way to do this is to refer to such attendance in appraisals and promotion procedures. Some universities are also covering inclusivity aspects in peer observation schedules (Clarke, 2007).

Another way is for Deans of Faculty to give a strong lead. Mandatory staff development tends to result in groups of colleagues with folded arms, but a message that 'we are all going to do this because we need to' can be powerful. At De Montfort University (United Kingdom), one Dean used to literally lead from the front, sitting in the front row at workshops on disability and learning difference.

There are useful resources available for staff development. See the end of this chapter for a list of UK national projects with a range of excellent online information. In terms of printed materials, Hurst (2006a) is a model of its kind, including as it does practical documents for workshop activities and a CD; it also models accessible practice in its physical appearance. Hurst (2006b) describes the development of this valuable resource. It is not as easy as it should be for university staff to obtain basic online information about disability and learning differences. In the United Kingdom, the University of Bournemouth has a set of web pages which are available to all; the BRAIN.HE web site contains links to information from all over the world (see list of national projects at end of chapter).

One final point in this section concerns the affective awareness referred to above. Like many other HEIs, De Montfort University (Leicester, United Kingdom) offers a half-day course for staff entitled 'Dealing with students in distress', delivered by the counselling team. It is offered several times a year and is always well attended, which shows that staff can be encouraged to take part in such sessions. As McCrea (Chapter 9) points out, numbers of students reporting mental well-being issues are increasing rapidly. This is evidenced by the number of universities in many countries which now have mental health advisors (or equivalent). Such people are doing excellent work with students, but they also have a vital role to play in delivering staff development.

Future Developments

The United Kingdom's Higher Education Academy (HEA, 2008) has published the Single Equality Scheme referred to above. The scheme sets out plans to promote equality and prevent discrimination with regard to age, disability, gender, race, religion/belief and sexual orientation; its development was motivated firstly by awareness that individuals often possess multiple identities (and thus may experience discrimination under more than one heading), and secondly by the fact that the UK government has passed an Equality Act (HMSO 2006), which begins a process of bringing such legislation under one heading. The HEA scheme contains the following:

55. *The disability legislation reflects the social (rather than medical) model of disability. The social model is defined as:*

> *The poverty, disadvantage and social exclusion experienced by many disabled people is not the inevitable result of their impairments or medical health conditions but rather stems from attitudinal and environmental barriers' (from Duty to Promote Disability Equality Code of Practice, England and Wales, 2005). The social model requires a shift of focus away from an individual's medical condition or impairment to the 'attitudes, systems and practices that create disabling barriers and prevent participation by disabled people' (Understanding the Disability Discrimination Act, Disability Rights Commission 2007). The Academy seeks to operationalise a social model of disability.   (HEA, 2008, pp. 23–24)*

The inclusion of the above text is a positive development, because truly inclusive approaches to learning and teaching depend on awareness of models of disability. However, there remains potential for tension between disability and inclusivity. It is possible that if people identified as disabled abandon an insistence on equality and accept a position on the difference and diversity agenda, structural inequalities may be allowed to continue under the heading of cultural recognition (Riddell and Watson, 2003).

There can also be an aspect of economic redistribution to this. In the United Kingdom at present, the Disabled Students' Allowance (DSA) funding system gives a student ownership of assistive technology. This individualized approach is helpful, because even at HEIs with excellent provision of assistive software on public computers, many of the students described in this book need to be able to access equipment and software at home. However, the British government is already trying to control the runaway cost of the DSA scheme by moving its administration from local areas to a central, national office. One reason why the cost is continually rising is that ever-increasing numbers of students are being identified with learning differences (see Chapter 1).

There is another way of looking at this, which is to recognize that neurodiversity – types of brain which are currently identified as disabled – is extremely common, so common in fact as to form part of the natural diversity of human beings. HEIs should be offered central funding to help them provide an inclusive learning and teaching experience for all. This should include loan schemes for such assistive items as laptops with the kind of software recommended by Draffan (Chapter 10). It is now regarded as standard provision to offer students counselling; alongside counsellors we are now seeing increasing numbers of mental health advisors; the next step should be the provision of central teams of mentors for Aspies (most of whom are currently funded in the United Kingdom by the DSA).

Assistive technology is not simply a matter of provision for individual students. Technological advances increasingly mean that courses can be made more accessible to all. For example, two programs have recently been published: Course Genie (Wimba, 2007) and the Articulate Studio suite (Articulate, 2007). They both enable the virtual learning environment to offer audio, video and animated material. This benefits not only those currently identified with learning differences, but all students who prefer to receive information through channels other than the printed word.

In the United Kingdom, copyright law until recently excluded dyslexic people from the kind of arrangements offered to the blind in terms of electronic versions of texts. This contrasts with the USA, where there has for many years been an organization called 'Recording for the Blind and Dyslexic' (RFBD, 2008). This has a national network of branches, offering digital sound recordings of academic books. In Canada, the University of British Columbia has a suite of recording booths; students can take printed material and be given a CD containing a recording of the text being read aloud by a volunteer. (In 2005, there were 120 volunteers.) Although this depends on the ability of the readers, it is superior to the way automatic voices generate reading (however, it is fair to say that this is constantly improving).

A small number of current British printed publications (Goodwin and Thomson, 2004; Jamieson and Jamieson, 2004; Hurst, 2006a; Hargreaves, 2007; Jamieson and Morgan, 2008) model accessible practice by providing CDs which contain the full text (and often additional material). This allows readers both to change the appearance of the text and to use assistive technology to hear it spoken. University libraries remain inaccessible to many students, because trying to extract meaning from printed pages (even where the text is not small and the page is not white) is extremely slow and laborious. A way forward must be found for students to be provided with scanned versions of key texts, and for all new acquisitions to come with CDs containing the entire book. At present (in the United Kingdom), students with the DSA are often given scanners; this is again a 'better than nothing' arrangement, but it obliges the student to spend time scanning books page by page. The fact that they do this is evidence of their determination and commitment, but the experience underlines the 'within-person' or 'individual adjustment' model of provision which currently obtains.

Two of the books referenced in the previous paragraph are for students, and two are for staff. The latter contain many valuable recommendations. As Hurst (2006a and Chapter 2 above) points out, there is an urgent need for a higher level of awareness, among all HE staff, of the kinds of student covered by this book. Griffin and Pollak (2008) found that although things seemed to be improving, plenty of negative comments – by school teachers and HE lecturers – were still being reported. As Riddell, Tinklin and Wilson (2005, p. 53) point out, 'lecturers may resent further calls on their time to produce accessible curricula or individualised forms of assessment'. The way forward is for such staff to be persuaded that inclusive learning and teaching practices, far from being an awkward imposition demanded by interfering disability legislation, in fact improve the retention and attainment of all.

Cooper (Chapter 4) makes this thought-provoking statement: 'The current challenge is not how dyslexic learners can be supported, but how a whole-organisational approach to university systems can enable all learners to learn.' Mortimore (2008) also alludes to the need for what is becoming known in the United Kingdom as 'mainstreaming' inclusive practice, i.e. removing it from the realm of disability and learning difference. This is vital. Adams and Brown (2006, p. 187) conclude their book with a 'manifesto for mainstreaming inclusive practice', based on a conference which took place in 2005. None of the 21 points in that manifesto has become any less important in the meantime. Here are the first three:

- Stop adopting practices which predominantly focus on adjustments and start thinking about inclusive curriculum and assessment design which offer all students choices that align with their abilities. All students are likely to benefit from the flexibility in time, mode and place that is often seen as the basis of making reasonable adjustments.
- Engage disabled students in the debate that goes into curriculum design, so that inclusive practices are informed by authentic voices.
- Think inclusively when designing assessment instruments, so that alternatives are built in at the outset which enable disabled students to have an equivalent assessment experience.

Riddell, Tinklin and Wilson (2005, p. 156) also end their book with comments on 'mainstreaming equality'. They point out that 'individual identity is complex, not unitary', and that 'the principles which underpin equality in relation to all aspects of identity are fundamentally similar'. This means that potential discrimination should be viewed as a whole, which is the thinking behind the UK government's creation of the Equality and Human Rights Commission out of what were previously several separate bodies (including one focused on disability). The present book demonstrates that there are many fundamental similarities between types of neurodiversity, a view supported by the student voices in Griffin and Pollak (2008).

However, Riddell, Tinklin and Wilson (2005) go on to observe that by definition, specific provision for students identified as disabled would be reduced under a mainstreaming policy; generic learning support would not carry any stigma, but would be likely to be less extensive than at present. Mainstreaming of inclusive practice will only benefit the students described in this book if there is a higher level of staff awareness, training and commitment than we find today. In the United Kingdom, future developments at the time of writing will partly depend on the nature of the national government. If the Labour party remains in power, inclusivity may have more chance of support than it would under a Conservative regime, which would be likely to allow institutions more freedom to make their own decisions (Riddell, Tinklin and Wilson, 2005). On the other hand, the situation in the USA may be about to change in the other direction.

Summary

Whatever they are identified with, in the current climate the types of student in this book:

- are increasing in numbers in HE
- feel different (and often pathologized)
- are usually working much harder than neurotypicals
- are undermined by prejudice and ignorance
- have a lot to offer academia (and creative industries and the professions)
- can be greatly supported by the mainstreaming of inclusive learning and teaching, but this is not a panacea.

There are several paradoxes (or tensions) involved in this:

- students both benefit from being identified and are disadvantaged by it
- identifying types of neurodiversity is needed for staff development, but can seem to run counter to 'inclusivity for all'
- the social model of disability and learning difference is a good thing, but it includes the fact that aspects of neurodiversity are often experienced as impairments, for example, dyspraxic awkwardness and dyslexic verbal/working memory
- disability legislation has led to good practices which might be lost in a new culture of single equality policies.

It is possible that the biggest challenge comes from the view that 'non-standard provision is incompatible within a mass higher education system' (Riddell, Tinklin and Wilson, 2005, p. 153), compounded by poor staff morale resulting from increases in student numbers and bureaucracy. The many and varied UK national projects listed below (and others, to whom apologies are due for their omission – and of course equivalent projects in other countries) have a great deal to offer. Their existence should be widely disseminated in all universities (as should the work of the Key4learning organization, because it is vital that workplace issues regarding neurodiversity are dealt with pro-actively).

Let us end with an illustration which throws light on the current position. Physical accessibility arrangements are now the norm; we have automatic doors, accessible toilets and ramps. Yet how many university web sites offer easy, up-front access to ways of changing the appearance of the page and a human voice to speak the text? How many have even one of the W3C logos, to prove that efforts are being made towards accessibility? The presence of such features can speak volumes about the level of awareness of an institution. If their absence is simply the result of ignorance, that can be remedied. If however it results from a belief that such provision in some way labels a university as a 'special needs' institution (and thus by implication less academically rigorous), it directly contravenes the spirit of equality legislation, let alone the legitimate aspirations of many thousands of students. Higher education across the world must respond to this challenge.

References

Adams, M. and Brown, S. (eds) (2006) *Towards Inclusive Learning in Higher Education*, Routledge, London.

Articulate (2007) *Articulate studio suite*, www.articulate.com (accessed 24 May 2008).

Biggs, J. (1999) *Teaching for Quality Learning at University*, Society for Research into Higher Education and Open University Press, Buckingham.

Chanock, K. (2007) How do we not communicate about dyslexia? The discourses that distance scientists, disabilities staff, all advisers, students and lecturers from one another. *Journal of Academic Language and Learning*, **1** (1), 33–43.

Clarke, J. (2007) *Peer Observation Schedule for Academic Staff*, Academic Professional Development Unit, De Montfort University, Leicester.

Cottrell, S. (2001) Developing positive learning environments for dyslexic students in higher education, in *Dyslexia and Effective Learning in Secondary and Tertiary Education* (eds M. Hunter-Carsch and M. Herrington), Whurr, London.

Cowan, J. (1998) *On Becoming an Innovative University Teacher*, SRHE/Open University Press, Buckingham.

Crow, L. (1996) Including all of our lives, in *Exploring The Divide: Illness* (eds C. Barnes and G. Mercer), Leeds, Disability Press. Cited in S. Riddell and N. Watson (eds) (2003) *Disability, Culture and Identity*, Pearson, Harlow.

DANDA (2005) *The Make-Up of Neurodiversity* (as edited by the BRAIN.HE project). www.brainhe.com/neurodiversity%20venn.jpg (accessed 20 May 2008) (see also www.danda.org.uk).

Denham, J. (2008) *Widening Participation*, Higher Education Funding Council for England conference, University of Warwick.

EHRC (Equality and Human Rights Commission) www.equalityhumanrights.com (accessed on 19 May 2008).

Ferguson, I. (2003) Challenging a 'spoiled identity': mental health service users, recognition and redistribution, in *Disability, Culture and Identity* (eds S. Riddell and N. Watson), Pearson Education, Harlow.

Frith, U. (2002) Resolving the paradoxes of dyslexia, in *Dyslexia and Literacy: Theory and Practice* (eds G. Reid and J. Wearmouth), John Wiley & Sons, Ltd, Chichester.

Goodwin, V. and Thomson, B. (2004) *Making Dyslexia Work for You*, David Fulton, London.

Grant, D. (2007) *Incidence of Synaesthesia and Its Diagnostic Implications*, www.brainhe.com/students/types/index.html (accessed 27 May 2008).

Griffin, E. and Pollak, D. (2008) Student experiences of neurodiversity In higher education: insights from the BRAIN.HE project. *Dyslexia* **14**(4) in press.

Hargreaves, S. (ed.) (2007) *Study Skills for Dyslexic Students*, Sage, London.

Hall, T. and Stahl, S. (2006) Using universal design for learning to expand access to higher education, in *Towards Inclusive Learning in Higher Education* (eds M. Adams and S. Brown), Routledge, London.

HEA (2008) *Single Equality Scheme*, www.heacademy.ac.uk/resources/detail/ourwork/tla/single_equality_scheme (accessed 16 May 2008).

HMSO (2005) *Disability Discrimination Act 2005*, Her Majesty's Stationery Office, London.

HMSO (2006) *Equality Act 2006*, Her Majesty's Stationery Office, London.

Horgan, J. (1999) Lecturing for learning, in *A Handbook for Teaching and Learning in Higher Education* (eds J. Fry, S. Ketteridge and S. Marshall), Kogan Page, London.

Hurst, A. (2006a) *Towards Inclusive Learning for Disabled Students in Higher Education – Staff Development: A Practical Guide*, Skill/UCLan/HEFCE, London.

Hurst, A. (2006b) Disability and mainstreaming continuing professional development in higher education, in *Towards Inclusive Learning in Higher Education* (eds. M. Adams and S. Brown), Routledge, London.

Jamieson, C. and Morgan, E. (2008) *Managing Dyslexia at University*, Routledge, London.

Jamieson, J. and Jamieson, C. (2004) *Managing Asperger Syndrome at College and University*, David Fulton, London.

Lawrence, D. (1996) *Enhancing Self-Esteem in the Classroom*, Paul Chapman, London.

Mortimore, T. (2008) *Dismantling the Glass Wall Between Learning Support and Academic Departments: Establishing Inclusive Practices Across a University*, Seventh British Dyslexia Association International Conference, Harrogate.

Oxford, E. (2008) *Adrift in Dark Waters*. Times Higher Education 10th April. www.timeshighereducation.co.uk (accessed 12 April 2008).

Parker, V. (2007) *Timetable for University of Middlesex Pre-admission Course for Dyslexic Students*, personal communication.

Pearson, E. and Koppi, T. (2006) Supporting staff in developing inclusive online learning, in *Towards Inclusive Learning in Higher Education* (eds M. Adams and S. Brown), Routledge, London.

Pollak, D. (2005) *Dyslexia, the Self and Higher Education*, Trentham Books, Stoke-on-Trent.

Pollak, D. (2006) *Dyslexia and Pharmacy: Chalk and Cheese?* Breaking down the Barriers in Pharmacy Education: Enabling Students with Disabilities. Conference at The School of Pharmacy, University of London.

Powell, S. (ed.) (2003) *Special Teaching in Higher Education. Successful Strategies for Access and Inclusion*, Kogan Page, London.

Price, G. and Skinner, J. (2007) *Support for Learning Differences in Higher Education: The Essential Practitioners' Manual*, Trentham, Stoke-on-Trent.

RFBD (2008) *Recording for the Blind and Dyslexic*, www.rfbd.org (accessed 17 May 2008).

Riddell, S., Tinklin, T. and Wilson, A. (2005) *Disabled Students in Higher Education. Perspectives on Widening Access and Changing Policy*, Routledge, London.

Riddell, S. and Watson, N. (eds) (2003) *Disability, Culture and Identity*, Pearson, Harlow.

Rogers, C. (1983) *Freedom to Learn for the 80s*, Merrill, Columbus, OH.

Rose, D.H. and Meyer, A. (2002) *Teaching Every Student in the Digital Age: Universal Design for Learning*. Association for Supervision and Curriculum Development, Alexandria VA. www.cast.org

Singleton, C. (ed.) (1999) *Dyslexia in Higher Education: Policy, Provision and Practice*. Report of the National Working Party on Dyslexia in Higher Education, University of Hull.

Stein, J. (2004) Dyslexia genetics, in *Dyslexia in Context* (eds G. Reid and A. Fawcett), Whurr, London.

University of Edinburgh (2006) *Competence Standards and Definitions of Discrimination*. www.disability-office.ed.ac.uk/legislation/ (accessed 27 May 2008).

Wimba, Inc. (2007) *Course Genie*, www.wimba.com (accessed 23 May 2008).

Winter, R. (2003) Contextualising the patchwork text: addressing the problems of coursework assessment in higher education. *Innovations in Education and Teaching International*, **40** (2). 112–122.

Some UK National Projects: Inclusive Approaches to Teaching and Learning

TechDis

The TechDis service aims to be the leading educational advisory service, working across the United Kingdom, in the fields of accessibility and inclusion. Its mission is to support the education sector in achieving greater accessibility and inclusion by stimulating innovation and providing expert advice and guidance on disability and technology. TechDis is funded by the Joint Information Systems Committee. www.techdis.ac.uk

Strategies for the Creation of Inclusive Programmes of Study (SCIPS)

A project aiming to support academic staff to improve access to the curriculum for disabled students. www.scips.worc.ac.uk

The Open University's inclusive teaching web site

The site has practical advice about teaching inclusively and will also help you meet the requirements of the Disability Discrimination Act. It gives an insight into what study is like for disabled students, and what you can do to make a difference. The site encourages you to adopt an anticipatory and pro-active approach, recognize and meet the learning needs of individuals, and thus create a learning environment that is inclusive by design. www.open.ac.uk/inclusiveteaching.

Accessible assessments – staff guide to inclusive practice

Practical support to academic staff in the design and delivery of inclusive academic assessments. www.shu.ac.uk/services/lti/accessibleassessments.

Staff–Student Partnership for Assessment Change and Evaluation (SPACE)

One output of this project is an Alternative Assessment Toolkit, applicable to the six disciplines of Arts, Education, Humanities, Human Science, Science and Technology. www.space.ac.uk/index.php

In 2007, it also published 'Inclusive Assessment in Higher Education: a resource for change' which includes case studies and provides raw materials for exploring the equity, validity and reliability of assessment regimes. www.plymouth.ac.uk/pages/view.asp?page=10494.

Promoting Enhanced Student Learning (PESL)

By making small adjustments and speaking to the students about the implications of their disability in the learning and teaching environment, many difficulties faced by students can be can greatly alleviated and the effectiveness of teaching for all students can be enhanced. www.nottingham.ac.uk/teaching/resources/issues/disability/.

Making research education accessible (PREMIA)

The Premia resource base offers awareness and development materials for research supervisors, managers, administrators, examiners, research and generic skills trainers, disabled students and graduates, staff developers, non-disabled researchers, careers advisers and others. The aim of all the materials is to make

the research environment more accessible to disabled postgraduate students.
www.premia.ac.uk/.

Teachability project

The Teachability project at the University of Strathclyde promotes the creation of an
Accessible Curriculum For Students With Disabilities through making freely available
informative publications for academic staff. www.teachability.strath.ac.uk/.

Accessible Curricula – good practice for all

A quick-reference manual for curriculum-related disability issues. Includes field trips,
work placements and laboratory practicals. www.techdis.ac.uk/resources/files/
curricula.pdf.

Inclusive curriculum project

The project aims to develop, disseminate and embed resources for supporting
disabled students studying geography, earth and environmental sciences
in higher education and to transfer the generic lessons widely to subject-based
academics, educational developers, learning support staff and disability advisers.
www2.glos.ac.uk/gdn/icp/gdlist.htm.

South West Academic Network for Disability Support (SWANDS)

A useful staff development resource which may be reproduced for auditing and
training purposes. It covers a wide range of accessible learning and teaching
practices: www.plymouth.ac.uk/pages/view.asp?page=3243.

Raising Aspirations, Inclusion, Success and Employability (RAISE)

This project produced a framework of support for students in higher education with
specific learning difficulties, especially dyslexia. It includes a self-assessment tool
that HEIs can use to assess their own provision with reference to the framework:
www.raiseproject.co.uk/site/index.cfm.

BRAIN.HE (Best Resources for Achievement and Intervention re Neurodiversity in Higher Education)

A project which brings together information for students and staff about a wide
range of types of neurodiversity, covering the nature of specific learning differences
and learning and teaching issues. The web site contains audio and video
interview extracts with a variety of students and people working at universities.
www.brainhe.com.

AchieveAbility

This is a UK national network formed to promote awareness of the needs of those specific learning differences in the pre-university learning environment. The purpose of the network is to ensure that there are appropriate learning opportunities to support and enhance the continuation rates of SpLD learners across the educational sectors. To this end it initiates and participates in discussion and research, as well as developing projects, in order to mainstream equality and access issues related to the involvement of SpLD learners across sector. www.achieveability.org.uk.

InCurriculum

A joint action research project between three HEIs in the United Kingdom. The ethos of the work is that the HE curriculum should be:

- assisting all students in achieving their full potential, irrespective of disability or learning difference
- ensuring that all students are treated fairly
- underpinned by the social model of disability
- offering everyone access to the opportunities provided by higher education and creating barrier-free learning. www.incurriculum.org.uk

Thinking about dyslexia: a staff resource for developing practice

How are staff developing their teaching practices in ways that suit the wide range of approaches to learning which dyslexia presents? What is the student perspective? This web site offers 33 video interviews, intermingled with quick help on inclusive teaching methods and reasonable adjustments, and supported by in-depth documents. www.nottingham.ac.uk/dyslexia/.

Key4Learning

Key4Learning is not an educational project like those listed above; it is a company which offers skills, resources and information to promote understanding of what it calls hidden disabilities (which includes the types of neurodiversity covered by this book). As well as offering staff development and support materials for a range of organisations, Key4Learning facilitates such organizations to develop specific workplace arrangements for individuals. www.key4learning.com.

Index

academic assessment, 79–80
Academic Quality Inspection, 248
accessibility, 28
accommodated assessment, 246
accommodations, 248
Accreditation of Prior Learning, 260
AchieveAbility, 247
Action on Access, 25
active learning, 76
ADDers, 6, 7, 38, 56–71, 69
  see also attention deficit
      (hyperactivity) disorder
addiction, see substance abuse
Adult Asperger Assessment, 154
  see also Asperger's Syndrome
AHEAD (Association on Higher
    Education and Disability), 253,
    256
Annual Course Monitoring Review, 250
anxiety, 110, 160, 161, 175, 196,
    200
  see also maths anxiety; mental well-
      being; stress
Asperger's/Asperger Syndrome (AS), 2,
    4, 9, 58–9, 149ff
  characteristics, 153
  diagnosis, 152–3, 154
  disclosure, 153
  DSM criteria, 154–5
  personal history, 154
  screening, 152–6
  self-assessment, 153–4

shared identity, 150
Aspies, 6, 9
  see also Asperger's Syndrome
assessment, 10
  academic, 79–80
  accommodated, 246
  choice, 248
  confidentiality, 46
  diagnostic, 33–4
  ethical issues, 46
  grading, 251
  for learning, 77–8
  psychological, 33
  reports, 156
  tools, 252
Assessment of Need, 71, 81
assistive technology, 9, 76, 80–1, 112,
    217ff, 279, 284
  bloated, 218
  electronic handwriting recognition,
      225
  optical character recognition, 222–3
  screen reading, 221
  tax-exempt, 219
  training, 218
  voice recognition, 221
  see also Disabled Students' Allowance
Association of Dyslexia Specialists in
    Higher Education, 246
  see also dyslexia
attention, 38
attention deficit disorder (ADD), 56–7

attention deficit (hyperactivity) disorder
   (AD(H)D), 9, 56–7, 169ff
   accommodations for, 180–1
   co-occurrences, 170, 172
   course selection, 177–9
   as development marker, 4
   DSM criteria, 169–70
   medication, 183, 185–7
   prevalence, 170
   screening, 176–7
   signs, 46
   social issues, 175–6
attention span, 204
Audio Notetaker, 224
   see also assistive technology
auditory memory, short-term, 47
Australia, anti-discrimination legislation,
   21, 24
autism, 2, 4, 34, 155
   triad of impairment, 155–6, 158–62
Autism Quotient test, 153
autistic spectrum, 2
   see also Asperger's Syndrome

behaviour
   inhibition, 171
   ritualistic, 58
binge drinking, *see* substance abuse
bipolar disorder, 201
Blackboard, 235–6, 258
   see also assistive technology
boredom, 174
   see also restlessness
brain gym, 257
BRAIN.HE, 3, 7
British Dyslexia Association, 52
Brown ADD Scales, 176
   see also attention deficit
      (hyperactivity) disorder
buddies, 178, 256
budgeting, 136
   see also financial literacy;
      independent living
bullying, 41, 151, 152, 156, 162

CapturaTalk, 222
   see also assistive technology
change, 159
Charters, G., 28
ClaroView, 229–30
   see also assistive technology
clumsiness, 43, 44, 91, 97, 98, 99
   see also development coordination
      disorder; dyspraxia; motor
      coordination
cognitive behaviour therapy, 187
cognitive function, 54, 171
cognitive profile, 36
Commission for Equality and Human
   Rights, 25, 26
communication, 156, 159–60, 276
competence, 279
computer technology, 226–34
   see also assistive technology
concentration span, 204
concept mapping, 78
confidentiality, 255
Conners Rating Scales, 176
   see also attention deficit
      (hyperactivity) disorder
counselling, 160, 212–13
   see also mental well-being; student
      support
course
   analysis, 84
   assessment, 138, 250–4
   design, 249–50
   selection, 46
   validation, 250
Creative Learning in Practice, 257
cultural change, 30
cultural diversity, 243
culture, cultural history, 40
curriculum
   design, 10
   development, 249–50

Dearing Report, 27
delinquency, 171

depression, 9, 41, 113, 160, 175, 197, 198, 200
    see also mental well-being
development coordination disorder 39, 91
    definition, 92–3
Developmental Adult Neurodiversity Association (DANDA), 35, 92–3, 170, 246, 271
developmental dyspraxia, 92
    see also dyspraxia
Diagnostic and Statistical Manual of Mental Disorders (DSM), 4
Digit Span test, 43, 47, 48
    see also dyscalculia
digital pens, 225
    see also assistive technology
digital recorders, 223
    see also assistive technology
disability
    medical model, 270
    social model, 36
Disability Discrimination Act 1995, 1, 18–19
Disability Discrimination Act 2005, 21–3, 202, 247, 270
disability equality, promotion of, 202–3
Disability Equality Duty, 10, 149, 247
    responses to, 247–9
Disability Equality Scheme, 19, 21, 270
    evaluation, 25
Disability Rights Commission, 20–1, 25
Disability Statements, 19
Disabled Students' Allowance, 14, 72, 152, 156, 284
    assessment, 220
    for part-time students, 13, 14
disclosure, 20, 22, 272, 276
    see also confidentiality
discrimination, 1, 19, 20, 280–1
    codes of practice, 24
distractibility, 57
due diligence, 39
duties, 21

duty of care, 39, 246
dyscalculia, 9, 39, 45, 125ff
    characteristics, 128
    co-occurrence with dyslexia, 129, 134
    course selection, 134–5
    difficulties, 127–32
    and mental well-being, 131
    prevalence, 126
    screening, 132–4
Dyscalculia Screener, 132
DysCalculiUM, 133–4
dyslexia, 9, 16–17, 34, 36, 39, 65ff
    cause(s), 65
    characteristics, 66
    as deficit, 65
    definition, 54
    disclosure, 84
    screening, 72–3
    as social construction or model, 64, 66–7
    support, 76–7
dyslexia staff, 261
dysorthographia, 52
dyspraxia, 2, 9, 33, 34, 39, 41, 43, 55, 91ff
    assessment for, 95, 99
    cause(s), 93
    co-occurrences, 95, 98
    course selection, 103–5
    incidence, 94
    indicators and characteristics, 96–8, 98–9, 100–2
    long-term implications, 95
    screening, 97
Dyspraxia Foundation, 55, 92, 246
Dyspraxia Student Screening Checklist, 100–2

eating disorders, 199, 201
    see also mental well-being
Education Act 1981, 1
Educational Testing Service, 51
e-learning, 279

electronic notetakers, 225
  see also assistive technology
emotional intelligence, 199
empathy, 149, 153, 277
empowerment and enablement, 3–4,
  220
EndNote, 220
  see also assistive technology
equality, 18, 21
Equality Act 2006, 3
Equality and Human Rights Commission
  (EHRC), 21, 249
  compliance notice, 249
Equality Challenge Unit, 22–3, 25
equity, 18, 21
essay writing, 78, 110–11
  avoidance, 46
examinations
  and anxiety, 207–8
  arrangements for, 112
executive function, 157, 171

FEDORA (European Forum for Students'
  Guidance), 253
feedback, 206–8
financial literacy, 136–7
  see also independent living
flexibility, 157, 160–1, 277
forgetfulness, 57, 174

grapho-motor difficulty, 42
gratification, 174
gross motor skills, 44
group work, 205

harassment, 21
Heads of University Counselling
  Services, 195, 196
higher education
  admission to, 258, 273–4
  barriers to, 28–9, 156–8
  social environment, 158
  transition to, 106, 135, 179–81,
    199, 201, 273–4; *see also*
    independent living

Higher Education Academy, 14
Higher Education Authority Centres of
  Excellence in Teaching and
  Learning, 25
Higher Education Authority Single
  Equality Scheme, 3
Higher Education Funding Council, 1,
  14, 15
holistic learning, 83
holistic processing, 67
hyperactivity, 174
  see also attention deficit (hyperactivity)
    disorder; restlessness

identification, 10, 274–6
  diagnosis as, 5
impact assessment, 21, 22
impairment, 5, 270
  deficit/medical model, 15–16
  social model, 16
  unseen, 22
Improved Access to Psychology Therapy
  Project, 197
impulse control, 175
impulsiveness, 170, 174–5, 187–8
inattention, 172–3
inclusion, 7, 10, 85
inclusive learning, 76
independent living, 17, 113–14
Index of Working Memory, 48
inspiration, 83
Institute for Learning and Teaching in
  Higher Education, 14
International Society for Education
  through Art, 257
international students, 259–60
Internet, 235–7
involvement, 22
Ireland, anti-discrimination legislation,
  24

Johnson, M., 30

labelling, 7, 33, 152, 269, 275
lateral thinking, 245

Layard Report, 197
learning
  active, 76
  barriers to, 107, 277
  environment, 71–80, 107
  holistic, 83
  inclusive, 76, 243
  kinaesthetic, 257
  multisensory, 181
  support, 182–3
  troubled, 243
Learning and Skills Council, 247
Letter-Number Sequencing test, 47,
  48
  see also dyscalculia
life coaching, 188–9
linear sequencing, 69–70

mainstreaming, 25, 30, 285–6
mathematical ability and disorder,
  125
  social issues, 141–3
mathematical skill, 55–6
Mathematics Support Centres, 143–4
maths
  anxiety, 128–32, 137–8, 143
  difficulty, 43
Meares-Irlen Syndrome, 228
memory
  auditory, 47
  olfactory, 257
  short-term, 173
  working, 37, 38, 41, 43, 47, 48,
    57, 144
  see also forgetfulness; time
    management
mental health advisors, 196
mental health disability
  disclosure, 195
  incidence, 195
  social model, 196
  see also anxiety; bipolar disorder;
    depression; mental well-being;
    schizophrenia; stress
Mental Health Support Services, 197

mental well-being, 2, 5, 6, 9, 195ff,
  282–3
  definition, 197
  promotion of, 203
mentors, 178, 256, 272
  see also student support
metacognition, 271
mind-maps, mind-mapping, 74, 78
  software for, 233–4
mistakes, modelling of, 71–2
mobile phones, 221
mobile technologies, 220–6
  see also assistive technology
mobility, 16
monitoring, 24
motivation, 84, 172
motor coordination, 91, 95
multi-sensory learning, 76
multi-sensory teaching, 181, 257

National Association of Disability
  Officers, 29
National Bureau for Handicapped
  Students, 13
National Bureau for Students with
  Disabilities, 250
National Disability Team, 24, 25
National Network of Assessment
  Centres, 250
neurocognitive profile, 34
neurodiversity, 34
  assessment, 35–6
  definition, 35–6
  diagnosis, 39
  in higher education, 4, 7
  overlap, 271–3
  prevalence, 3
  and unemployment, 18
neurotypicality, 36
neurotypicals, 150
New Zealand, anti-discrimination
  legislation, 23–4
nonverbal learning disorder, 40,
  46
note-taking, 110

number
  processing, 127
  representation, 127
  see also dyscalculia; mathematical
      ability and disorder;
      mathematical skill
numerical reasoning, 139–40

Office of the Independent Adjudicator
    for Higher Education, 26
olfactory memory, 257
orientation, 136
otherness, 245
overlays, 37, 228
  virtual, 230; *see also* assistive
      technology
  see also visual stress

participation, 108–10
PDFs, 232
  see also assistive technology
pedagogic change, 249
perceptual processing, 69
perfectionism, 152, 206
personal digital assistant, 221
  see also assistive technology
personal histories, 39–45, 48–50
  ethical issues, 46
  see also confidentiality
podcasts, 221
PowerPoint, 236
prejudice, 162–3
presentation skills, 213–14
prioritization, 157, 171
problem-solving, 74–5
processing speed, 57
Professional Association of Teachers
    of Students with Specific
    Learning Differences (PATOSS), 51,
    246
professional staff development and
    training, 10, 17, 27–8, 138,
    184, 245, 247–8, 261,
    281–3

Quality Assurance Agency, Code of
    Practice, 14, 24

Rammell, B., 14–15
ReadAble, 230
reading
  comprehension, 42
  speed and accuracy, 37, 37–8, 244
  and visual stress, 51
  see also dyslexia
reasonable adjustments, 1, 19, 20,
    107, 262, 272, 280
recreational drugs, *see* substance abuse
resources, 115–20
respect, 5
restlessness, 56, 57, 170, 174
  see also attention deficit
      (hyperactivity) disorder
Riddell, S., 27
right hemisphere function, 45, 59
rights and responsibilities, 20
risk assessment, 20
  see also work placement

schizophrenia, 201
Schwarz Report, 258, 261
Scotland, 24
  Scottish Higher Education Funding
      Council, 28–9
Screen Ruler, 228–9
  see also assistive technology
Screenshot Reader, 233
  see also assistive technology
scribes, 111
  see also student support
self-assessment, 245
self-control, 171
self-efficacy, 140
self-esteem, 33, 113, 142–3, 181,
    199, 206, 207
  see also depression
self-harm, 201
  see also depression; substance abuse;
      suicide

self-management, 179, 182–3
self-negativity, 33
    see also self-esteem
sensory overload, 49–50, 157
sensory world, 47
sequencing skills, 69
service delivery, 160
Simpson, A., 28
single equality legislation and schemes,
    249
Single Equality Scheme, 283
Skill: Bureau for Students with
    Disabilities, 13
skills
    gross motor, 44
    mathematical, 55–6
    presentation, 213–14
    sequencing, 60
    social, 71
slowness, 56
Smart Hal, 221, 222
Smart Phone, 221
    see also assistive technology
social environment, 161–2
social interaction, social skills, 71
social isolation, 142, 143, 156, 162,
    199
social networking, 235
Special Educational Needs and
    Disability Act 2001, 19–21
specific learning difference, 2, 34
    birthing history, 40
    co-occurrence, 6, 39, 40
    DSM criteria, 38
    HE students with, 13
    incidence, 38
    medical model, 4, 16
    social model, 5
    staff awareness of, 3
speech recognition, software for, 234
    see also assistive technology
spell checkers, 224–5
    see also assistive technology
spelling, 52

stereotyping, 149
    see also labelling
stress, 41, 71, 198, 200–1
    see also mental well-being
Student Enhanced Learning through
    Effective Formative Feedback, 249
student support, 208–9
    see also accommodations; assistive
        technology; buddies; counselling;
        Disabled Students' Allowance;
        mentors; reasonable adjustments
students, part-time, 14
subitizing, 132
substance abuse, 171, 179, 199, 201
suicide, 201
Swan, W., 24
Sweden, anti-discrimination legislation,
    24
synaesthesia, 43, 49–50, 271
    incidence, 48
    see also sensory overload

Tag Cloud, 237
    see also assistive technology
Teachability programme, 28–9
teaching
    environment, 108
    multi-sensory, 181, 257
    strategies, 256–9
    style, 204–5
    time, 108
    see also professional staff
        development and training
Teaching and Learning Research
    Programme, 27
tests, diagnostic, 51
text-to-speech software, 231–2
    see also assistive technology
time 173
time management, 67–8, 81–3, 136,
    157, 271–2
time-keeping, 67–8, 81–3, 135–6, 204
Tourette's Syndrome, 7
Towards Learning Creatively, 253

302 *Index*

underachievement, 199
underperformance, 41
United States, anti-discrimination
    legislation, 23
Universal Design for Learning, 278–9
university admission
    barriers to, 68
    choice, 17
    course selection, 68–9
    criteria, 72
    grounds for exclusion, 17–18, 20
    rates of, 1, 3
    see also higher education

verbal reasoning, 37–8, 139
    see also visualization
verbal thinking, 74–5
virtual learning, 10, 258, 284
virtual learning environment, 235, 258
visual stress, 37, 41, 42, 77
    and reading speed, 51

visualization, 43, 47, 48–9, 66, 74,
    156, 271
viva voces, 252–3

Wechsler Adult Intelligence Scale
    (WAIS), 47, 51
    WAIS-III, 60
work
    group, 205
    placement, 84, 105–6, 138–41,
        184–5
    presentation, and anxiety/stress,
        205–6; see also essay
        writing
Work-based Learning and Placement,
    255
working memory, 37, 38, 41, 43, 47,
    48, 57, 144
    and maths anxiety, 130
Writing Pad, 253–4, 257
    see also assistive technology